PEREGRINE BOOKS
The Informed Heart

Bruno Bettelheim, one of the world's most distinguished contemporary psychoanalysts, is the founder of the Orthogenic School at Chicago University and until his retirement in 1973 was its Director. Born in Vienna in 1903, he received his doctorate at the University of Vienna. During the Second World War, he was interned in the concentration camps of Dachau and Buchenwald, and it is about this that he writes in *The Informed Heart*. After moving to the USA he became Professor of Education, and then Professor of Psychology and Psychiatry at the University of Chicago. His other books include *The Children of the Dream, A Home for the Heart, On Learning to Read, the Child's Fascination with Meaning, Surviving and Other Essays, The Uses of Enchantment* (also in Peregrine), and *Freud and Man's Soul.*

Bruno Bettelheim

The Informed Heart

Penguin Books

PENGUIN BOOKS

Published by the Penguin Group
27 Wrights Lane, London W8 5TZ, England
Viking Penguin Inc., 40 West 23rd Street, New York, New York 10010, USA
Penguin Books Australia Ltd, Ringwood, Victoria, Australia
Penguin Books Canada Ltd, 2801 John Street, Markham, Ontario, Canada L3R 1B4
Penguin Books (NZ) Ltd, 182–190 Wairau Road, Auckland 10, New Zealand

Penguin Books Ltd, Registered Offices: Harmondsworth, Middlesex, England

First published in the USA by The Free Press, A Corporation 1960
Published in Peregrine Books 1986
Reprinted 1987, 1988

Made and printed in Great Britain by
Richard Clay Ltd, Bungay, Suffolk
Typeset in Baskerville

To Trude

Contents

Acknowledgments

MY APPRECIATION GOES TO THE publishers who graciously granted me permission to include material from my articles which originally appeared in the following publications:

American Journal of Economics and Sociology, for permission to quote from, "Remarks on the Psychological Appeal of Totalitarianism," Vol. XII, No. 1;

Europäische Verlagsanstalt, for permission to quote from "Individual Autonomy and Mass Control," which appeared in *Sociologica,* 1955;

Frederick Fell, Inc., for permission to quote from my preface to Miklos Nyiszli's *Auschwitz: A Doctor's Eyewitness Account* (New York, 1960);

Journal of Abnormal and Social Psychology, for permission to quote from "Individualism and Mass Behavior in Extreme Situations," Vol. XXXVIII (1943).

I would also like to gratefully acknowledge the publishers and authors who granted permission to quote from other sources referred to in this volume:

The American Jewish Committee, for permission to quote from, "The Criminal as Public Servant," by Edouard Roditi, in *Commentary,* Vol. XXVIII (November, 1959);

Deutsche Verlagsanstalt, for permission to quote from, *Kommandant in Auschwitz,* by R. Hoess (Stuttgart, 1958);

Eugen Kogon, for permission to quote from *Der SS-Staat,* (Frankfurt, 1946);

The Psychoanalytic Quarterly, for permission to quote from E. P. Bernabeu's article, "Science Fiction," Vol. XXVI, (1957);

Time, Inc., for permission to quote from, "War Crimes—Subject: Women," in *Time,* November 24, 1947.

Preface

WE ARE IN GREAT HASTE TO SEND and receive messages from outer space. But so hectic and often so tedious are our days, that many of us have nothing of importance to communicate to those close to us.

Never before have so many had it so good; no longer do we tremble in fear of sickness or hunger, of hidden evils in the dark, of the spell of witches. The burden of killing toil has been lifted from us, and machines, not the labor of our hands, will soon provide us with nearly all we need, and much that we don't really need. We have inherited freedoms man has striven after for centuries. Because of all this and much more we should be living in a dawn of great promise. But now that we are freer to enjoy life, we are deeply frustrated in our disappointment that the freedom and comfort, sought with such deep desire, do not give meaning and purpose to our lives.

With so much at hand that generations have striven for, how bewildering that the meaning of life should evade us. Freedoms we have, broader than ever before. But more than ever before most of us yearn for a self realization that eludes us, while we abide restless in the midst of plenty. As we achieve freedom, we are frightened by social forces that seem to suffocate us, seem to move in on us from all parts of an ever contracting world.

The tedium and dissatisfaction with life are becoming so great that many are getting ready to let freedom slip out of their hands. They feel it is all too complicated, too difficult to hold on to it, and to themselves. If meaning has gone out of their lives, then at least they wish not to be responsible for it, to let society carry the burden of failure and guilt.

Just how to achieve self realization, to preserve freedom, and adapt society to both, seems increasingly harder to know; it is felt as a central, overwhelming problem of our days.

Later in this volume, in discussing the discomforts of our civilization, I have alluded to how we are having to change. From finding security in a repetition of sameness, of only slight and slow variations, we are having to live with a very different kind of security; one that must rest on achieving the good life, with very little chance to predict the outcome of our actions in a fast changing world.

To manage such a feat, heart and reason can no longer be kept in their separate places. Work and art, family and society, can no longer develop in isolation from each other. The daring heart must invade reason with its own living warmth, even if the symmetry of reason must give way to admit love and the pulsation of life.

No longer can we be satisfied with a life where the heart has its reasons, which reason cannot know. Our hearts must know the world of reason, and reason must be guided by an informed heart. Hence the title of this book: for the rest it must speak for itself.

Introduction
to the Penguin Edition

I AM VERY GLAD THAT THIS BOOK WILL now again be readily available to British readers. It represents one man's efforts to try to cope with totalitarian terror in general and with the horrors of the German concentration camps and the Holocaust in particular. These events have occupied my mind for over forty years. This suggests how difficult it is to try to comprehend these phenomena, to come to terms with man's inhumanity to man, which made them possible. It also shows that mastering the emotions which such inhumanity arouses can easily require a life-long struggle, the goal of which is not to let such events destroy one's belief in mankind. What follows presents one person's efforts at mastering the trauma of the past, so that it can be put to rest and will no longer haunt the coming generations. It is a serious effort at attempting to comprehend the wider ramifications of these events for our times, events which when they happened were so overpowering and upsetting that the question "How is this possible? How can people do this to one another?" overshadowed all other considerations.

My approach to this task has been guided by Freud's insights into the role which our unconscious plays in motivating human actions, and by his discovery of the darkest aspects of our minds. Only if we do not close ourselves to these but accept their existence will we be convinced of how important it is to control these our destructive tendencies; thus we may be able to prevent catastrophes such as that from which my generation suffered. Without such controls, some men's destructive tendencies will induce them to victimize others; this has happened from time to time all throughout man's recorded history. What is new in our times, which makes it all so extremely dangerous, is the mechanization of destruction produced by modern technology. The door to a mechanization which may destroy us all is wide open.

This explains my underlying motive for writing this book: the conviction that only a greater humanization of human relations offers the promise that no future Holocaust will engulf us. Only if we truly love life—our own and that of others—will we be able to preserve it and look forward with confidence to the future. If we do, we shall have dispersed the shadows which events of the recent past have shed over our lives.

Thus my business is not with the dead but with the living. My concern is not with the past, but with the present. The Nazi concentration and extermination camps are by now appropriate subjects for the historian. My interest here is based on their significance for the present. This is the reason we ought not to forget or distort the meaning of Nazi terrorism and genocide; not because of the terrible things which were done by average people to average persons a generation ago, but because of the warning these events hold for man of today. Now that more than forty years separate us from what led to the writing of this book, it is time to ask what may be learned from these events for now and the future; what additional insights into the workings of the human psyche are necessary to understand what happened then, why it happened, and how we may be able to protect ourselves from such things happening ever again.

It is understandable that we wish to avoid coping with the deeply perturbing perspectives on man which these awful events open up: man as a wanton destroyer, and as a victim shorn of all defenses. So we tend to view what happened in Hitler's Germany as belonging to a past which is gone and over with; thus we may deny its lessons for the present. This is by no means a new attitude or defense against that which is too dreadful to consider. The same defense of denial was also used when it all happened. We protected ourselves then by denying that it was happening, as we defend ourselves today by believing these are past events of history which have no pertinence for the world of today. What is needed instead is an understanding that, in today's world, destructive totalitarianism is an ever-present danger.

We do not need to think back to the Holocaust to realize what is involved, and that survival requires continual watchfulness: the Viet Nam boat people of yesterday, the Khmer Rouge of Indochina, the starving people of Ethiopia make this amply clear. All too many perish trying to make their escape. But whether or not their desperate attempts to stay alive will result in their survival really depends on whether others are willing to make their survival possible. Exactly the same was true for the Jews of Europe. Had there been willingness on the part of the free world to take them in, a great many more would have resisted, many more would have tried to escape in time, and many, many more would have survived. The fact that the rest of the world closed itself to the Jews sapped them of the strength they needed to try to stay alive; robbed them of their will to resist.

It requires inner strength to try to stay alive under the most destructive conditions, and whether or not one can muster this strength depends to a very important degree on whether one feels that others wish one to stay alive, whether they are willing to help. For example, many Jewish children in France might have survived had their parents felt that some Frenchmen were willing to help them stay alive. The stories of the all-too-few children who survived indicate that their survival was the result of their parents finding some French family who were ready to help save a child. Those whose parents despaired, because they did not know anybody who would be willing to help them or their children, did not live to tell their stories. Thus the inner will to stay alive depends to a large measure on the help one receives from the outside; these are inextricably interwoven.

The strongest motive for staying alive is that one has something for which one is determined to remain alive at all costs, at all risks. This is no problem as long as one has strong attachments to others, for whose sake one wishes to remain alive. In the German concentration camps the thought of one's parents, spouse, children, and all other loved ones was the strongest incentive to try everything possible to remain alive, even under the most devastating conditions. Herein lies a crucial difference between the camps before the beginning of the extermination policy, and after it was instituted. In the extermination camps little hope was left that, if one survived, one would be reunited with those whom one loved. Even if one was temporarily spared in the selection process which determined who would be murdered right away, and who was destined to be murdered later, one knew that one's spouse and children would also be sent to the gas chambers. It was very hard to struggle to stay alive when the conditions were so utterly destructive.

The sheer will to live cannot take the place of the strength one derives from outside support, real or imagined. This is why those on the outside of any catastrophe who lovingly work for one's return to the living are the strongest lifeline imaginable, the most powerful motive for staying alive. The absence of such a lifeline weakens one's determination to the degree that little or no strength is left to carry on the desperate fight to remain alive. One of the lessons of the camps was that, contrary to what I expected and thought Darwinism taught, the will to live—the life drive, the élan vital, or whatever other name it is given—provided little support unless it could attach itself to some loved person or some all-important idea, such as communism or religious conviction.

Murderers can only kill; they do not have the power to rob us of the will to live, of the ability to fight to stay alive. Conditions such as the Nazis imposed on Europe's Jews—degradation, exhaustion, utter debilitation through torture, starvation, sickness—all seriously weaken our will to live, undermine the life drive and thus open the way for death to come. When such conditions are worsened by the feeling that the rest of the world has forsaken one, then the person is totally deprived of the strength needed to fight to stay alive. Then he no longer has the strength to refuse to dig his own grave, to refuse to walk to the gas chambers.

Genocide has been perpetrated all throughout history. However, survival has always depended on the individual's will to live, on his strength to fight for survival. Yet survival has always also required that others be willing to help. Only to the degree that we are ready to help, to exert ourselves to help, devote ourselves to helping in time, will those who are threatened by destruction be given a chance to survive. And there was time and opportunity to help those threatened by death through Nazi persecution, but the help was not forthcoming.

The Nazis murdered the Jews of Europe and millions of others whom they considered undesirable. That nobody but the Jews cared for the Jews, and that even many Jews on the outside did not care very much, that the free world did not care—this was why the will to survive of so many European Jews became first weakened and then extinguished. One of the last messages from the Warsaw ghetto said: "The world is silent; the world knows and stays silent. God's vicar in the Vatican is silent. There is silence in London and Washington. The American Jews are silent. This silence is incomprehensible and horrifying."

We cannot fully grasp the nature and the implications of what happened in the concentration camps if we shy away from facing the destructive tendencies in man, the aggressive aspect of our animal inheritance which in man has assumed its specifically human and peculiarly destructive form. Freud called it man's death drive, and Konrad Lorenz, "the so-called evil." Freud believed that in man the life and the death or destructive drives wage continuous battle against each other, and further that we can truly accept ourselves and relate positively to others only when the life drive is in ascendancy within ourselves, so that it manages to neutralize or at least adequately control the death drive and its derivatives.

I think we cannot understand the Nazi phenomenon, nor genocide or mass extermination of men by men—and there were other monsters like Hitler in history—unless we recognize that in such people the death drive has overpowered their life drive. Hitler's belief that his cherished superior man of pure Aryan blood could flourish only when the lower races were completely exterminated created a death mania which, while it began with the Jews, did not stop with them. Many others were also exterminated: the Gypsies, the mentally or physically defective; while the Poles, Russians, Blacks and members of other so-called inferior races were to be radically reduced in numbers in Hitler's 1000-year Reich.

Had Hitler not been so obsessed by the conviction that other races had to die for the Germans to live, he might well have won the war, and with it much of the world. Not only German Jews, but vast numbers of Polish, Ukrainian, and even Russian soldiers might have joined the German armies and might have brought it victory, had Hitler's wish to exterminate some and to enslave the rest not prevented him from integrating them into his army.

So it happened as it must: those beholden to the death drive in the end also destroy themselves. Hitler's insistence that his army at Stalingrad let itself be killed rather than save itself is but one example. Another is Hitler's continuing the war long after it had been lost, trying to have every German fight until death rather than making peace.

Further, the behavior of those Jews who, without offering resistance, permitted themselves to be walked to the gas chambers, cannot be comprehended either without reference to the death tendencies which exist in all of us. After the terrible transportation into the death camps, after the tortures and degradations they had suffered, confronted by the gas chambers and crematoria, these Jews, having been deprived of all that had given meaning to their lives, robbed of all hope for themselves and, worst of all, having been deserted by the entire world, were no longer able to keep their death drive in bounds. In their case the death tendencies were not directed against others, but turned inward, against the self.

This is why it is our obligation, not to those who are dead but to ourselves, and to those dear to us today, to strengthen the life drives. We must make certain that never again will the life-enhancing tendencies be so totally destroyed in so many millions of people, least of all by the power of a government. A true understanding of Hitler's or any other concentration camp state ought to imbue us with the determination that never again shall men, overcome by their desperation and enslaved by their death drive, walk themselves to their deaths, as their murderers would wish.

June 1985

THE
INFORMED HEART

1
The Concordance of Opposites

IN THIS VOLUME I HAVE TRIED TO PRESENT those aspects of my thoughts and work that have to do with the human condition in modern mass society, and with the psychological impact of totalitarian tendencies. Small but significant portions of this book have been published before, though in quite different form. All that follows was newly written or rewritten with this book in mind.

I have been sifting the ideas presented here for the last twenty years, since they emerged only slowly in their present form. Ordinarily, the development of an author's views of man and life are his private affair, particularly when he considers his publications scientific reports. Still, a writer whose work depends on observation, introspection, and the scrutiny of motives wonders what inner links bind together his life's work as he sits down to select what from his writings is worth being rethought and brought up to date, what of it still meets his present opinions, what deserves to be forgotten, and what calls for radical revision. Perhaps the reader too is interested in knowing what deeper unity binds the thoughts of a book together beyond the fact that they were set down by one person and relate to a single broad subject. In an effort to sketch this inner coherence I have set down some personal history that I hope will connect more intimately what might otherwise seem just another miscellany of social psychology.

But I have another, more important reason, deeply connected with the main thesis of this book. It is my conviction that to withstand and counteract the deadening impact of mass society, a man's work must be permeated by his personality. Just as his choice of work must not be due to mere convenience, chance or expediency, but should directly reflect how he reaches for self realization in this world of ours, so the results of his work, beside being objectively purposeful, should also reflect his own purposes in life. Out of this conviction I discard a conventional reticence and begin this book by relating how I came to be involved in the problems to which it addresses itself.

The generation of my parents raised their children in a climate now vanished—a western and central Europe that wished to believe in an age of permanent progress and ever greater security and happiness. Though contradicted by fact, this creed was accepted with firm belief, particularly by what we would now call the upper middle classes who benefited most by developments of the late nineteenth and early twentieth centuries. For them, such comfortable beliefs were easily held, because supported by experience. In their lifetime they had witnessed a continuing and ever accelerating social, economic, and cultural progress, along with the more rational and equitable politics and social practices that characterized western Europe before the first World War.

But one August day Lord Grey remarked with deep sadness and clairvoyance, "the lamps are going out all over Europe; we shall not see them lit again in our lifetime." His prediction not only came true but extended far beyond his lifetime and into ours. Northern Europe ceased being "the workshop of the human race," hard as that was for my generation to accept before Hitler made it obvious to all.

The formative years of my generation of Viennese intellectuals stood under the deep impact of the psychological and social crisis of the first war. For us, the personal crisis of adolescence and early maturity was compounded by the social and economic chaos that followed the war and culminated first in Russian Bolshevism, then National Socialism, and finally in a second World War. While this was true for the younger generation all over Europe, for the Viennese it was further aggravated by the collapse of the Austro-Hungarian empire. The central intellectual and emotional problems this posed to me make up a highly personalized instance of the now dead but then very lively "nature-nurture" controversy.

The misery of the war and postwar years in a suddenly no longer imperial Vienna, the collapse of the existing order of paternalistic autocracy at exactly the moment when the adolescent revolted against the world of his parents, all this brought its special problems and led to particular solutions. It is hard to revolt against a parent whose whole world has suddenly fallen shattered to pieces. Revolt is the less avoidable because the adolescent feels even more betrayed at suddenly realizing that the parent he thought an oppressive but protective hero is just a clay god. He can no longer test his new values against those of his parents, because they turned out to have no value at all. And how can he even test his new and still untried way of life against something so unstable, so in flux, as parental ways now seemed? All of a sudden he feels deprived of the firm support, not of his parents, but of the values they instilled in him; and this happens just when he needs them most as a safe harbor from which to venture on his new and anxious moves into semiadult independence. Such a defection by his individual parents is the more keenly experienced by the adolescent because it deprives him of the security with his parents that alone lets him rebel safely against the world his parents stand for.[1]

---

[1] It was this psychological situation and a reaction to it of total hopelessness that forms the background for much of Kafka's writings.

Quest for certainty

All this and much more led to the fervent wish to create a permanent and satisfactory society. The wish fathered the belief, and since the wish was intense, the belief soon became easy conviction: a new and different society could readily be created, a "good" society that would guarantee the good life for all. This society was to be both very stable and secure, while at the same time permitting, even guaranteeing, greatest freedom of personal development and self realization.

It took me many years—from the end of the first World War until nearly the beginning of the second—to recognize intellectually and against strong emotional resistance, the contrary nature of these requirements. Further struggle was needed to acknowledge what was rationally arrived at, and still more time and effort before I could fully accept it emotionally.

Since this adolescent crisis took place in Vienna, against a family background of assimilated Jewish bourgeosie, the influence of Freud and his teachings soon made itself felt. These interfered with the wished-for belief that if only society were more rationally organized, no such crisis or the discomfort it brought would ever perturb another youth. Psychoanalysis suggested that maybe it was not society that created all these difficulties in man, but rather the hidden, inner, contradictory nature of man that created difficulties for society.

This, then, was the particular form in which the nature-nurture conflict presented itself to me: in order to create the good society, was it of first importance to change society radically enough for all persons to achieve full self realization? In this case psychoanalysis could be discarded, with the possible exception of a few deranged persons. Or was this the wrong approach to the problem and could only persons who had achieved full personal liberation and integration by being psychoanalyzed create such a "good" society? In the latter case the correct thing was to forget for the time being any social or economic revolution and to concentrate instead on pushing psychoanalysis; the hope was that once the vast majority of men had profited from its inner liberation, they would almost automatically create the good society for themselves and all others.

Most of my small group of intimate friends (the concept of peer group and its importance for the adolescent had not yet been formulated, or if it had, it certainly had not reached postwar Vienna) strove for certainty at all cost, as adolescents of all ages are apt to do. Trying to escape their inner struggles and contradictions, they embraced unquestioningly one of these two sets of theories, blinding themselves to the merits of the other. Some of them joined socialism and likely as not early communism—which a few years later was superseded by either blind or uneasy partisanship to official communism (Russian), or to splinter group communism (Trotsky, etc.)—totally rejecting what Freud had taught them. Others chose the opposite solution and devoted themselves just as singlemindedly to the pursuit of psychoanalysis. Still others, and they were the majority of this group of by then University students and their fringes, retired to a private world of art, scientific pursuit, or bohemia, while many of my gentile friends embraced either orthodox or neo-catholicism (and many, later on, national socialism) thus denying any validity to either side of the controversy. Of course, there were some members of the first two groups who changed sides, at one time fully embracing one persuasion such as communism, at another time, flatly convinced of the merits of the other solution, psychoanalysis.

Much as I, too, would have liked to live in certainty, I felt unable to join either persuasion with a whole heart. Many aspects of each seemed attractive and convincing to me at one time or another, while most of the time each one seemed empty without the other. The solution of a very few who tried to graft psychoanalysis onto communism (the best known of whom was Wilhelm Reich) seemed from the beginning, and soon turned out to be, not viable; for this there were many reasons, the most obvious being the contradictory nature of the union.

At times I, too, tried to get around the problem by escaping into privatization, though this concept too was still unknown. The particular form it took was a preoccupation with literature and art and, to a lesser degree, music, along with concentrating on a few intensely intimate relations. But though my interest in art and literature had preceded my interest in psychoanalysis and social problems, they proved discouraging since they did not seem to answer my quest for a better man in a better society. But I was not ready to discard them yet. I thought if I could only plumb deep enough, I might find the one right answer.

Philosophy seemed to plumb deepest, so it was that discipline I turned to at one period. There I encountered the theory of the concordance of contraries, but since I was still looking for unilateral solutions, it helped me little in my search. I did not then realize how it could be applied to understanding the dynamic interdependence of the organism and its environment, and how life consists of struggles to reach higher stages of integration within a basically irreconcilable conflict. To accept this last as fact was not possible for me at the time. As a young man anxious to find himself I was convinced that any environment—in this particular case viewed less as nature and more as society—simply needed to be reorganized in such a way that self realization would follow. But this self realization I could not yet see as existing within a *conjunctio oppositorum*.

So again I found myself asking whether it was the good society that would automatically, or with some effort, produce the good men who would then perpetuate it; or whether it was hopeless to think that presently existing man could create the good society and live the good life in it, because his very nature would interfere with and finally destroy it. If the first were true, then at all cost, even at the cost of great suffering to generations, the good society had to be created, because it alone would automatically breed the good man. This was the promise which, in the early years after the first war, communism seemed to hold out. But Russia, it was apparent by the twenties, was not creating the society that would guarantee full self realization to man. Social democracy was the next best bet and I joined, but with hesitation and misgivings. It was clear enough that it was not going to create a better society until its ranks and leadership were first peopled by better men.

If, on the other hand, only the good man could create the good society, then the problem was how to change existing man so that he would become the good man who would then, in his image, create and perpetuate the good society. Of all the known ways of influencing people, psychoanalysis seemed to hold out most promise for a radical change for the better among existing men. By that time some of my friends had undergone psychoanalysis to become analysts; persons who were psychoanalyzed without wishing to become (and becoming) analysts were hardly to be found among my friends at that time; the vogue of analysis among young intellectuals barely started before the early thirties. The personality changes I could observe in them did not seem to encourage the notion that it was apt to create the good man who then would create the good society. But this could be, and always was, ascribed to the fact that these people had simply been too sick to begin with to show the full benefit of their psychoanalysis.

The promise of psychoanalysis

In the end it was psychoanalysis that I turned to more hopefully than to political reform. Nor was it only disappointment in the chances for the good society creating the

fully untrammeled man that decided me. I entered psychoanalysis partly for personal reasons, and partly to find solutions to problems that bothered me, some of which I have
just sketched. I did not start out intending to practice the
profession, though I hoped to derive from it, besides personal benefit, a deeper comprehension of the theoretical,
social, philosophical, and aesthetic problems that I wished
to understand, problems that in my youthful arrogance I
was probably sure I would be able to solve with the help of
psychoanalysis.

It took several years of intensive analysis, and many more
years of its practice, to teach me how far psychological experiences can change the personality of a man living in
a particular society, and where its influence stops. The
lessons of Hitler, the concentration camp, and then the immigration and adjustment to the New World, were required
for learning to what degree society can, and to what degree
it cannot, change the personality and life pattern of the
individual. These lessons were finally taught me some twenty
years ago. But it took another fifteen or twenty years to
understand what was implied in those lessons.

First, I realized that however much psychoanalysis can
help the adult with his personal difficulties, it is not apt to
change him enough to assure the good life. To achieve this
for the vast majority, and not just the few who at all times
managed to gain it through deep personal struggle, called
for reform of the entire education of man and of society.
Not only infant rearing and formal education, but most experiences of the young had to be different to achieve the
good life for the many and not just the all too few. But
before one could advocate reform, one had first to understand what present methods of child rearing did to the child,
how they conditioned his later life in society, and thus society
itself. Certainly in my case, the pendulum had to swing back
and forth many times between the two assumptions (that

society, or that the child, is father to the man) before I could emotionally accept what I had realized intellectually years before: that what counts, or what constitutes the good life, under normal conditions, is living a subtle balance between individual aspiration, society's rightful demands, and man's nature; and that an absolute submission to any one of them will never do.

The next lesson I needed to learn had to do with man's nature and society's impact on it. Here I am approaching the essence of my life's work, which centers on the application of psychoanalysis to social problems, and to the bringing up of children in particular.

That psychoanalysis was not all it possibly could be, and that its theory and practice needed improvement had come to my awareness through observing what it did and did not do for two autistic children whom I lived with for several years, as part of their treatment. Trying to understand what happened to them, and also how and why living conditions had to be modified over and above their daily psychoanalysis to achieve any improvement, led to an obvious conclusion. For very disturbed persons the impact of classical psychoanalysis is not enough to promote the necessary personality changes; the impact of psychoanalysis itself, or of a life organized on its basis, had to be in effect all the time, not just one hour of the day—or so it seemed at the time. This effort was made with the two youngsters, but with limited success. Still, that was as far as I had gone at the time. I did not then recognize that what they needed most was to live in a human environment that was not yet existent, and which had therefore to be specially designed for the purpose. It had to be an environment that offered meaningful human relations, satisfying living conditions and significant goals, not simply an application of psychoanalysis to the life they already knew.

Some further reservations about psychoanalysis came from closer to home. About a decade before Hitler's occupation of Austria brought radical changes in my external life, I realized vaguely that I was approaching or living in an inner crisis in my personal life, though socially and professionally all appeared well ordered and successful. Relatively late in life I was living in what Erikson named and described decades later as a psycho-social moratorium. It was this condition that neither years of analysis nor the several years that followed it had resolved.

All the same, up to the time I was imprisoned, I did not doubt the merit of psychoanalysis in general, and of my own in particular. I was convinced it had done as much for me as it could, and that no more was possible; so I had settled down, more or less uneasily, to live the way I then was, and I tried to like it.

This is no reflection on either my analysis or my analyst, since both did much for me. Among many other things I owe it to them that I can understand, live with, and help the most withdrawn, deteriorated or psychotic children, and organize for them the particular social and human environment they need for achieving their human potentialities.

The impact of the concentration camp on the other hand, within a few weeks, did for me what years of a useful and quite successful analysis had not done. (I realize that with this admission I lay myself, and my analyst, open to the criticism that my analysis provided me with insight, but did not lead to working through. Perhaps it is to the credit of my analysis that the prospect does not trouble me.)

New viewpoints

Through my own analysis, the study of psychoanalytic literature, and the application of such theories to practice, I was still searching for an understanding of the "true" nature of man. Though I was no longer convinced that psycho-analysis as a therapy would produce the "good" man, I still thought it the best way to effect significant changes in personality.

In respect to these, as to so many others of my ideas, my year in the German concentration camps of Dachau and Buchenwald in 1938-39 came as a great shock. It was to teach me much; so much, that I am not at all sure I have even now exhausted what was implied in that learning experience. Since a psycho-social study of the concentration camp forms a good portion of this book, I need not repeat here what those experiences were. How largely my work has been influenced by realizations still being derived from the experience may be seen, for example, from my paper on schizophrenia as a reaction to extreme situations.[2] What were these realizations, and how did I come to make them?

When I speak here about what I learned in the concentration camps, it must be viewed in the context of that experience. The extreme deprivation and fear for life that the camps imposed on all prisoners, particularly Jewish inmates, did not make for clear thinking. But maybe what was lacking in reasoning power was made up for by the deep feeling impressions one receives in an extreme situation. Such impressions engrave themselves permanently on the mind and can lead—when not repressed—to a re-evaluation of all values, even if the mind is unable to sort them all out at the time, or to understand their far-reaching implications.

While in the camp, I was little concerned with whether psychoanalytic theory was adequate, and only with the problem of how to survive in ways that would protect both my physical and moral existence. Therefore, what struck me

[2] *American Journal of Orthopsychiatry*, 26, 1956, pp. 507-518.

first was probably more urgent and more shocking in terms of my immediate needs and expectations. It was the realization that those persons who, according to psychoanalytic theory as I understood it then, should have stood up best under the rigor of the camp experience, were often very poor examples of human behavior under extreme stress. Others who, according to the same body of theory and the expectations based on it, should have done poorly, presented shining examples of human courage and dignity. I also saw fast changes taking place, and not only in behavior but personality too; incredibly faster and often much more radical changes than any that were possible by psychoanalytic treatment. Given the conditions of the camp, these changes were more often for the worse, but sometimes definitely for the better. So one and the same environment could bring about radical changes both for better and worse.

I could no longer doubt that environment can and does account for important aspects of man's behavior and personality. This, in a way, was a throwback to earlier, pre-psychoanalytic convictions that only the good society could create the good man, though in reverse form; because I saw before my eyes how a bad environment so obviously evoked evil in men. But the same bad social conditions also brought into the open, perhaps even evoked new meritorious qualities in some who never evinced them before. If one and the same society, in this case the world of the concentration camps, could create deep reaching changes in man, then it seemed that society accounted for personality; but since it produced wide varieties, and sometimes radically opposite personality changes and types of behavior, then it stood to reason that it was man who was the decisive factor in what he is and will be like within it, irrespective of society. And psychoanalysis by no means assured that a man would become a better or worse person under the impact of a better or worse society.

Such realizations were not easy for me, but I had to
arrive at them quickly if I wished to survive, and in ways
I could approve of. The psychoanalytic notions by which I
had tried to guide my life had fooled me in this respect,
fooled me radically. They failed at the moment when I
needed them most. So new viewpoints were needed. Most
important of all was to arrive at a clear conception of what
could be given to the environment without compromising
the inner self. Some prisoners tried to give the environment
all; most of them were either quickly destroyed or became
successful inmates, "old prisoners." Others tried to maintain
their old selves unchanged; but while they had a lot better
chance to survive as persons, their solution was not flexible.
Most of them were not up to living in an extreme situation and if not freed soon, they did not survive.

This realization of the tremendous impact of the environment did not come as easy as it came soon. I was imprisoned
in the camps at about the time when my convictions derived
from psychoanalysis were at their height: that the personality shaping influence of the immediate family is all
important, and that society in the broader sense is relatively
negligible by comparison. I also believed firmly that nothing
compared with psychoanalysis when it came to freeing the
individual and guiding him toward higher integration.

My experience in the camps taught me, almost within
days, that I had gone much too far in believing that only
changes in man could create changes in society. I had to
accept that the environment could, as it were, turn personality upside down, and not just in the small child, but in
the mature adult too. If I wanted to keep it from happening
to me, I had to accept this potentiality of the environment,
to decide where and where not to adjust, and how far. Psychoanalysis, as I understood it, was of no help in this all
important decision.

Most surprising of all, psychoanalysis which I had come

to view as the best key to all human problems offered no suggestions or help toward the solution of how to survive and survive halfway decently in the camps. For that I had to fall back on qualities that in my psychoanalytic experience and thinking were of little importance, if not of negative valence, while those qualities I had learned to stress were often as much of a hindrance as a help.

Certainly psychoanalytic theory and experience helped me to understand the problems I was up against: unintegrated, asocial tendencies are always present in man; under certain circumstances the inhibitions controlling them break down and they appear openly, unrestrained; having to be in the concentration camp leads to a breakdown of these inhibiting forces; if different persons react differently, if the inhibitions of some stand up while those of others fail, if some even strengthen their defenses against behaving asocially, it can all be ascribed to their different life histories or personality make-up.

Such explanations—and I could and did apply much more subtle applications of psychoanalytic reasoning to the problem—could shed light on what happened to some individuals. But my central problem was not whether or not psychoanalysis could explain things, but whether and how well these explanations could help me and others to survive as human beings under extreme conditions. Experience with both analyzed and unanalyzed persons in the camps was convincing demonstration that when the chips were down, it was utterly unimportant why a person acted the way he did; the only thing that counted was how he acted. While psychoanalysis could explain the why best, the environment was more effective in conditioning the actions of some—but not of all.

Only dimly at first, but with ever greater clarity, did I also come to see that soon how a man acts can alter what he is. Those who stood up well in the camps became better men, those who acted badly soon became bad men; and this, or at least so it seemed, independent of their past life history and their former personality make-up, or at least those aspects of personality that seemed significant in psychoanalytic thinking.

It just would not do under conditions prevailing in the camps to view courageous, life endangering actions as an outgrowth of the death instinct, aggression turned against the self, testing the indestructibility of the body, megalomanic denial of danger, histrionic feeding of one's narcissism or whatever other category the action would have to be viewed from in psychoanalysis. These and many other interpretations have validity in terms of depth psychology or the psychology of the unconscious, and they certainly did apply. Only viewing courageous behavior by a prisoner within the spectrum of depth analysis seemed ludicrously beside the point. So while psychoanalysis lost nothing as far as it went, it went unexpectedly, and in terms of my expectations, shockingly short of the mark.

The way a person acted in a showdown could not be deduced from his inner, hidden motives which, likely as not, were conflicting. Neither his heroic nor his cowardly dreams, his free associations or conscious fantasies permitted correct predictions as to whether, in the next moment, he would risk his life to protect the life of others, or out of panic betray many in a vain effort to gain some advantage for himself.

As long as the actions of others did not directly endanger my life and were mostly of theoretical interest to me, I could indulge in viewing their unconscious processes as equal in importance to their overt behavior, if not more so. As long as my own life was running its well ordered course, I could indulge myself by believing that the working of my unconscious mind was, if not my "true" self, certainly my "deeper" self. But when at one moment my own life, at the next moment that of others, depended on my actions, then I concluded that my actions were much more my "true" self than my unconscious or preconscious motives. Since these actions, my own and those of others, so often ran counter to what could be deduced from the working of the unconscious mind, I could no longer accept that what is uncovered by means of depth psychology is what constitutes the "true" nature of man. What goes on in his unconscious is certainly true of man, it is part of him and his life, but it is not the "true" man.

Again, it is simple to state and accept that only id, ego, and superego in their entirety form man; that only unconscious thoughts and overt behavior in their totality are man. But the issue is not whether or which of these aspects exist, but which of them need to be most considered and in what combination, in order to live the good life, to create the good society; in order to adapt the environment, the educational procedures, so that justice is done to a correct balance.

What, then, were the lessons I learned from my experience in the concentration camps?

Firstly: psychoanalysis is by no means the most effective way to *change* personality. Being placed in a particular type of environment can produce much more radical changes, and in a much shorter time.[3]

Secondly: the then existing psychoanalytic theory was inadequate to *explain* fully what happened to the prisoners; it gave little guidance for understanding what makes for the "good" life, the "good" man. Applied within the appropriate frame of reference it clarified much. Outside of its

---

[3] A later consequence of this realization was the use of milieu therapy; that is, the creation of a purposefully designed total environment, apt to help in achieving radical personality changes in persons who could not be reached by psychoanalysis.

particular frame of reference, or applied to phenomena outside its province, it distorted their meaning instead of clarifying them.

While it told much about the "hidden" in man, it told much less about the "true" man. To use one example: it became obvious that the ego was by no means just a weak servant of the id or the superego. Some men revealed astonishing ego strength that seemed derived from neither id nor superego.

All this is by now common knowledge, ever since Hartmann developed the concept of ego autonomy and later, together with Kris, stipulated the existence of neutralized (ego) energy. These theoretical formulations, carried further by Erikson and Rapaport, were not available when I was experiencing life in the camps and what it did to the prisoners' personalities. My original paper on behavior in extreme situations I had couched (or felt I had to) in the then available psychoanalytic concepts that could not do justice to my topic. Both the data and their interpretation transcended the theoretical framework I tried to force them into.

Not to give an erroneous picture, I want to stress that this goes mainly for psychoanalytic theory and the views on personality that derive from it. Psychoanalysis is really at least three different things: a method of observation, a therapy, and a body of theories on human behavior and personality structure. They are valid in descending order, the theory of personality being the weakest link of the system, quite in need of revision.[4] But there was this first aspect of psychoanalysis, as a way of observing, that more than proved its value and was most helpful to me. It gave me a deeper understanding of what may have gone on in the unconscious of prisoners and guards, an understanding

---

[4] See my *Symbolic Wounds*, Glencoe, Illinois: The Free Press, 1954, pp. 69 ff.

that on occasion may have saved my life, and on other occasions let me be of help to some of my fellow prisoners, where it counted.

So my camp experience also taught me two seemingly contrary lessons: firstly, the deficiency of psychoanalytic theory when applied outside the framework of its practice; and its shortcomings in certain practical applications to which it is not germane, such as what constitutes a well integrated personality. Secondly, the great value of the practical applications of psychoanalysis where it is germane, such as learning to understand, by observation, the unconscious motives of human behavior (apart from which behavior is preferable, or which personality more adequate).

Perhaps another example may be best here. According to psychoanalytic convictions then current, the test of the well functioning, well integrated personality, the goal of psychoanalysis, was the ability to form freely intimate relations, "to love," to be in ready contact with the forces of the unconscious, and to sublimate in "work." Aloofness from other persons and emotional distance from the world were viewed as weakness of character. My comments in Chapter 5 on the admirable way in which a group of what I call "anointed persons" behaved in the concentration camps suggest how struck I was with these very aloof persons. They were very much out of contact with their unconscious but nevertheless retained their old personality structure, stuck to their values in the face of extreme hardships, and as persons were hardly touched by the camp experience.

Similar behavior characterized another group which, according to psychoanalytic theory, would have had to be viewed as extremely neurotic or plainly delusional, and therefore apt to fall apart, as persons, under stress. I refer to the Jehovah's Witnesses, who not only showed unusual heights of human dignity and moral behavior, but seemed protected against the same camp experience that soon destroyed persons considered very well integrated by my psychoanalytic friends and myself.

Much later and in an entirely different (or perhaps not so different) context, came some parallel events that were more widely recognized. I refer to the study of persons raised in communal children's houses in the socialist Kibbutzim of Israel. Many of them knew childhood experiences which, according to psychoanalytic theory, should have produced very unstable personalities. They too were aloof and somewhat unrelated, at least in the psychoanalytic sense. Psychoanalysts viewed them as very neurotic. But they were also persons who withstood incredible hardships without any disintegration during the war for liberation, and again in the short campaign against Egypt; not to speak of the hardships of continuous living in the border settlements subject to Arab infiltration. These very persons who, according to existing psychoanalytic theory, should have had weak personalities apt to readily disintegrate, turned out to be heroic leaders, mainly because of the strength of their character.[5]

Pictures out of context

The question then became why psychoanalysis, which in so many ways had proved its value for understanding man and modifying his personality, proved so disappointing in other respects. Why was it not the key to understanding the "true" nature of man, when it revealed so much more about him than any other method we knew? Why, when it could achieve personality changes that relieved some persons of distress and enabled them to lead a richer life, as it had

---

[5] I do not wish to suggest that aloofness or keeping one's emotional distance are desirable human characteristics, nor that rigidity makes for the good life. I only wish to suggest that the psychoanalytic theory of personality is deficient in suggesting what makes for a "desirable," well integrated personality; and this because it overstresses the importance of the inner life to the neglect of the total man as he deals with his human and social environment.

done for me, did it not gain for others the integration that would enable them to stand up well in extreme situations?

It took me a long time to understand the reasons for this. One of them is that despite its great propensity for resolving inner conflicts, and its great value as a tool for penetrating surface behavior and understanding some of the innermost recesses of the mind, the practice of psychoanalytic therapy, as conceived by Freud and practiced by his followers, is basically no more than a powerfully conditioning social situation; as such it can elucidate only some and not all aspects of the human mind, can modify some but not all aspects of personality, and cannot fail to impose limitations both on patients, practitioners and theory.

Psychoanalytic therapy then is essentially a very special environment with its unique consequences. It is not Archimedes' point outside the world of social phenomena; it cannot serve as the fulcrum for a lever that will lift man out of his social environment and give us his "true" picture. To be in the psychoanalytic situation is tantamount to having exchanged one's usual environment for a very special one. Therefore to study man's reactions in this particular environment can lead only to such attitudes and discoveries as are germane to it. One could easily arrive at erroneous opinions if findings made in the psychoanalytic setting were applied outside the context of that particular environment without being modified.

Let me give a short and oversimplified example. We will assume that two students want to try to understand society, man and his nature. The first decides to do it by studying a group of scientists and observing them only during their research activities. Likely as not he will find each of them (and man) devoted to his social tasks, giving all he has unselfishly, unquestioningly, and without any reluctance or misgivings in order to achieve his self chosen goal, namely furthering the interests of society.

Now our second student, quite the contrary, decides to arrive at an understanding of the scientists, and thus of man, by observing the same people only during the fifty minutes when they congregate after work in a bar across the street. There they have a few drinks together, too fatigued by their efforts to leave directly for home. Aggravated either by small setbacks met in furthering their research goals, or with each other, their director, or their wives, they let loose. This is their time for letting off the steam that piles up during many hours of hard work. It is the period of total relaxation. They even incite each other, boys among boys for these few minutes, to talk wholly irresponsibly about their work, themselves, their wives, and each other.

Let us further assume that each one of them knows quite well this is an "as if" situation, without any bearing on the work reality. Trying to overcompensate for the strain they have put themselves under voluntarily, they may go so far as to say that their work does not make any sense, knowing well that it forms part of the essence of their lives. Boastfully they may declare they are only in it for the money they can make, or to get even with their wives. They may proclaim how much they hate the slavery of work, some of their co-workers, or what not else.

Now let us further assume that our second observer, for one reason or another, arrives at the conclusion that in listening to such conversation at the bar, he has discovered not the correlate to hard work, but the "true" motivation of these men, their real nature. He will then conclude that all the hard and useful work they do during the day is nothing but a clever screen for their "real" desires, a cover-up for the true nature of their selves. Such an observer may soon come to view the things that form impediments to the men's work (petty gripes and jealousies, frustrated hopes) as the true or only motivation for the many hours they spend in working toward important goals.

Obviously both observers have seen important, though different aspects of man in society. Neither view is untrue, but neither does the one or the other give a "true" image of man. The true man consists of a combination, in reality an integration of both pictures. He is the same man, only in the first case at work, in the second at the bar after a few drinks.

During psychoanalysis, the patient deals mostly, of course, with what disturbs his successful living. This is so because the patient does not go to an analyst to give a total account of his life, but to get help with particular difficulties. Were he to engage in long reveries about all the things that were and are good in his life, the analyst would sooner or later have to point out that while this is all very fine, he hardly needs help with them; so why waste scarce and expensive time on things that are all right anyway. It then might appear that talking about the positive aspects of one's life was a device to avoid thinking about the unpleasant ones, or because of a need not to seem ungrateful to those who provided good experiences, etc. This might be construed as suggesting that good experiences are less important, or only a pretext in life. Actually they are very real and very important in life, however much of a pretext in psychoanalysis.

The healed man and the healthy man

Returning to my concentration camp experience, psychoanalysis had helped me to understand some of the more hidden motives of prisoners and guards, even to understand why prisoners' personalities broke, and why they broke in certain ways. Strangely enough, and to my sharp disappointment, it did not help me in any specific ways to protect myself from that danger, nor to understand why those who stood up well under the experience were able to do so. Re-examining psychoanalysis in this light, it becomes apparent why, and to what degree, it has investigated destructive influences, and why and how it has not done the same for the constructive. The single important exception is the constructive influence of psychoanalysis itself.

Without any deliberate intention by psychoanalysts, and often contrary to their stated beliefs, the emphasis of nearly all investigations is on what went wrong in people's lives, and what can be done to correct the mishaps. Since psychoanalysis deals with these problems mainly or only, this is entirely legitimate. But it does not then offer a theory of personality giving positive guidance toward the good life. At the same time, it is more and more being pressed into service as a guide in life, both directly and indirectly, since it now provides theoretical structures for many of the behavioral sciences.

Psychoanalysts would be among the first to say that the import of their theories and practices now goes well beyond the narrow field of psychotherapy; they are well aware of its importance in sociology, education, aesthetics, life. But when psychoanalysis is thus applied outside the limits of psychotherapy, then serious hazards may appear if its original point of departure, and its continual emphasis on the morbid, the pathological, are not tempered by equally careful attention to the healthy, the normal, the positive. Through such concentration on the bad and its correction, one could easily arrive at a theory according to which overcoming the morbid, rather than its absence, becomes the norm of the healthy personality.

In this neglect of the positive lies still another danger. We could come to believe that for all men, as for patients in psychotherapy, the goal of self-realization, of individuation, is achieved by ridding man of what ails him, or failing that, by compensating for gross pathology through great intellectual or artistic achievement, like Beethoven. While lasting works of art may thus be created, those persons closest to the artist may be destroyed in the process.

To prefer compensation for pathology to the normal (similar to the religious attitude that heaven rejoices more in a repenting sinner than a good man) is a dangerous moral position both in psychotherapy and society. It emphasizes the tragic and spectacular and slights the salt of the earth—what makes for common happiness and the good life—namely, living a sane and relatively happy life with one's family and friends. It is a philosophy which, by centering its interest on the destructive instincts, by being fascinated with pathology, ends up (without really wishing to) by neglecting life. The nonspectacular man living a good life may not create works of art or be plagued by deep neurosis or compensate for his emotional turmoil by great intellectual or artistic achievement; but neither will he destroy his nephew or make life miserable for his brother for want of a family.[6] Instead he will try simply to make a good life for his own. But if pathology is the frame of reference for all human action, then such a life may seem devoid of achievement or value.

Freud was well aware of all this; witness his insistence that there is no psychoanalytic *Weltanschauung,* and his silence, by and large, on what constitutes the normal personality or how children should be brought up to achieve it. But since psychoanalysis is the most valid body of theories we have on human behavior and personality, it is made to serve a job for which it is still only partially equipped.

Taking undue advantage of some remarks Freud made in passing, he believed that the signs of the healthy personality are the ability to love and to work. But though he developed a superb theory of the libido (sex, aggression) he left us too small a theoretical frame of reference for understanding the nature and importance of lasting human attachments, and of work, within his system.

---

[6] See R. and E. Sterba, *Beethoven's Nephew,* New York: Pantheon Books, 1954.

How inadequate psychoanalytic theory is for understanding the positive "work" forces in life shows up in the psychoanalytic literature on great men. Starting with Freud's study of Leonardo, many psychoanalytic studies of famous persons have appeared: those on Beethoven, Goethe, Swift, to mention only some of the most recent. In each one the emphasis is on the hero's pathology and how it influenced certain aspects of his work. All three emerge as near schizophrenic personalities; all three are convincing studies in psychopathology. But the real enigma is not the psychopathology, but the creative contributions.

These contributions are fully recognized; they are why their creators were studied in the first place. But as Freud had to state, his analysis of Leonardo's childhood experiences (and here it is irrelevant whether his data or their analysis were valid) sheds no light on the problem of why Leonardo became a great inventor and artist when the same experiences might have led to empty scribbling or purposeless gadgeteering in others; therefore, he felt, his analysis did not and could not shed light on why Leonardo was a genius. And so with the others who have written about Beethoven, Goethe and Swift. They present us with fascinating sidelights on the lives of their heroes, but fail to make at all plainer why their work, that is, their positive contribution to mankind, took place.

Each of the three analyses only emphasizes again that psychoanalysis is the best method for uncovering and understanding the hidden man, but by no means an especially good tool for understanding man in his entirety; least of all for understanding what makes for "goodness" or "greatness" in him. The conclusion then seems warranted that while psychoanalysis can explain the psychological upheaval, the pathology that got something started, it is much less successful in explaining why and how, from such starts, positive developments take place.

Elsewhere[7] I have tried to show that the psychoanalytic interpretation of circumcision as symbolic castration takes into account only the pathological aspects of this ritual (mutilation of the genitals) without mention of its constructive aspects (magic manipulation of the genitals in order to bear children). Viewed only in a negative way, this rite is purely destructive of life. Viewed in its totality, it centers, quite the contrary, on fertility and new life. This raises the possibility that when men failed in their magical efforts to procreate as women do, they turned to creating the larger forms of society and to modifying the physical world. If all this were so, then to consider the "sexual" meaning of circumcision as its only or main significance would do extreme tort to its great "work" achievement.

Between insight and practice

The same danger prevails when things concern us more directly than the meaning of circumcision. Typically, when psychoanalysis deals with the bad results of certain childhood experiences, it tends to be concerned with mistakes made in bringing up children, rather than with positive values that derive from the very same type of education.

Thanks to psychoanalytic insight, for example, it is now easy to see how swaddling, or the cradle board, interferes with the infant's free motility and in this way curbs spontaneous development of his bodily movements. It is almost as simple to understand that while swaddling inhibits mobility, it also gives security, because the swaddled infant is not so apt to make a sudden move and fall off the bed or otherwise hurt himself.

It is much more difficult to fathom the radical consequences when new insights about freedom and restraint are put into practice. What happens, for example, when this very freedom we give our infants to crawl around in the

[7] *Symbolic Wounds.*

crib, play pen, or on the floor of our living rooms is unexpectedly and severely curbed in isolated but significant situations? This occurs typically when the infant is held down firmly for cleaning or diapering, and later when he is suddenly confined in the high chair at feeding time. Such sudden change from a great freedom to move about to utter restraint asks for a very complex adjustment to the environment. The infant must achieve both an inner permission to move about freely and an inner inhibition of random movements. This is a much more complicated lesson than accepting, once and for all, that movement is restricted, as it is for the infant in swaddling clothes.

Thus modern infant rearing practices do not pose a simple dichotomy between motility-and-insecurity versus immobility-and-security. According to theories derived from psychoanalysis, life is supposedly easier and pleasanter for infants when restraint is removed. In reality what the infant gets, along with the new freedom, is the need to adjust to opposite types of behavior and an opposite set of inner commands. And this, likely as not, when he is much too young to master such complicated shifts in behavior and hence to succeed in personality development. It is premature for two reasons: first, because it expects the infant to make subtle distinctions so soon; and second, because the parent must appear too early in contradictory attitudes, when a uniform picture of him might still be needed for deeper security, or stronger identification.

But even this is not all. The infant does not simply have to learn that in one situation he has great freedom of movement (when he crawls most of the day) and in another no freedom to move (when he is cleaned and when he eats). He must also learn that this sudden and radical interference with freedom takes place around two of the most important bodily functions his life depends on, namely intake and elimination. The net result is that the small child is teased with the promise and some practice of freedom, as symbolized by motility in relatively unimportant situations. Then his freedom is more effectively dashed where it counts most, in the essential interactions with his parents around important physiological processes.

Though I have elaborated this example I have not dealt at all fully with the problems posed by just this one type of impact by the environment on the child. All I wanted to show was how very complex are the issues that arise if we try to apply insights derived from psychoanalysis (here, the patient's discomfort at parental interference with his bodily freedom) to everyday life situations.

The really practical problem is to find out which and how many restrictions can be reduced, or how one life situation or another must be changed to permit the removal of inhibitions with safety. Or to put it differently, how should the great contributions of psychoanalysis best be put into practice.

Struggling with theory

Both that problem and my extended example belong to the particular set of life activities that interest me most, namely, the rearing of children in general, and education in particular. I met and settled on both of them, more or less by chance. First I encountered the two autistic children mentioned earlier. Living with them forced me to rethink psychoanalysis so that it could be used for creating a milieu that was totally therapeutic and still a real life setting.

Later I began to work at the Sonia Shankman Orthogenic School of the University of Chicago with the easy assumption that what kept child psychoanalysis from taking full effect was children's living with their parents.[8] But soon

---

[8] I simply disregarded the fact that the two autistic children with whom I had lived for years were not living with their parents and that child analysis even within a benign environment that met their instinctual needs was not enough to rehabilitate them.

it became apparent that though the children at the Orthogenic School were now away from their parents, they did not improve enough. And this though they now lived under conditions that not only did not interfere with psychoanalytic efforts, but supported them strongly. The living situation was not only as benign as human efforts could make it, but also derived from what we then considered the best child rearing practices, based directly on psychoanalytic theory and practice.

As a matter of fact, some children even deteriorated, while others made even less use of their psychoanalysis than before placement because the comfort they now lived in removed much of their incentive to change. Several simply dropped their analysis because they felt they had gained all they wanted, namely, placement in a seemingly "ideal" environment. And this would have been all right, too, had they improved in personal integration or effective living. But this they did not do, or only inadequately.

Only then did I realize that my initial efforts to create a total treatment setting based on "love" and on appropriate considerations of the unconscious, of the life and death instincts, of sex and aggression, were erroneous. I had to learn once again that love is not enough; that the good life can be achieved for individual and society only if, in addition to "love," it is also based on the constructive, healing, personality building (not just "ego" building) propensities of work.

Prior to this, my efforts to understand the concentration camp experience through classical psychoanalysis had broken down and only then was I willing to accept the need for revising that frame of reference. Similarly, my efforts to create a total psychoanalytic treatment institution based on classical psychoanalytic premises proved wanting, and only then did I fully apply what I had learned in the camps to this so different situation and problem.

In a strange way the two situations forcing new lessons on me, a reluctant learner, were related though diametrically opposed. In the first of my two great efforts to apply psychoanalysis outside its frame of reference, my goal was to prevent, to mitigate, slow down, in short to counteract the personality disintegration forced on the person by the environment. The goal of my second attempt is the building up of disintegrated personality through the impact of the environment.

The awkward way in which I first expressed some of my ideas on these and related matters came from trying to stay within the framework of psychoanalytic models, though they proved less and less suitable for the purpose. My own development in psychoanalysis had been guided by these models and I had gained so much from it, that personal experience, loyalty and gratitude to those, most of all to Freud, who had opened new possibilities of thinking and feeling, all combined to suggest first that these were the only models for expressing my thoughts adequately and later, that they should not be lightly discarded.[9]

By that time, others proceeding from different observations and experiences had also grown dissatisfied with existing psychoanalytic theories. The first to suggest important revision based on theoretical considerations and practical experience was Hartmann. The first comprehensive revision

---

[9] How difficult it was for me to give up these models may be seen from the fact that in two books on the work of the Orthogenic School, *Love Is Not Enough* and *Truants from Life,* though my purpose was to recount a radical venture away from the practice of psychoanalysis, I tried as best I could to couch them in the theoretical language of psychoanalysis.

My own breaking away from these theoretical models came only with the writing of *Symbolic Wounds.* There I tried to show that the observation of facts, based on exactly that consideration of motives which psychoanalysis has made possible, convinced me that in many instances prevailing psychoanalytic theories do not fit the facts they are supposed to explain, and that therefore a considerable revision of this body of theories is required.

of the pertinent theories, in ways that fit my own experiences better than anything published up to then, was Erikson's *Childhood and Society*. To them and many others I owe important thoughts expressed in this book and elsewhere, an indebtedness I gladly acknowledge. Of course, so many have influenced my work and thinking that I cannot even begin to enumerate them. I have long since expressed my intellectual discipleship to John Dewey. Here, too, I would have to repeat that many of my ideas and practices were formed thanks to many long and intimate conversations with Fritz Redl over the years; so much so that with the best of intentions I could not say which of my thoughts germinated in him and which in me. In my early years at the Orthogenic School, Emmy Sylvester provided many and always stimulating ideas.

Much, too, was clarified for me through my conversations with Ruth Marquis; most of my ideas took the final form in which they were committed to print thanks to her. She not only edited this book, as many other of my publications, but she helped me plan it, from the title down to the last entry of the index. But often the ideas themselves came out of efforts at teaching, mostly the staff of the Orthogenic School and my students at the University. I am grateful for the stimulation they provide and the pleasure that teaching them gives me.

All these are influences I am distinctly aware of. Beyond that I would be at a loss how to continue. I am what I am and I do what I do because of what I have learned from many people, some alive and others long dead. But above all it remains the Orthogenic School staff and the children who continuously force me to reexamine the theoretical models I use. Many of them were found wanting in the very process of using them to explain difficult points to my staff or students, or in trying to apply them toward shaping the institution. It was often on such occasions that it hit me, with the shock of recognition, that the theory did not fit the case; that a different and better one had to be worked out either to convey to others what I felt they should understand, or to make the School a better institution.

Given my interest in a better society and a better life in it, I could not rest with exploring the validity of theoretical models just within the microcosm of the School. I always had to ask if they would also stand up when applied to society at large. For me, the societal area that appealed most as a testing ground was the one I am most familiar with: the education of the young, both in and out of school. But as the reader can see, I sometimes went beyond this to speak of certain aspects of society in general.

However much I may be deviating from classical psychoanalysis, the deviations seem small in my mind, compared to the vast intellectual debt I owe it. Most of my deviations came from dissatisfaction with the critical, perhaps even negative bent that has entered psychoanalytic theory from its practice or practitioners, with their too scant attention to the positive powers of life and to how much they predominate over the crippling influence of neuroses.

Still I shall probably always, to some degree, remain under the spell of the psychoanalytic models, which overstress the suffering man experiences when society puts curbs on his natural aspirations, while neglecting, by comparison, the incredibly greater benefits he derives from society. Despite my reaching for models that avoid this error, I may still be short of the mark. To reach firm middle ground between a somewhat jaundiced pessimism and a too naive optimism is difficult, perhaps because theoretical models tend to do more justice to the one or the other, and in any case do more justice to extremes. The conjunction of opposites, and the absence of certainty, are not comfortable or firm bases for building theoretical models.

What I do try to show is that with any further progress,

the balance becomes more and more subtle and harder to achieve. The example of the swaddled infant shows that the balance between security and freedom gets more complex when new freedom in some areas is balanced by restriction in others. In general, I think that the difficulties we are witnessing, the ones that create the discomforts of civilization, the anxiety of our time and age, all pivot on the present character of change. We are having to shift from tradition, that is from a security based on a repetition of sameness, to a much less certain security that can only be based on efforts to live the good life without any ability to predict the outcome of our actions in an ever changing context. But with change a persistent condition of life now, this seems to be the only security we can have in our modern technological society.

This problem I have tried to examine in later chapters. Here I would like to add that the problems of modern mass society and fast technological change, of which the concentration camp was only one outgrowth, threw into relief for me why psychoanalysis alone cannot account for all pertinent phenomena, and why its premises must be reshaped more dynamically than they were when originally conceived.

Relevance of the environment

By and large, it is still the work of Freud and the early analysts that psychoanalysis remains based on, and from which it derives its theoretical framework. These men and women dealt with patients in a society that appeared very stable and only in slow evolution. What evolution there was seemed only to bring to fruition what was already there and had long been accepted by the patient. No radical changes in society, morals, style of life, were expected, held possible, or desirable.

To all this I have already alluded when I spoke of the world of my parents. In any case, the world of Freud's early patients changed so slowly, and what changes there were had so little effects or only benign and supporting ones, that the social matrix of life for the individual could be called a constant. Witness, for example, the advice that the patient in analysis should not make any far reaching decisions about his external life until the analysis was over. This reflects both a disregard for the importance of the external life, as well as a conviction that it would be exactly the same after years of analysis and that changes would be just as easy to make then as earlier. I need hardly comment on the pattern of life nowadays which alters so fast that it might be hard for a patient to freeze his external life for three, five, or more years, unless his life is already in a decline, or devoid of the challenge to make decisions.[10]

If society, and the adjustment required to live well in it changes slowly, organically, and according to what man can expect and prepare for, then for understanding personality dynamics this constant can be disregarded. All personality changes will then be due wholly to inner processes and will show up as if on a neutral screen.

This was my own assumption, too, only it was twice invalidated; the first time traumatically, the second benignly. The first was the sudden change to living in the concentration camp, the second to living in the New World. Coordinating, or trying to coordinate, how these radical changes

---

[10] Several biographers of Freud have remarked on his reluctance to leave Vienna, although he claimed to be deeply dissatisfied with living there. I have disputed his stated dissatisfaction with living in Vienna, and showed why it is subject to doubt. (See the review of E. Jones' *The Life and Work of Sigmund Freud* in *Am. J. Sociology*, 62, 1957, p. 419.) Here I would like to add that by not stepping out of the confines of that world and culture until almost the end, Freud long remained shielded from the realization of what far reaching changes can be brought about in a person when he moves from one environment to another, a realization that might have led him to consider the influence of the environment on the person as neither negligible nor constant.

in social environment and in my personality were related to each other led me to the conviction that neither is society as irrelevant for understanding personality dynamics as psychoanalysis suggested, nor is personality development as rooted in biology and early life experiences, or as independent of the current environment, as was assumed.

If, on the other hand, society can have such far reaching influence on personality, then its influence must be better understood. More important, man must be better protected, through education or otherwise, against its potentially destructive influence. He must be better equipped to change society so that it will not be an obstacle to living the good life, but a setting that facilitates and encourages it. In short, man must do both: live the good life in society, and create anew in each generation the good society for himself and all others.

It seems to me, then, that we should never again be satisfied to see personality change as proceeding independent from the social context. While the irrelevance of environment may still hold for some, it certainly does not hold for all any more, and it may hold less and less for the few if social changes follow more rapidly; witness recent developments in China and the radical changes it is claimed to have wrought in the Chinese personality which, more than others, once seemed frozen in traditional and permanent patterns.

What psychoanalysis has already achieved for the personality within a stable social context must now be done for personality and social context in their interaction, when both of them are changing.[11]

---

[11] There are, for example, very few psychoanalytic remarks dealing with the impact of the outbreak of war, of immigration, and so forth, on the patient. But it is true, and we have seen it again and again in our work at the School, that when staff members start out with the conviction that events happening within the social environment of the School or in the outside world have no influence on shaping the personality of the child, the child tends to fall in with the con-

Interplay

From here on, the rest is much easier to explain. Having started out with the conviction, derived from World War I and the postwar chaos, that society had to be changed first before man could live the good life, having then derived from my own psychoanalysis the conviction that only psychological work for and with man could assure the good life for the individual and with it the good life for society, I was projected into the concentration camp and the realization of how deeply the environment can influence the individual, while at the same time being unable to change certain aspects of his personality.

All this was further crystallized for me by emigration. After the concentration camp experience, the experience of leaving Europe and making my home in the United States raised the issue once again and forcefully: to which degree do living conditions and the adjustment to them change personality, and which aspects of the personality remain relatively untouched by such a radical change in environment. Here the issue was not so much the degree to which man can be manipulated by the environment. It was more a question of which areas of freedom he retains and does not adjust to, but instead manipulates the new environment according to

viction. But with each such experience the child becomes less flexible, less responsive to his environment, less trusting in his ability to observe and react; more withdrawn from reality, more beholden to his unconscious alone, and consequently less master of it. So too, the adult patient may be conditioned by his environment (the analytic situation) to become unresponsive to the external world, and respond only to his inner world. Just as the concentration camp had its good "old prisoners," psychoanalysis may have its perfectly adjusted practitioners and patients; perfectly adjusted to the world of psychoanalysis where reality counts for little, and the unconscious for all. This, under special conditions, may be justified by the requirements of psychoanalytic therapy. But it is circular reasoning to then assume that because the powerful impact of a particular environment (analysis) prevents other environmental influences from exercising deep influences, these other influences have (or should normally have) little or no impact on personality.

his needs, and to which degree does his frozenness prevent him from doing either.

Here again, watching those of my friends who shared this experience, and whom I could observe closely as I had watched fellow prisoners in the concentration camp, I came to realize that there is a wide spectrum of behavior. At one extreme, the individual holds on rigidly to values and attitudes that are no longer useful or germane to the environment; he does this simply because they were imprinted on him early in life. At the other extreme is a total adjustment to a new situation where the new environment is permitted to take over, as it were. Only rarely could I watch the subtle interplay between personality and environment with higher integration as a consequence.

Having several times experienced the destructive impact of societal conditions on my life, I was then fortunate in being able to take advantage of the healing influence of a new and freer environment in the United States. These experiences then, in a not always easy emotional and intellectual development, led to the conviction that as much as environment can destroy, it can heal; particularly when to the healing impact of the environment is added the healing impact of psychotherapy.

This conviction I tried to translate into practice by creating a setting in which the therapeutic impact of psychoanalytic treatment would be enhanced by an environment as conducive to living the good life as we could fashion within existing society. Little did I know, when I began the experiment, that these two could not simply be added to each other; that their addition led to its own contradictions with new problems and drawbacks. Having created the microcosm of the Orthogenic School[12] I had to realize that

---

[12] It goes without saying that this very special environment, the Orthogenic School, could be created and can be maintained only through the generous and understanding support of the University of Chicago, within the framework of which it exists, and through the devotion of its staff.

in some respects this world interfered with the success of psychoanalytic treatment. Hard as this was to accept, it was even harder to accept that psychoanalysis in its turn can have a harmful impact, even on an environment created partly in its image. I think only these last realizations led me to fully recognize how subtle the balance is between environment, personality, and psychotherapy.

Since then, the following problem has occupied me: to which degree can the environment influence and shape man, his life and his personality, and to which degree can it not; how and to which degree can environment be used to shape life and personality; and how must personality be developed so as to stand up in any environment or, if need be, to change environment for the better. These have remained the underlying concerns of my work and of this book, even if the connections seem vague at times.

In particular my task became and remained to learn more about how the findings of psychoanalysis could and should be freed from parallactic distortions—those coming directly or indirectly from the special analytic situation, and from an overemphasis of the unconscious that came with it. To do this we had to stop applying directly to real life situations those findings based on what happens in the analyst's treatment room, and to replace them by an understanding of man in real life where he is scrutinized as carefully, and with due consideration of the unconscious, as the patient on the couch. Nor could we stop with observations and the conclusions drawn from them; these had to lead to carefully planned changes in the environment, and after that we had to evaluate the changes all over again. Sometimes the reasoning that led to a change was supported in the practice, sometimes not, while most often what was indicated was some further revision in our thinking, planning, and actions.

So in a continuous process of learning and testing we devote ourselves to the practical question: what changes in the environment are needed to bring up children so that their chance to lead the good life is greater; and what methods of bringing up children are necessary to help them live the good life whatever their environment may be.

Since we have rehabilitated children at the School who were once thought of as hopeless by all concerned, and since some persons managed to retain their humanity in the German concentration camps even after ten years or more, these tasks, though difficult, do not seem more than man can do.

2
Imaginary Impasse

GIVEN THE GENIUS OF A GREAT ARTIST it is possible to recreate between the covers of a book that subtle interplay between environment and human being which is the substance of life, as of art. Since I am neither genius nor artist, I can only deal with them somewhat separately. Therefore in this chapter I shall try to look mainly at our environment—what it does to modern man and what we fear it does—and in the next chapter mainly at ourselves.

Certainly the fear that ours is an age of neurosis haunts modern man, and adds to his personal unhappiness. Feeling acutely the discomforts of our civilization he grows discontented with it and often overlooks the fact that each age and society has its typical conflicts, its typical forms of discomfort and hence of neurosis. Concerned as we are with the difficulties we encounter in our civilization, we worry about those of its features that make for anxiety and mental illness. But in a hunting society it is the hunter, much as he enjoys the hunt, who worries about falling prey himself, about being hunted down. That is the price he pays for living in a society based on hunting. The farmer has different fears to mar his life; he worries about sandstorms, drought and flood. Those are discomforts that go with an agricultural way of life.

Sometimes it seems that as society evolves, every step forward may reduce old discomforts but not all the old anxieties. At the same time, each new development seems to bring new anxieties to add on to old and still active ones. These new fears coming with each higher step in social growth seem to develop in a continuum from animate to inanimate to abstract. The hunter must be wary of human enemies and wild animals; the farmer adds the vagaries of climate to his fear of hostile creatures. All these together plague modern man, whose civilization aggravates the old fear of animate and inanimate dangers by compounding them with anxieties about abstract or symbolic issues like morals.

The modern mother still has the age old fears for her own survival and the physical well being of her child; but now, much as she enjoys motherhood, she is also haunted by the fear of being a failure as a mother. In brief, whatever forms the essence of our life's activity also tends to become its most pervasive fear. In the machine age man is afraid of being robbed of his humanity by his own handiwork, the machine; witness the social fear of the evils of mass society and the psychological anxiety about losing one's identity.

As early as a century ago, a poet voiced this anxiety when confronted with the new industrial age. Heine, on visiting England, remarked: "The perfection of machinery, which is applied to everything there, and has superseded so many human functions, has for me something dismal; this artificial life on wheels, bars, cylinders, and a thousand little hooks, pins, and teeth which move almost passionately, fills me with horror. I was annoyed no less by the definiteness, the precision, the strictness, in the life of the English; for just as the machines in England seem to have the perfection of men, so the men seemed like machines. Yes, wood, iron, and brass

seem to have usurped the human mind there, and to have
gone almost mad from fulness of mind, while the mindless
man, like a hollow ghost, exercises his ordinary duties in a
machine-like fashion."

I do not know what the ancient nomad felt as he watched
others settling down to agriculture in slow steps. Maybe he
could not have put into similar words his feelings of anxiety
as he watched those of his fellow men who gave up, for
greater economic ease and security, a relative freedom to
roam. But the modern Arab nomad certainly pities those
who gave up their condition of freedom to settle down to
the comforts that agriculture could give them. He feels that
the only truly human existence is to be free as the wind.
Strangely enough the desert wind, which is his symbol of
freedom, is also the curse of the nomad who can scarcely
protect himself against it. Still he is right; a certain bondage
comes with settling down, certain freedoms and satisfactions
have to be given up to win some comforts and a measure
of security.

However it may have been in other times, modern man
suffers from his inability to make a choice, as he sees it,
between renouncing freedom and individualism, or giving
up the material comforts of modern technology and the
security of a collective mass society. This, as I see it, is the
true conflict of our times.

Compared with this central conflict those individual
neuroses based on a denial of the problem are peripheral.
They are of minor importance, even though they plague
many people today. Such denial may take the form of asserting individuality at all cost, as the Bohemian does, or of
giving up all individuality in a wholly other directed adjustment—this "other," likely as not, being the requirements of
technology and a life geared to further it.

When confronted with this seeming impasse, instead of

examining to see if any new types of analysis, new techniques, new attitudes can resolve it, the Bohemian or the extremely other directed man has a tendency to deny that an impasse exists by his neurotic and essentially simple minded choice. Many who are less disturbed and less extreme try to escape it by rushing off in one single direction or an entirely different direction, in short by evasive maneuvers. Some of them, in psychoanalytic terms, are relying on repression, others are acting out or regressing, again others suffer from delusions.

Denying the problem

Alcoholism is a graphic example of how society showed one such irrational attitude in dealing with a social impasse. Faced with the predicament of alcoholism, the U.S. decided to legislate the whole problem out of existence. Like repression on an individual basis, this denial of the complexity of the problem, and the suppression based on it, not only failed to solve the problem, but had even less desirable results. The body politic, weakened by the repressive maneuver, was invaded by criminality, violence, and sometimes even worse forms of alcoholism. Although the prohibition law was abolished, we are still not quite rid of the after effects of this attempt at a nation-wide repression, since the crime syndicates are still with us.

This example falls far short of making a difficult point about the machine age. No one yet has seriously asked that we prohibit mechanical contrivances, although repression was suggested by imaginative authors such as Butler in *Erewhon*. More often there is just a tendency to deny that the problem exists. Or else, like the person suffering addiction, our society seems to be rushing ahead unthinking into an ever greater mechanization of life, expecting more extensive technology to solve the problems it creates. Here we operate like the alcoholic who tries to escape from his hangover by going on a new binge.

Another evasive maneuver, that of escape into primitivism, is symbolized by those men of the machine age who are so discontented that they look for comfort to simpler types of civilization. These, being centered on a different life activity, do not know the discontent of our machine-made culture. Captivated by this alone, they overlook the fact that earlier civilizations suffer, in their turn, from discontents inherent in their own mode of life.

For example, many intellectuals now look for comfort to what seem like the simple beliefs of their forefathers. In doing so, they may only acquire new fears about hell and damnation, without necessarily getting the emotional relief their forefathers got from revival meetings.

Nor will twentieth century man find a cozy home in an eighteenth century setting. If we are beset by the neurotic consequences of a toilet training based on the odium of dirt and smell, we will not find relief by living in the stench of dung-heaps and outhouses in a colonial Williamsburg. A restored Williamsburg, sporting modern plumbing, sewers and running water, is a nice weekend plaything but no abode for man of the technical age.[1]

Wistful side glances at the comforts of other civilizations will only distort our views, and interfere with finding a viable solution to the problems of our culture. The pleasures of hunting, diverting as they may be, will not heal the damage man can incur in a technological age. Nor will leisure time activities do away with bad features of the machine age; at best they can make us forget for stretches of time, and seduce us into avoiding the search for redress. Repeated

---

[1] I owe the example of Williamsburg to Daniel J. Boorstin's perceptive "Past and Present in America," *Commentary*, 25, January 1958. Boorstin also points out that Williamsburg only became fully popular after a vast motel with swimming pool, etc., was added.

honeymoon trips will not save a bad marriage by improving what is wrong with it, but may lead to its continuing without purpose and in growing discomfort.

The way to avoid the machine taking command is not to take more and longer vacations from a life dominated by machines, or from a machine regulated existence. The solution lies in finding ways to make this an age where humanity dominates despite the usefulness of machines, and to do this by making fullest use of their convenience. While every civilization creates its own type of discomforts and the emotional disturbances germane to it, it must also find its own solutions, both to the real needs of man and the neurotic ones typical for the age. Unless we keep this simple fact in mind, we may advocate remedies having no bearing on the special needs and stresses that ail man and society at any particular time.

To survive well under the preaching of hellfire and damnation, we need a correlary belief in revival and salvation. What is needed to survive well in the modern machine age, with its alienation of man from man and man from nature —that is the question we face in our own times. To this question I do not pretend to have discovered final answers. But the struggle to approach a solution to some of its aspects is what binds this book together.

Unwitting bondage

In my daily work with psychotic children, and in my efforts to create an institutional setting that will induce them to return to sanity, I have come face to face with this problem of how to take best advantage of all the conveniences of a technological age, of all that modern science offers toward the understanding and well being of man, and to do it without entering a bondage to science and technology.

At no time did it occur to us that we could do more or

better without the "machines." On the contrary, by using them judiciously we managed to live a freer life than is possible without them. To say this may seem to belabor the obvious. After all the machine was invented to free life of bondage. But things are not quite so simple.

Whenever we introduced a new technological convenience, we had to examine its place in the life of our institution most carefully. The advantages we could enjoy from any new machine were always quite obvious; the bondage we entered by using it was much harder to assess, and much more elusive. Often we were unaware of its negative effects until after long use. By then we had come to rely on it so much, that small disadvantages that came with the use of any one contrivance seemed too trivial to warrant giving it up, or to change the pattern we had fallen into by using it. Nevertheless, when combined with the many other small disadvantages of all the other devices, it added up to a significant and undesirable change in the pattern of our life and work.

This is what I mean by "seduction." The advantages of the machines are so obvious and so desirable, that we tend to become, small step by small step, seduced into ignoring the price we pay for their unthinking use. The emphasis here is on *unthinking use*, because they all have their good uses. But the most careful thinking and planning is needed to enjoy the good use of any technical contrivance without paying a price for it in human freedom.

If an example were needed, TV is certainly a case in point. Much has been said about the contents of television programs. But my concern here is less with content and much more with what persistent watching does to a child's ability to relate to real people, to become self activating, to think on the basis of his own life experience instead of in stereotypes out of shows.

Many children, four to six years of age, communicate mainly in terms of their favorite shows and relate much better to the TV screen than to their parents. Some of them seem unable to respond any more to the simple and direct language of their parents because it sounds unimpressive compared to the suave diction and emotionally loaded idiom of TV professionals. True, for such far reaching consequences, not only the children, but their parents have to spend too much time in front of the set, or talk so little to each other that their adult conversation cannot offset the talking down or overemphatic voices of the programs.

Children who have been taught, or conditioned, to listen passively most of the day to the warm verbal communications coming from the TV screen, to the deep emotional appeal of the so-called TV personality, are often unable to respond to real persons because they arouse so much less feeling than the skilled actor. Worse, they lose the ability to learn from reality because life experiences are more complicated than the ones they see on the screen, and there is noone who comes in at the end to explain it all. The "TV child," expecting events in his own life to follow in sequence with a beginning, a middle and a predictable solution, all of it explained and made plain by one of the chief actors (as in Westerns) or by a master of ceremonies (as in comedies) ends up feeling discouraged because life is too complicated. Conditioned to being given explanations, he has not learned to puzzle for one on his own; he gets discouraged when he cannot grasp the meaning of what happens to him and is thrown back once more to find comfort in predictable stories on the screen.

If, later in life, this block of solid inertia is not removed, the emotional isolation from others that starts in front of TV may continue in school. Eventually it leads, if not to a permanent inability, then a reluctance to becoming active in learning or in relations to other people. By adolescence, this inability to relate is apt to have even more serious consequences because then the pressure of sexual emotions begins to unsettle a personality that has never learned to internalize or sublimate them, or to satisfy them through personal relations.

This being seduced into passivity and discouraged about facing life actively, on one's own, is the real danger of TV, much more than the often asinine or gruesome content of the shows. But "TV passivity" is only one aspect of the overall "let the machines do it."

Despite all this, I am by no means suggesting that we do away with the TV sets in our homes. But if we wish to enjoy their advantages without paying too high a price, we too will have to take action. If we let our children watch TV passively we must at other times provide them with active experiences, and not just physical activity. They must be helped to experience life directly, to learn to draw conclusions and to take a stand on their own, not to accept whatever is told them as correct.

Maybe something less controversial than TV can make the point more concretely: I cannot imagine a housewife not being glad to come by a dishwashing machine. But for some couples the electric dishwasher eliminated the one thing they did together every day; one of them washed while the other dried. As one woman put it, she now enjoys not only less fatigue but a pure gift of time. Yet she added wistfully, "But it *was* cozy, just the two of us together for that little while every night, after we got the kids to bed."

This necessary chore brought husband and wife together. Obviously having a dishwasher is preferable to having to do them by hand, and more hygienic, to boot. The comfortable intimacy that went with the chore was hardly noticed until it vanished. But just as obviously, the arrival of this machine in the home meant the couple would have to find some other occasion for spending their brief while together. Only then would the machine truly add, not detract from their lives with each other. This, as I say, is obvious. But in how many families does this "obvious" become an actuality?

At the Orthogenic School we had no choice here. Prodded by necessities that grew out of our task, we found it quite possible to create and keep going, in this time and age, an institution that made use of the most up to date science and technology without entering into compromise with them. What made it easier to avoid errors was the realization that struck us again and again, of how much neurotic symptoms and their causes can tell us about what is apt to disturb the individual in a particular civilization. Realizing this helped us to eliminate from our setting such obstacles to human freedom and spontaneity.

Delusions for moderns

While any neurotic or psychotic breakdown is rooted in the inner difficulties of man, the outer form it may take, that is the external symptoms, reflect back the nature of the society. Psychotic disturbances are particularly revealing, perhaps because of the extreme anxiety they are based on, and the total breakdown in functioning they signify and are meant to overcome. Often their exaggerations show up more clearly what ails all of us in some measure at present, and warn us of things to come. Far more than neurotic behavior, they can also inform us about which forces an age looks to for solving the difficulties it is failing to master.

In the Middle Ages when a man could not deal with the problems before him and escaped into a world of delusion, he felt possessed by devils. But once possessed, he took comfort in the thought that he might be saved by the heavenly intercession of angels or saints. At all times and in all civilizations there are persons who feel possessed or persecuted by outside forces they feel are beyond them. We recognize that this need to ascribe inner conflict to some external force arises when the individual feels he cannot solve the difficulty within his own psyche. It is less well understood that what he feels possessed by tells us a great deal about what features of society disturb him.

Sexual seduction by the devil is not often experienced unless utter chastity is required by the mores, and accepted by the individual as an inner goal to strive for. So the delusional belief that it requires a devil to seduce a woman reflects an inner standard of chastity so stringent that it takes a superhuman power (bad demons) to break it down. But the same delusion shows what forces the society looks to (good demons) for settling inner contradictions it seems unable to deal with.

In another time and age it was the great man that people turned to for solutions to their difficulties. A prevalence of the megalomanic delusion of being Napoleon, etc., tells us that an age was looking to the great man to solve its difficulties. Angels and devils were no longer superhuman, but seen in the image of man. Yet the great man is only the apotheosis of the average man. Even if a person feels "hounded" as we say, the image of his persecutor is still a dog or some other living creature. But what of a time that trusts neither angels nor great men to solve its problems, but only mechanical 'brains' or guided missiles?

Modern man no longer seeks his nirvana, his escape from the unsolvable problems of life, in heaven, but in outer space. To the extent that he relies for security on guided missiles and nuclear fusion, the fear of atomic bombs must haunt him.

What is so new in the hopes and fears of the machine age are that savior and destroyer are no longer clothed in the image of man; no longer are the figures that we imagine can save and destroy us direct projections of our human image. What we now hope will save us, and what in our delusions we fear will destroy us, is something that no longer has human qualities.[2]

This new development has other aspects. Formerly it was not just that savior and destroyer were clad in human likeness, it was also that they were conceived as supernatural or at least superior to man, never as man's servants. Machines and scientific discoveries, on the other hand, were and are conceived of as rational creations of man, existing only for man's use. The transition from the useful but mindless machine to the manipulator if not the killer of man is viewed not as a change in kind, but a change in quantity or degree.

A typical example is what (for good reasons) was first given a name in Germany: the *Karteimensch,* freely translated as punch-card-existence. The punch card, with the sorting machine that makes it useful, seems to turn each of us into a mere conglomeration of useful characteristics. Singly, or in certain combinations, these traits allow persons in control to use us first and foremost as owners of such traits, and only incidentally (if at all) as total persons.

A probably apocryphal story in the *New Yorker* illustrates the point better than any long discussion. There we are told that after a lady's subscription to a book club ran

---

[2] The rational argument that the atomic bomb really can destroy, while the devil was a relatively harmless fantasy is fallacious. When the devil was real to people, he destroyed hapless victims just as the bomb does. Those burned at the stakes because they or their fellow men believed in the devil died no imaginary death; they were as dead as the victims of atomic warfare. The prophecy of the world coming to an end in the year 1000 was not only as widespread, but led to more suicides, percentage-wise, than our fear of atomic bombs destroying the world. In a religious age, man believed and feared out of religious knowledge: namely, the 1000th anniversary of Christ's birth. In a scientific age, man fears on the basis of scientific knowledge: the atomic bomb.

out, she discontinued it. Nevertheless she continued to get a punch card at regular intervals with the request to send in payments, though none were due. She repeatedly returned the card with notes explaining that she had dropped out and did not owe anything. Still the cards continued to come in the mail, until one day she took her son's punch and punched a few holes in the punch card. That settled it; she was no longer bothered. The machine run organization could respond best to a machine like reply.

This is an amusing story. But our readiness to obey requests not to fold or bend a punch card should give us pause. Most of us do not hesitate to fold or bend a personal handwritten letter; we treat the machine and its requirements with greater respect. I realize that a valid answer is that we do not expect a machine to be able to adapt itself to human vagaries. But it still augurs poorly for a future when more and more we will have to react to punch cards and less and less to handwritten letters, inquiries or even paychecks. Not being able to react freely (with folding if we like) to such items, interferes with our general ability to react spontaneously. The more we have to keep our spontaneity in check when responding, the more extinct it may become for lack of use.

This, again, is a minor example of how a mechanical device, invented strictly to simplify tasks and save human labor, forces human beings to conform to the requirements of the machine. A change in the *degree* of difficulty in decision making seems to have changed the *nature* of the decision making process and deprived it of its human qualities. It is so much easier to route a punch card, or the number it corresponds to, than it is to direct a person. Many manipulations of men that would ordinarily arouse great resistance in the manipulator, if not open refusal, are carried out without qualms, because all the manipulator has to do is feed anonymous cards into a pre-set sorting machine. Once the cards are sorted out, it seems so simple to assign tasks to men and women whom the machine sort indicates are best suited for them. This is very different from deciding whether you, the reader, or I myself should be discharged from our jobs or sent on a difficult mission.

In a strange psychological process persons who are viewed by those in authority as numbers on punch cards, tend to view themselves as numbers rather than persons, unless they deliberately guard against it. As G. H. Mead has pointed out, the image others have of us also shapes our own image of ourselves. Psychoanalysis indicates that whatever the rational causes of an action, they also have an unconscious meaning. However rational the use of punch cards—and it is a purposeful, rational way of doing things, avoiding errors due to human shortcomings or the pressure of time—it also has irrational, unconscious effects.

Here, as in many other cases, the answer is neither to do away with the punch card and its proven advantages, nor to submit to seeing ourselves and others as the punch card describes us. The answer again is what psychoanalysis prescribes for restoring the disturbed individual to fuller human functioning: not to deny or neglect the dangers of a situation; not to run away from it by destroying it and depriving oneself of its advantages; but to realize the dangers and meet them with conscious action based on personal decision. This neutralizes the danger, and lets us enjoy the advantages of technology without letting it deprive us of our humanity.

In the same context, and again according to psychoanalytic theory, whatever the rational causes of an invention, there is also an unconscious meaning and origin.[3] If

---

[3] Sachs, H. "The Delay of the Machine Age," *Psychoanalytic Quarterly*, 2, 1933, pp. 404 ff.

this is so, then if machines are invented for their usefulness, their invention too is unconsciously influenced by the inventor who externalizes and projects either his whole body, or isolated parts of it. Maybe with even greater specialization of the mechanical process, it will happen less and less often that the whole body and its functions or movements will be the unconscious starting point for the inventor's imagination. More and more often will an isolated part of the body or an isolated bodily function serve as the unconscious underpinning for the rational process of designing new machinery.

In modern mass production we find a human corollary. There the worker is often viewed, and views himself, as being a "cog" in the machine rather than someone who runs it. He repeats a few isolated work tasks, is theoretically unable to deal with or shape the whole productive process, never confronts the end product or end decision, or only in a manner incidental to his work.[4]

Just as modern machines can no longer be recognized as obvious extensions of our bodily organs, or as performing bodily functions more efficiently—though that may have

---

[4] I do not know whether and to what degree automation will change this by freeing the worker from having to repeat the same task over and over again. It should certainly do away with much drudgery in the productive process. But as less of man's labor will be needed for survival, more of his time and energy will become available for other tasks. Unless he finds ways to expend this time and energy on tasks deeply meaningful to him, his personal agony will increase to the degree that less of his physical and mental energies go to assuring survival for himself and his family. It is relatively easy to find life meaningful if most of one's energy is constructively spent in securing the essentials of living for oneself and one's own. It is quite difficult to find that much meaning in less essential, or less obviously meaningful tasks. We can all derive a great deal of self respect and deep satisfaction from the knowledge that we are helping others and ourselves survive; very little meaning can be wrung from the ability to provide ourselves and others with ever less essential conveniences.

been their origin—so in modern delusions we find more and more nonhuman projections. For example, a characteristic feature of modern insanity is the "influencing machine," a device that supposedly puts thoughts into a person's head as if they were his own, or forces him to act against his conscious will.

As one might expect, the influencing machine as a form of delusion appeared only after electrical machines were not only a basic feature of daily life, but also what many looked to as the answer to important social problems. Today, when man turns so often to the psychological skills with his personal problems, we should expect some delusions to take the form of feeling overpowered by psychological influences against one's knowledge or will. The term "brainwashing" and the widespread notion that thoughts and convictions can be put into a person's mind by psychological techniques —as well as the irrational anxiety this evokes in some people —suggest that we have reached such a point. An intensified belief in the "saving" and destructive powers of psychology has thus replaced saints, devils and even influencing machines, as the preferred content of delusional feelings of helplessness, of being overpowered and manipulated against one's will.

It can be shown that the influencing machine, too, began as a projection of the human body,[5] but the essential point is that it does not retain this image; it becomes ever more complex and the psychotic person ends up feeling controlled by mechanical devices that no longer resemble anything human or even animal-like. Thus modern man, when he is

---

[5] See Tausk, V., "On the Origin of the 'Influencing Machine' in Schizophrenia," *The Psychoanalytic Quarterly*, 2, 1933, pp. 519 ff; Kaufman, M. R., "Some Clinical Data on Ideas of Reference," *ibid.*, 1, 1932, pp. 265 ff; Linn, L., "Some Comments on the Origin of the Influencing Machine," *Journal of the American Psychoanalytic Association*, 6, 1958, pp. 305 ff.

haunted, whether sane or profoundly disturbed, is no longer haunted by other men or by grandiose projections of man, but by machines. This, while at the same time relying for his protection or salvation on machines.

Machine gods

These developments are often expressed in popular science fiction, the prefabricated daydreams of a technological age. If the machine can do so much, man by contrast can do so little. Some of the earliest philosophers recognized that if pigs and cows had gods, they would conceive them as glorified, godlike pigs or cows. The characteristics they would ascribe to them would be the ones found or desired in themselves, only magnified and made perfect. A man created in God's image, or a god created in man's image, no less than a devil created in man's image, tells us much about the fears and aspirations of man. A machine god thus tells us about the fears and aspirations of man in a machine age. If we look at science fiction in this perspective, we find it concentrating on "problems of space and time; the individual's sense of reality and identity; problems of prolonged isolation and individual existence in mortal combat with machines."[6]

Compared with other popular daydream material such as the Western—with its fantasies of sexual and aggressive desires being acted out and conflicts around them being dealt with—the modern scientific daydream, contrary to the highly developed technology we live in, deals with more primitive emotional problems. For example, space ships are completely enclosed structures in which the person is immobilized and isolated for long periods of time; all his needs are provided for, as with the human foetus. Problems of

[6] Bernabeu, E. P., "Science Fiction," *The Psychoanalytic Quarterly*, 26, 1957, pp. 527 ff.

living in space, of gravity, disturbances of equilibrium, orientation, and locomotion—all these are important elements in the infant's struggles with orientation, equilibrium, and movement.

Ideas about the limitless quality of space and the magnitude of once unimagined dangers also lead to feelings of insignificance and a dread of losing one's identity. It seems that if we project our wishful and anxious fantasies not on manlike objects but on complex machinery we run the risk of losing our psychological identity as man. Whether we do or not seems to depend on our ability to conjure up images that are bigger but not radically different from man.

Others who have approached the same phenomena differently have reached similar conclusions: "Comparison of these [science fiction] myths indicates that the dazzling speed of technological innovation in the present generation has psychological effects to which the rapidly increasing vogue of science fiction may give some tentative clues. In an age in which mechanical 'brains,' satellites, and flights to other planets exist, or are impending realities, the fantasies of science are vehicles for expression of far greater anxieties and more deeply regressive defenses even than those which evoked the demigods, devils, and witches of other times."[7]

I am no expert on science fiction, so I may be in error here; but it seems that this type of escape literature appeals to many educated and discriminating persons, including serious scientists. There also seems little doubt that some of the more startling of recent scientific developments were anticipated in these writings. What is interesting here is less the authors' acuteness about future scientific developments, than about the developments in man they may bring about. Apparently, authors who can anticipate new mastery over nature are also able to foresee what such progress may

[7] Bernabeu, *loc. cit.*

do to man. Or to bring it closer to what interests me here, those whose hopes lie in the extreme outposts of science are haunted by equal anxieties about how this may spell the destruction of man.

Since science fiction presents as already achieved what the authors hope for and dread about the future, the accompanying changes in man are also described as already existing. And the heroes of these stories abound in nonhuman qualities. Their depersonalization is often symbolized by their names, such as Og, or M-331, by an absence or disregard for their bodies, and by a lack of intimate human relations. More important, to the degree that the stories abound in marvels of progress, they also entail fantasies of world destruction. In some stories, after the robots or whatnot have destroyed man, they recreate him. But usually this is done synthetically, not by refashioning man in his own image, through procreation. Love relations are virtually absent; most of the heroes are basically minds without a body. Apparently science fiction writers, though motivated by a desire for scientific progress, seem to feel that the inherent danger of such progress is an end to our biological existence as man.

A reasonable thing to do

Nevertheless, while our progress can be measured by the fact that the machine is clearly recognized as the servant of man and not his better, the fear is now widespread that it could become our master. Since this is so, we must understand those potentials within us that we project into the machine, and which could make it our master in reality as it already is in our delusions. To escape into anxious nightmares and condemn the machine will not do, whether we frighten ourselves with brave new worlds or with 1984.

The modern schizophrenic enslaved by his influencing machines is no worse nor much better off (short of access to psychotherapy) than was medieval man who felt persecuted by the devil. But we were saved from former evils not by believing in angels but by creating modern science. What we now have to face is the potential evil of the machine, though its sole origin is the image of the machine in man's mind. From this exploration we must then draw a lesson about what needs to be done to prevent the machine from overpowering us.

In closing this chapter, I want to return to some initial remarks. The seeming impasse of having to give up freedom to gain comfort, as it confronted the early farmer, is basically the same one alluded to when we moderns speak of our civilization and its discontents. We can state and accept the truism that every way of life has its own discomforts, and leave it there. We can bemoan this fact and condemn civilization. Or we can do the only reasonable thing: arrange our lives so that the comforts of civilization are so used as to reduce discontents to a minimum, while securing for each citizen the maximum possible of human satisfactions. When posed as a dilemma between freedom and bondage, the impasse is insoluble. This is how the Arab nomad poses it who can find no alternative except to choose freedom with discomfort and insecurity, or bondage with discontent and more security. And this is how modern man, worried about the machine age, about mass society and the danger of atomic destruction, still poses the problem too often.

A solution can be found only by opposing inner to outer freedom; emotional freedom to the freedom to roam or discharge aggression. The greatest danger of our machine made wealth grows out of this: that for the first time we are living in an age when material comfort is possible for almost everyone. But if this, because it is so much more available, is sought not in addition to emotional contentment but in lieu of it, then there is danger of our becoming addicted to it. We will need more and more technological progress to cover up our emotional want and discomfort. This, as I see it, is the only danger of the machine age. But it is neither necessary nor inherent in it.

3
The Consciousness of Freedom

JUST WHERE DOES ONE DRAW THE LINE beyond which others must not be allowed to influence one's inner life? This question is as old as civilization and has bedeviled man from the moment he became aware of himself as a human being within a society. It is even harder, once we draw such a line, to keep it securely in its flexible place; flexible, because we have to keep adjusting it to the legitimate needs of society (which are not static) and to our inner requirements (which also vary in the span of a lifetime).

At certain times in history it was religion that epitomized the sum of man's consciousness. Then the conflict occasionally erupted as a war between church and state for the custody of man. At other times the battle was temporarily stalemated in an uneasy truce, with man's body entrusted to the state and his soul to religion. But as soon as man's dominant view of himself lost such duality, this dubious split became untenable. And when religion stopped being the essence of man's awareness of himself as a human being, he henceforth had to rely on himself alone to set up the barriers against encroachment by society.

Western man has grown unwilling to entrust his consciousness to others any more, be it to priest, philosopher, or party leader. He is convinced that he alone can develop, own and guard it. But then the problem of how much to let the state modify one's life becomes a very personal one that everyone has to solve for himself. And this just when modern science has provided the managers of society with the means of control—political, economic, social, and psychological— which in their potential consequences would have seemed fantastic a few decades ago. Also, modern technological developments ask for the cooperation of many, and so do advances in the social services which we think are desirable, or else plainly necessary. But cooperation by large groups cannot be achieved without imposing controls. Unfortunately, these controls are often evaluated for their immediate technical advantages, without due regard for the emotional well being of those they are supposed to serve.

Techniques as such lend themselves equally well to good or bad purposes. Therefore, it is often felt that control for desirable ends (the rule of the philosopher kings) is good, or at least not bad. But this is a dangerous belief. It neglects the complex and often serious effects of any external control of man; also the fact that when the area for free decisions grows too restricted, it reduces the scope of man's personal responsibility and thus his autonomy. It assumes that all else counts for little, as long as "right" decisions are arrived at, and that it makes no difference how you reach them.

Basically, this notion derives from the conviction that if man is not a wholly rational animal, he ought to be; and since he ought to be motivated solely by rational considerations, we might as well proceed as if he were. But the well being of man depends much more on his emotional life than this view is willing to accept. Otherwise he would find relative contentment only in the most rationally organized society, while actually all societies, whichever way they function, have their share of happy and unhappy persons.

Decision making

The historic statement, "Taxation without representation is tyranny" includes more wisdom about this issue than is commonly supposed. It does not question what taxes should be levied or how, nor for what purposes the so collected money should be spent. Nor does it simply say that taxes infringe on private property rights and should not be imposed without the owner's consent. Property and income, after all, derive from society and depend on its structure. Hence they are never quite as private as many who quote the statement like to think. On the surface it seems to safeguard property rights, and consciously it may have been meant that way. But on a deeper level its importance lies in the close connection it establishes between decision making on decisive matters, and tyranny. That this is the statement's true significance shows up in the way we remember it; for in the actual text ("No parts of His Majesty's dominions can be taxed without their consent") there is no mention of tyranny.

Consent to a tax levy is one thing, and basically of little import. But barring an individual from a part in decision making on matters that deeply concern him tends to create a feeling of impotence which we call being subject to tyranny. The particular actions or decisions that can make a person feel tyrannized when he is no longer free to determine them for himself—these change with time, society, and the individual. At one time and place they were obviously decisions about money and property, as the quotation suggests. At other times, what taxes a man had to pay mattered little to his sense of independence, compared with such issues as freedom of thought, speech or religion; or to cite freedoms looming larger today, those from want and from fear.

As a matter of fact, a good case could be made that the particular freedoms of action and decision we must have so as not to feel subject to tyranny tell us which issues are decisive for a particular society, or group of people in it. "The history of the world," wrote Hegel, "is none other than the progress of the consciousness of freedom." Obviously there are levels of consciousness, and at any given time and place in history there are areas of human action where the consciousness of freedom is acute, others where it is dormant.

The statement about taxation and tyranny reveals that at the time of the American Revolution, property rights were foremost in the consciousness of the colonists. At other times and places, other issues took this central place.

As a matter of fact, revolutions and wars (cold or otherwise) have been fought just because groups within a society (or different societies) had achieved different levels of consciousness. Perhaps much of what ails us today is that in one part of the world the consciousness of freedom from want takes precedence over that of freedom of thought, while in other parts of the world economic want has been so reduced that man is less acutely conscious of it than of his freedom to move about, to pick and change occupations, or to choose freely his political or aesthetic opinions.

Whether or not a societal organization is experienced as tyranny seems to depend mainly on whether its members are assured relative free choices and a part in decision making about issues that for them are the sum of their consciousness of freedom. One might then think that the more important areas of life to enter this consciousness, the greater the progress a society has made. But, alas, who is to decide which are important areas, and which unimportant? What may be experienced by one man in one society as tyranny, may seem only an inconvenience to others or a silly issue to again others. Still, this is only true within limits. While it varies with men as to which are important areas of freedom in decision making, a sense of autonomy depends everywhere on the conviction that one can make important decisions, and can do it where it counts most.

Whether in childhood or adulthood if one finds it impossible, first to influence one's social and physical environment, and later to make decisions on how and when to modify it, this is harmful if not devastating to the human personality. But not everything that later turns out to have been good is at first easy or pleasant. Decision making is a risky and demanding process so it is often avoided, even where it is theoretically possible. Yet however restrictive or oppressive an environment may be, even then the individual still retains the freedom to evaluate it. On the basis of this evaluation he is also free to decide on his inner approval or resistance to what is forced upon him. True, in an extremely oppressive environment these inner decisions can lead to little or no practical consequences. Therefore the more man is geared toward achieving "practical" results, the more he may view the making of inner decisions that lead to no practical end as a total waste of energy, and hence avoid making them.

At the opposite end of the scale, the more everything is arranged by others to one's best advantage, the less justified seems the expense of spirit involved in decision making. Therefore the child whose parents make all important decisions for him in his best interests, as well as the utterly deprived child or the child in an oppressive environment, all these will fail to develop a strong personality. Many of them will either be driven to senseless revolt (because pointless, or against their best interests), or they will give up all decision making because in their experience it makes no difference and is just a waste of energy.

Taking a stand—whether an inner stand without tangible consequences or, much better, a stand that finds open expression in action—is energy consuming. So if it leads to no benefit for the individual, it seems, offhand, to his advantage to save his energy; that is, as long as he is unaware of any need to maintain a "consciousness of freedom." As indicated, the two commonest situations in which a person may find it pointless to make decisions are an extremely oppressive situation where his decisions must not be acted on lest they endanger his life, or where all important decisions are made by others in what seem like his best interests (by the parents for the child; by religion or the government for the adult).

Unfortunately decision making is a function which, like some nerves or muscles, tends to atrophy when it lies fallow. Or in terms of psychoanalytic theory, decision making is not just an ego function; on the contrary, it is the function that creates the ego and, once created, keeps it going and growing.

If this is so then any external control, even for the good of the individual, is undesirable when it interferes too severely with ego development; that is, when it prevents first decision making, and then action, in those areas most important for developing and safeguarding autonomy.

It is easy enough to state this theoretically. In practice it is almost impossible to draw a line up to which the management of a person's own affairs by others is still possible without interfering with his autonomy, and beyond which no infringement on personal freedom can be allowed.

What I have just put in general terms may have some universal validity, but I am not here concerned with societal inroads on autonomy as a theoretical problem, nor whether and how this may apply elsewhere, such as in a primitive society. Individuals there may possess autonomy in our sense, and it may seem important to them, but both assumptions are open to doubt. What interests me are the dangers to autonomy in our society. Perhaps this is more of a problem to us because the more complex a society becomes, the greater the need for individual autonomy, because both reflect more advanced stages of a "consciousness of freedom." Also we are quick to feel our emotional sufferings when this complex society eats into our inner and outer freedom; we are less quick to realize that only the elaborate development of our society enables us to seek, find and cherish these values, and to dread their loss so acutely. Society is not the villain, nor is man born free. Both of them grow up together, if this crude analogy may be used.

Obviously modern Western man has not acted without reason in allowing certain areas of his life to be managed by society, nor has he carelessly deputized a selected few to make all-important decisions for him. Modern technology, mass production, and mass society have brought so many tangible benefits to man, that only in self defeat could he turn his back on them simply because they also involve dangers to personal autonomy. On the other hand, because he has gained so much by entrusting large areas of his life to experts, it has grown very seductive to let them take over more and more of what could remain areas of personal freedom.

It is not that modern man is so much quicker to surrender his freedom to society, nor that man was so much more autonomous in the good old days. It is rather that scientific and technological progress has relieved him of having to solve so many problems that he once had to solve by himself if he meant to survive, while the modern horizon presents so many more choices than it used to. So there is both: less need to develop autonomy because he can survive without it, and more need for it if he prefers not to have others making decisions for him. The fewer meaningful decisions he needs for survival, the less he may feel the need, or the tendency to develop his decision making abilities.

It is just as in psychoanalytic theory where the undeveloped ego is helplessly pushed around by the id and superego it ought to be able to control; so man, if he is not using and strengthening his decision making faculties, is apt to be pushed around both by his instinctual desires and by society; by instinctual desires because he cannot organize and control them (and then he feels cheated because society does not cater to his irrational wishes and rush to satisfy them—witness the typical "beat" attitude to life); and by society which will run his life for him if he does not do it himself.

But if man stops developing his consciousness of freedom it tends to weaken for lack of exercise. And here I do not mean busy activity, but decisions about attitudes. The simplest example might be the decision: "I want to live in this manner," as opposed to "What's the use of trying to be different," though both may result in exactly the same behavior. Therefore too much management of human affairs without personal decisions, even for the best of purposes, is bad because human autonomy is too apt to wither away.

Autonomy

I hope by now it is clear that the concept of autonomy used here has little to do with what is sometimes called "rugged individualism," the cult of personality, or noisy self assertion. It has to do with man's inner ability to govern himself, and with a conscientious search for meaning despite the realization that, as far as we know, there is no purpose to one's life. It is a concept that does not imply a revolt against authority *qua* authority, but rather a quiet acting out of inner conviction, not out of convenience or resentment, or because of external persuasion or controls.

Probably the simplest example is obeying speed limits because one likes one's own body and therefore likes orderly traffic, but not because one is afraid of the traffic police. Autonomy does not imply that the individual has or should have free reign. All society depends for its existence and growth on a balance between individual self assertion and the general welfare. If man's instincts were unchecked, society could not exist. The continuous balancing and resolving of opposing tendencies within oneself, and between self and society—the ability to do this in keeping with personal values, an enlightened self interest, and the interests of the society one lives in—all these lead to an increasing consciousness of freedom and form the basis for man's deepening sense of identity, self respect and inner freedom, in short his autonomy.

One's sense of identity, the conviction of being a unique individual, with lasting and deeply meaningful relations to a few others; with a particular life history that one has shaped and been shaped by; a respect for one's work and a pleasure in one's competence at it; with memories peculiar to one's personal experience, preferred tasks, tastes and pleasures—all these are at the heart of man's autonomous existence. Instead of merely allowing him to conform to the reasonable demands of society without losing his identity, they make it a rewarding experience, quite often a creative one.

The man who can afford rich food and drink, who enjoys it and hence consumes it, may need a much better stomach than the fellow who has to get along on simpler fare. By the same token the citizen enjoying an economy of plenty and great freedom in arranging his life, needs a much better integrated personality in order to choose well and restrict himself wisely, than the citizen who needs no inner strength to restrain himself because there is very little around to enjoy or abstain from. True, in any society there will be some who simply do not enjoy rich food or drink and hence need no strong personality or even a strong stomach for their continued well being. But such men are no problem to society in this sense, nor does a society of plenty tempt them beyond what they can handle. Obviously, in this simple-minded example, a society of plenty is a problem only to the person who has neither a strong stomach nor the inner strength to control his desires, but who also loves rich food and too much drink.

Perhaps my everyday practice may further illustrate why today, because of scientific progress, man needs a much better integrated personality. At all times there are a minority of parents who reject one of their children, and quite a few more who sometimes feel ambivalent about one of them. So far so good. If neither situation is too drastic, most children manage to survive fairly well, though they experience a loss.

A better understanding of psychology has taught us that such parental attitudes are, or can be, quite damaging to the child. So the educated parent of today who has negative or ambivalent feelings about his child feels quite guilty and wants to do something about it. As likely as not, having to feel guilty about his attitude toward one of his children aggravates the negative feelings, and the child now suffers doubly. In addition to the parent's ambivalence he also suffers now from the parent's annoyance with him for causing pangs of guilt.

Thus having learned that it is bad for one's child to have negative feelings about him, the parent needs a much stronger personality and greater inner security to integrate his guilt. This was not true for yesterday's parent who did not know that his negative feelings could be damaging. He may have been convinced that he did enough by feeding and otherwise providing for the child; about the rest he felt easy in his mind. Now, in order to rid himself of guilt feelings, a parent may even convince himself that the child is defective; that his own negative reactions are based on defects that no one is to blame for. So I face many parents who at other times would have rejected their child and simply left him alone but who now, in order to shake off their sense of guilt, are insisting he is brain damaged, or otherwise defective.

The lesson to be learned from such experiences is again not that we should condemn our new knowledge, but that each step toward greater consciousness—in this case recognition of the potentially damaging nature of some human emotions—requires that much stronger and better integrated a personality before it can represent true progress.

Both a rejecting parent and his child are better off if the parent does not feel guilty about his rejection, but the situation is still not desirable. Nevertheless, where before such a parent had no choice, now various possibilities are open to him, all of them for the better. He can integrate his guilt and not burden the child or anyone else with it. He can find out about the origins of his rejection and remove them, so that he will neither have to reject or feel guilty. Either solution would help everyone concerned. But when the parent simply responds to the more advanced knowledge (that rejection is damaging) and does not move on to achieve inner changes (integrating his guilt; removing the cause for rejection) then scientific advances lead to a deficit instead of the great benefits we can derive from them.

This one example must stand for many to indicate that social, scientific or technological progress, in order to better, not worsen man's lot, requires a more elaborate consciousness and an integration of personality that reaches into deeper levels than heretofore. Personal autonomy and a consciousness of freedom are only other aspects of these higher stages of personal integration.

It is this need for inner growth that leads some students of social and technological progress to take a dim view of the future. They despair of man's ability to achieve, with each step of external advance, a like progress in personal integration; thus their fear for man's future in our age of technology is really nothing but a consequence of their original low opinion of man.

We have, in fact, taken many such steps toward external progress, each one becoming viable only as we achieve the higher integration that our changed environment called for. But this is usually overlooked by those who hold a pessimistic outlook on the future. Their *a priori* low estimate of man and his potentials keeps them from realizing that from the time he became a social being, man has been meeting this problem and meeting it successfully.

In the preceding chapter I mentioned the attitude of the modern nomad toward dwellings and dwellers of the city. And it is true, the former nomad will not make a successful citizen unless he learns to control his tendency to take up and move away at whim or the slightest frustration; until he masters the wish to take bloody revenge at any offense. Nor will he achieve this control over himself until such time as close and permanent relations to a group larger than his family or tribe becomes meaningful to him, until the economic and cultural advantages of the city become very attractive. For the sake of these desired benefits he may be willing to restrain himself and to develop new social abilities; in short, to achieve a higher personal integration.

Most formerly nomadic tribes have been willing and able to do this, and to do it in a few generations. So there seems little doubt that today too, man can achieve the higher integration he needs if his new living conditions are to become freeing, not oppressive; provided, of course, that they offer him as many worthwhile advantages as city life offers the nomad. That technology offers great advantages we do not doubt. What may be in doubt is whether and how much these advantages add to the successful living together of man with his fellow men; because that alone will make further integration seem so worthwhile that he will readily achieve it.

This book was written mainly to suggest the direction I believe this higher integration will have to take, and to sensitize the reader to some aspects of modern mass society that hinder the process.

An imbalance

At present external progress has far surpassed a matching integration. This lack of balance affecting many citizens in the modern mass state also bears on emotional disorders. As most of us know, emotional disturbances are due to unresolved conflicts. But solving conflicts depends on an integrated personality that can handle them successfully. This ability comes with the repeated experience of having solved one's difficulties in the past. Hence the seeming "neurosis" of the adolescent. He is simply too young to have had enough experience at solving inner and outer conflicts to feel confident he can master them successfully. Hence also other adolescent problems.

The modern adolescent is also exposed to many more choices and temptations than the adolescent of former days; hence he needs much greater maturity to meet them without danger than was needed when life offered fewer temptations. As a boy I needed no strong personality or morality to resist stealing a car; nor did any other boy I knew ride around in one, nor did my girl friend expect me to provide a ride for her. There were just no cars around. At present car stealing is still the most frequent offense of adolescents; an everyday example of how modern progress compounds emotional problems and hence requires higher personal integration.

If a person keeps failing to solve his problems, those within himself, and those between him and society, he loses faith in being able to meet new ones successfully. The challenge of repeated choices as to which of many unsuitable jobs to select, which of several imperfect party platforms to support, which of many tempting but often not too essential gadgets to buy, confronts the modern citizen with his own lack of decision. Rarely do these choices really satisfy his deeper needs. Therefore, the psychic energy spent in reaching a decision is wasted and the individual feels drained of energy without purpose.[1]

Basically, reaching a decision on any matter and solving any conflict depends on a man's ability to eliminate, first, all solutions clearly not in line with his values and personality. Then very few solutions remain possible and to choose the correct one is relatively simple. A person who is not well integrated, who does not follow a consistent set of values, cannot correctly test a vast number of choices against his values and interests, and then cannot cut the problem down to manageable size. Such a person feels overpowered by any new need for decision.

Strangely enough, when a person faces many possibilities that are equally attractive it is theoretically an expression of freedom to choose one of them; but psychologically he does not experience it that way. If anything, it leaves him vaguely dissatisfied. On the other hand, to know definitely that you do not want this one or this one, and then to select that one as being best or most appropriate for you, is a satisfying experience. Though less actual choice making may be involved, it leaves the individual with a feeling of accomplishment and well being.

The experience of growing vagueness about who one is, the sense of restricted autonomy, is fostered by modern mass society in other ways too, including the following: (1) by making it harder for man to develop, and therefore live by, his own standards; because if so many choices are possible, if so many ways of life are viable, then one's own way is not

---

[1] Incorporated in this chapter are parts of an article titled "Individual Autonomy and Mass Control" which appeared in: Frankfurter Beiträge zur Soziologie; T. W. Adorno and W. Dirks, editors, Vol. I: *Sociologica*, Aufsätze, Max Horkheimer zum sechzigsten Geburtstag gewidmet. Europäische Verlagsanstalt, 1955, Frankfurt am Main.

so important and the ability to follow it need not be developed; (2) by at the same time fostering an illusion of greater freedom; which makes the experience of failing to satisfy one's desires still more damaging; (3) by presenting man with many more choices than anyone can reasonably be expected to handle well on his own; (4) by failing to provide in his early and later education, examples or guide lines on how and which of his instinctual desires may be gratified. Later on in life when he must gratify these desires or otherwise deal with them, his personality may have been formed without his having mastered the problem, and this then happens to someone who has come to depend on society for guidance in most of his life activities. So he relies on the clues society offers in deciding how, for example, to satisfy his sexual desires; and then not even his sexual life can give him the feeling of being a unique individual.

When social change is rapid, there is not enough time to develop the new attitudes needed for dealing with an ever changing environment in terms of one's own personality. This makes the individual "confused" and uncertain. The more this happens, the more he watches to see how others meet the new challenge and tries to copy their behavior. But this copied behavior, not being in line with his own make-up, weakens his integration and he grows less and less able to respond with autonomy to new change.[2]

What we now fear is a mass society in which people no longer react spontaneously and autonomously to the vagaries of life, but are ready to accept uncritically the solutions that others offer; we fear also that those solutions are geared only to technological progress, disregarding the greater in-

---

[2] Much that is said here of the autonomous individual versus the person subject to mass control has been more fully discussed, though with different emphases and conclusions, by David Riesman in *The Lonely Crowd*, New Haven, 1950, where he compares the autonomous with the other directed person.

tegration it requires. While the process of uncritical acceptance usually starts with externals, it does not often stop there
because external and internal life are too closely interwoven.
So once a person begins to rely on others for decision making
in externals it can soon extend to inner conflicts as well.
When such a state of personal disintegration characterizes
the majority there are no further brakes on rapid social
change; and the faster changes come, the harder it gets to
achieve the new integration needed to keep up with them.

Integration itself is a slow process. By the laws of psychic
economy, once a type of behavior is habitual, new types are
built up only after a person is sure they are either vastly
superior to the old ones, or his only way of handling a new
challenge. It takes time to achieve this feeling, and more
time and effort to develop and perfect new types of behavior.
It takes still more time and hard work to make them a
genuine part of the personality. Only then is man ready to
meet the next challenge autonomously; that is, in a way
wholly in keeping with his total personality. Therefore a
rapid rate of change in economic and social conditions makes
it very hard to achieve and maintain an autonomous personality. On the other hand, persons who have little autonomy can readily accept a fast rate of change. So there is a
serious problem we must be aware of: that fast change in
important social conditions may create more persons lacking
true autonomy, and this in turn may make possible a still
faster rate of change.

The less a man is able to solve inner conflicts, or those
between his desires and what the environment demands,
the more he relies on society for the answers to any new
challenge it may offer. And here it makes little difference
whether he gets his answers from the editorial writer, the
advertisements, or the psychiatrist. The more he accepts
their answers as his own, the less he can meet the next chal-

lenge independently and the more solutions must come from the outside. It is hard to say where exactly in this evolution of the mass state we now stand.

The work world

If we look first at externals we find that the more stratified society becomes and the more technology "assigns tasks to the individual," the less able he becomes to decide for himself on the sequence, execution and importance of activities. Yet a major support of any society is the ability of its citizens first to decide, and then to accept personal responsibility for their own actions. This is quite difficult when too much of what we do depends on the cooperation of others, or is regulated by them.

Whoever works without concern for the purpose of his labor or its final product is in this sense a dependent person; in effect, he accepts other people's decisions as the basis for his own actions. This holds equally true for all classes of workers, the skilled and the unskilled. Some physicists who worked on the first atomic bomb later showed concern. They questioned as irresponsible their willingness to perform tasks without considering, or being able to influence, the results of their work. The concern and frustration of factory workers who have little freedom in selecting their work, or power over its result, differ in no way in their impact on personality. They are just not always ready to give words to their emotions, or else lack the influence to have them recognized as important.

In our society, many wage earners choose their occupation for neurotic reasons rather than true inclination. Worse, many do not even consider the latter, because in their minds what one wants to do has become separated from earning a living. This leads to a contradiction that is psychologically dangerous. It undermines a person's self respect, his enjoyment of what he does much of the time, and his feeling that he works at a meaningful, important occupation.

To put the contradiction as simply as I can: such people are convinced, as they should be, that work, earning a living, is important. It is important to them because it provides sustenance for themselves and their families, and enables them to do what they want to the rest of the time. But it is also a fact that their "work" often appears tedious, unrewarding, out of kilter with their true interests. So their work is important and unimportant at the same time. Matters are further complicated because their afterwork life too is meaningful (it is what they work for) and at the same time unimportant (because what truly counts is earning a living, or they could not exist). Where the contradiction exists it creates serious dissatisfactions and conflicts that devour much of a person's vital energy; and it exists for many, though often they are not aware of it, or not consciously so.

A ready parallel is the youngster who hates school but still tries for good grades because he needs them for later advancement. But nobody can do really well at what he dislikes or has a low opinion of. So most of these youngsters fail to make the good grades. Another example is that of the many middle class parents who are highly critical of existing schools but still want their children to do well in settings which, according to them, are not fit to do well in. The miracle is that in spite of being projected into such contradictions some of our young people do quite well. Only one wonders: at what needless emotional expense?

The preference for jobs offering greater "security," spurious as it may be, is also neurotic, since experience has shown that when security is most needed—during severe depressions, or political upheavals—such jobs do not usually offer more security than others. Selecting jobs for the pseudo independence that higher pay seems to offer, instead of for autonomous reasons—i.e., the job offering deepest satisfaction because it has intrinsic meaning for the person and adds to his self respect—is likewise due to neurotic tendencies, namely the unrecognized equation of money with true status. Here, too, the outer security (what money can buy) is accepted in lieu of inner security; the impersonal coin of exchange is given more relevance than the particular product of one's labor. Matters are, of course, much worse when not even a semblance of freedom exists in choosing occupations.

In all societies the forces of environment can seem overpowering through their pressure and complexity, real or imagined. To this, modern technology has added man's physical weakness compared to the power of machines, his insignificance in a process where it takes hundreds to form and distribute the final product, and his ready exchangeability, not only on the assembly line but often in the vast research labs—to mention only some of the blows to his feeling of whether (or how much) he or his particular abilities matter in the overall process of production.

Once, in talking with a group of foreign service officers about the frustrations they experience, I was told that one of the hardest things for them to accept is the many orders they get from Washington to do things without being given the reasons underlying them. They know that it happens in part because the reasons are often so complex it would take a minor treatise to explain them, and often there is not enough time. Another factor is that any particular reason given would expose the person responsible for the order to varieties of criticism, in and out of Congress, which the order itself would not. That is, both his superiors and the public are much less apt to judge whoever gave the order for the order itself, than to take him to task over one or another of his reasons for giving it.

Here, then, are persons in important positions, representing their government in foreign countries, in an occupation whose intrinsic meaning few would question. All this would seem to breed a healthy pride in their calling. Still, the immensity of the enterprise they serve, and the complexity of the world we live in, finds them being used as mere means toward an end which they do not know. This, I was given to understand, is one of the major frustrations of their work.

Remote control

The vastness of the political system and its bureaucracy, and the bigness of most modern technological enterprises, now add still another factor—distance. Each one fosters personality disintegration because just at the point where man begins to feel he is losing control of his destiny and may be spurred to do something about it, he is offered a convenient excuse for evading the responsibility. Mass society is so complex that a man can justify his saying helplessly that he does not understand his role in the political or productive process. The trouble is that the justification does not help; it just lowers his own confidence in himself. His distance from the managers adds the often valid excuse that he is powerless to reach them, let alone influence anyone directly.

Without clear notions of these psychological phenomena, many Germans made use of them after the war when confronted with the horrors they supposedly consented to. They said (unless they disclaimed any knowledge of the horrors): "I was only a little man, what could I do?"[3] But if the excuse was heavily justified by reality, it marked another step toward personal disintegration. It was contrary to what

[3] Hans Fallada's book, *Little Man, What Now?* (*Kleiner Mann, was nun?*, Hamburg, 1932/1950) was widely read before the ascent of Hitler, and also presented as a movie. Even those who did not read it were familiar with the title which became a slogan of the pre-Hitler epoch. The story emphasized the individual's inability to decide his own fate, which was then to be decided by totalitarian control.

we like to consider man's greatest pride: maintaining his independence in the face of outside pressure.

Significantly, similar statements were made by workers on the atomic bomb projects in denying their responsibility. The atomic bomb brought into relief some of the social and psychological problems people face in the mass state. Public reaction in the U.S. was first one of pride in the power of the state and its managers, with whom most citizens identified. On further thought the terrifying power of whoever owned the bomb roused anxiety in the individual and a feeling of utter helplessness. Since he could not cope with his anxiety, he turned to society and its managers for protection, willing to grant them even greater power in exchange for protection against the new danger. A battle then began between the rational control of emotional fear ("there's no protection from atomic death except world cooperation") and mechanisms of compensation that are aggressive in nature, namely, reliance on the managers' power to offer security ("let's use it first!").

The feeling of helplessness, of being "only a little man," just an object of manipulation, brings about a need for compensation. The child who depends on his parent for survival must believe in his parent's goodness because only then can he feel sure of being cared for. Critical or aggressive feelings toward the parent create guilt feelings because the child is so dependent to begin with. Similarly, the more powerless the individual becomes in the mass state, socially, economically, politically, the more important appear those who seem to hold the power; therefore the individual needs to believe that these powerful managers will look after him. Only in this belief lies his psychological security. Lack of justice, when experienced in reality, is then blamed on the ill will of the middleman—on the foreman in the factory or the straw boss.

Here, too, modern man finds himself in a strangely con-

tradictory situation. While he sees himself as hopelessly enmeshed in, and at the mercy of the vast enterprise of modern
society, there is no doubt in his mind that this, his society,
is by far the most powerful known to man. The more powerful society grows, the more powerful (he rightfully feels) he
should become, as a part of it. But actually the opposite is
true, so that emotionally it adds insult to injury.

This might, in part, explain the anxiety and resentment
many feel about nuclear power. Such a tremendous advance
in science and technology should have given everyone a
feeling of greater security and strength. Actually it has increased our feeling of being helplessly at the mercy of powers
beyond our comprehension, or at least beyond our control.
As an advance in making nature serve man it should have
given us immense satisfaction, but what we enjoy is almost
negligible compared to the vast new anxiety created. Once
again, as society became so much more powerful, the citizen
got the short end of it. With society wielding more power
than ever, and himself more anxious than before, the individual must rely for his very survival on the wisdom of the
managers of society.

Physical distance from the managers keeps a man from
testing against reality his belief in their good will, a process
that might prove disastrous to his sense of economic and
social security. It also protects the pipe dream of managerial
wisdom and correctness on which he bases his psychological
security. This psychological process is as old as civilization.
Throughout history, the conqueror's power has made men
invest him with virtue, at times even to transfigure him into
a demigod or hero. It seems almost inevitable as a mental
process. The greater an individual's power over others, the
greater the evil that might possibly originate with him. The
greater the threat, the greater the need to deny it by believing in his virtue.

Distance which prevents reality testing of the manager's

virtue was used to advantage in the Hitler mass state. The leader appeared in public only on great occasions and then surrounded by his guards, speaking to large masses. This put a double distance between him and the individual: the guards who were close to the leader, and the tremendous audience preventing personal contact.

Another kind of distance was also used for intimidation: distance in time. The masses waited hours for the leader to appear. During this time their tension was increased to an insufferable degree by demonstrations, exciting music and the sheer physical exhaustion of standing for hours. The leader's appearance and the ending of tension that followed, was experienced as the great emotional relief it actually was. The experience of the leader's appearance bringing relief and the end of tension left an impression of some inherent power he had for relieving stress. This inspired gratitude and a belief in his "magic" power over the individual.

Because the contents of his speech bore no relation to the relief from tension, any one of his speeches had the desired effect on those present. This divorcement of effect from content increased the belief in the leader's charisma. The shallowness and unexciting quality of Hitler's or Mussolini's speeches, when heard over the radio without exposure to the events that preceded them, was for most persons in stark contrast to the impact of the leader's appearance on the physically present audience. With no previous tension built up in the radio listener, the leader's presence brought no relief, and the speech fell flat.

Consciously or unconsciously, distance in time is used by the boss in our society who lets an inferior wait before seeing him. This impresses the person with the boss' power and his own inferiority. Conversely, seeing the inferior immediately helps to establish direct, personal contact on a friendly, equal footing. This example also shows the inner forces at work: the waiting person becomes tense and anxious as time passes. He cannot deal with the accumulating anxiety about seeing the manager, his feeling of impotence grows and weakens his position. Only the very secure person (or someone who does not care about the outcome of the meeting) can stand the tension without getting anxious, and then insecure. Thus the ability to "be oneself" in the managed society is, again, largely a matter of personal integration and not entirely dependent on the structure of society.

The demoralizing effect of using time instead of intrinsic merit for gaining security can also be recognized in how wage earners try to compensate psychologically. Although they know better, they try to counteract fears of losing a job in which they are easily replaceable, by referring to how long they've been working on it. Irreplaceability due to quality of performance, as in the craft shop, is replaced by the pseudo security of time. Stable inner security based on a conviction of knowledge and skill is replaced by a reliance on outer security that can be shattered at any moment.[4]

After hours

A result is man's growing need to look for self respect and autonomy in the private sphere. Where there are slim chances for self realization in his work life, it becomes even more important to find it in his private life so as to acquire there a sense of identity. But for this he must be free to arrange his private life according to personal needs and desires. Here, modern technology seems to offer relief from automatism by shortening the time spent in "earning a living."

Unfortunately, this relief is often more apparent than real. Here it is less important that even leisure activities are frequently just offered to people, not self created. I do

---

[4] This, of course, does not fully apply where seniority on the job does provide security through union contracts.

not believe that painting a mediocre painting necessarily deepens self respect more than watching a good movie. Only good movies are so rare. By good movies I do not mean here movies that meet some esoteric standards, but those presenting situations and ideas that induce the spectator to reexamine his life and its purposes. Out of the experience, he may arrive at spontaneous new decisions about himself and his way of life, decisions that awaken in him, or encourage him to persist in, the elusive search for meaning and the widening of his consciousness of freedom.

Most movies, TV shows and other types of leisure time activities are so planned as to prevent such experiences from taking place. They are devised and prepared by people who do not allow themselves (or are not allowed) any free play of ideas; they are not supposed to have that effect. But short of it, choices among movies, juke boxes, or TV shows are so limited or meaningless that they are pseudo choices. They are so empty or so fixed that they evoke no emotional or intellectual participation and cannot serve the need for enriching one's life. Then after hearing and watching the same programs people often read the same book club selections chosen by persons representing the publishers who publish them in the first place. In exchanging opinions they enjoy the comfort of conformity until suddenly they feel the emptiness of a life offering too few experiences particular to themselves.

Even in the more active use of leisure, many tend nowadays to follow patterns suggested by the mass media. Having lost the ability to self regulate his work, man is equally dependent at play. Yet a life may be full of variety and still seem barren if activities and experiences do not bear the flavor of personal preference, do not spring from a meaningful, individual style of life. To pattern one's way of life on that of others is not a truly free choice, even if nothing is openly forced on the individual. Activities taken up because they are readily available, or "the thing to do," remain a miscellaneous collection of experiences. Since they have no common intrinsic qualities they can hardly be added, even less will they form an integral field which is more than the sum of its parts. Such a life is therefore fragmented and experienced as "empty," even if its lack of meaning is obscured by great busyness.

Most of us buy much the same clothes as our neighbors, much the same car,[5] much the same furniture. As a matter of fact, only mass production enables so much of Western society to buy these goods. The ability to provide oneself with material goods and many important services is a permanent advantage of mass society, one of the great achievements of our age. Nor should the initial increase in pride they offer be sneered at. But the fact remains that it is precisely because the experience of feeling worthwhile, on acquiring a new car, new furniture, a new house, is so satisfying, that the issue "What price such gains?" is not met. Who can afford to buy a house to meet his taste? not to speak of having such a house built for him? But how wonderful that so many of us can now buy our homes.

Because man wants a home of his own, he lives in naked housing developments or enormous apartment buildings where the arrangement of rooms, the inner plan of the dwellings are more or less uniform, thus imposing a uniformity on the way of life, of the pattern of rooming together. Unfortunately, instead of his home being the castle of his intimate world, it has picture windows exposing his privacy to one and all. This is not inherent in mass production, nor

---

[5] The recent interest in smaller foreign cars is an interesting exception. But in a strange way it too fails to enrich individual experiences because contemporaneous with it is the spreading of the superhighways which take the driver farther away from the countryside and both invite and require a greater, more uniform speed. So what is gained on the one hand (an expression of personal taste) is often lost on the other (less direct touch with regional variety in living and nature, no sensitive adjustment to the differences in the roads).

is it cheaper or more efficient. It also imposes one of the
most negative features of mass society: to look out at others
and be looked in on by them; they being concerned with
how we manage and we looking out to see how they do it.[6]
Some window or gable of these houses, having no impact
on the way of life, is shaped differently from unit to unit,
to make one home seem different from another. A semblance of individual taste is thus used to deny its absence
in all essentials.

Suburban life which so many now choose as an escape
from mass living imposes its own uniformities. Sometimes it
is even more constricting than city life because it lacks the
anonymity still available in the large urban setting. It does
not matter much if people are told how and what to eat
and drink, and when, or if they choose to eat and drink as
their neighbors. But it matters terribly if they are told how
to bring up their children or treat their mates, and if they
allow these external advices to sway them in the most intimate areas of living. The advice may be no more outspoken
than the astonishment of neighbors, or ridicule from children on the block toward those brought up differently, but
it works effectively.[7]

---

[6] This watching and being watched is very different from the intimate
living together in a group that was common in the villages and small
towns of the old world. There, too, everyone knew what went on in other
homes; but these were not strangers watching and copying or competing
with each other. They were people who lived together most intimately,
as if in a very large family. All was not love or mutual helpfulness there;
on the contrary there was often much ambivalence and pettiness. But
there were always strong emotions, however mixed, binding the group
together intimately. We have lost this emotional intimacy which is built
on associations stretching over generations, and in doing so have gained
a much higher degree of potential freedom. But as long as we pattern our
lives on that of our neighbors this potentiality has not become reality, and
we have lost a great deal of emotional intimacy without having gained an
equal measure of freedom.

[7] Nature, too, can be controlled for good or bad. Suburban land-
scaping is pleasant until it imposes unwelcome controls on man's free
time (after commuting). Mowing, watering and pruning can be a pleasure

When control of one form or another finally reaches the intimacy of sexual relations, as it did in the Hitler mass state, hardly anything is left that is personal, different, unique. When the sexual life of man is as regulated by external controls as his work and his leisure, he has finally and totally lost all personal autonomy; what identity is left him can only reside in his inner attitude toward such emasculation as a person.

Fortunately, total control is alien to the Western world. Free choices are still open, but by now they are seriously threatened; very little by laws, and only to a very limited degree by managed mass persuasion; but mass persuasion would never gain much of a foothold were it not for the deep inner anxiety of uncertain man.

The development and satisfactions of intimate living, including the sexual life, with greater spontaneity, richness and freedom—by which I do not mean dissoluteness—these are some of the inner developments man needs as a counterpoint to the growing complexity of social and technological development. Unfortunately, there are many reasons why enrichment in his intimate life, either as a person or as a member of a family, is not easy nowadays. Despite a far more liberal attitude toward sex in principle, the satisfaction of his sexual desires in practice often seems harder for modern man than knowing what to do with his aggressive tendencies.

---

when self chosen, or a drudge when neighbor imposed. One man moved to the suburbs to get away from city pavements and enjoy a more natural setting. The first summer his front lawn was full of dandelions and he rather liked the color and naturalness they added. But his neighbors had spent money and care to have perfect lawns and they objected to the weeds that would soon go to seed and spread to their lawns. After several experiences of this kind the man ruefully moved back to a city apartment. A formal garden or velvety lawn does not yield more comfort, shade, leisure, space or privacy than one closer to a natural woodland. They are just different kinds of gardens. But few suburban dwellers feel free to depart from pattern and choose what appeals most to themselves.

For one thing, in the less urban settings of the past, the animal world was not so clearly separated from that of man. On the contrary, it was part and parcel of the family's life experience and vital to its economic well being. The mating of animals was highly important, freely discussed, and readily observed, without the child being expected not to watch it or know about it. In the towns, even love making among adults was not the closely guarded secret it is today. Such a way of experiencing sex, both in its being viewed practically, and its psychological immediacy, is rarely available to most children today.

But it is not as simple as if just watching others make love (which I do not advocate) were a desirable solution. What counts is not what can be seen in the overt act but the inner attitudes that go with the love relation. When the intimate relations of parents are accompanied by hostility, guilt, or shame it is a more powerful obstacle to the child's ability to have successful intimate relations in his own later life than any other single factor. The issue is not so much whether or not some action is so overt that the child can easily grow familiar with it. Much more important are the attitudes and emotions that characterize the parents' relations to each other, to their children and to their work, all the days of their lives. And these things children can and do readily observe.

Most important of all in preparing for successful intimate relations later in life is the experience of having known good emotional care as a child. As one of my children (age 13) put it when her camp counselor was doing a poor job of taking care of her: "*Her* parents didn't take good care of her, so of course she couldn't take good care of herself, and now she can't take good care of me."

The variety of distractions that face modern parents often tempts them to devote less time, energy, and emotion to taking good care of their children, though technological progress makes the task easier than it used to be. But not having known good emotional care as a child (as distinct from physical care, though that counts too), the adult is poorly equipped to manage his love relations.

Confronted with the very difficult, demanding, and complex problems he must face in his most intimate relationships, he then does what society has taught him to do in all other respects—namely, look to the outside for direction and guidance. The result is that what could have been the core of spontaneity and self assurance enabling man to move about freely in a mass society without losing himself in it entirely, becomes an area that others are invited into by looking to them as examples to be emulated.

Many try to love by copying from examples out of magazine fiction. But this turns out to be useless because the stories tell what is already known, how to court, but fail to help with the unknown, how to love a mature sex partner. So the next best thing is tried, namely, finding out from others. This may in part explain the custom of double dating and necking. It gives the conviction that one does as well as others, and offers both permission and examples of behavior in an area where one is not too sure of being adequate. Thus, society, in the person of another couple or their example, invades the privacy of young people's intimate relations and keeps it from giving them a sense of identity, while at the same time robbing the relation of spontaneity.

As a matter of fact, much that passes for promiscuity has very little to do with sexual desire for the new partner. Often it is largely one more effort to learn how others manage their sex lives and thus find out if one's own is up to community standards. Only rarely is it a unique love relation (I love you because you meet my needs and desires as nobody else can—love me because I am uniquely worthy of your love, or shall try to be so). Most often the driving impulse is to find out if here, too, one can keep up with others. (I'll show you I'm as good or better than the other man—meaning: Assure me that I compare favorably with all my competitors; in return I'll provide you with identical assurance.)

Where does this leave many citizens of the mass state? Already too dependent on outside examples and too uncertain to meet the challenge of their environment in a way uniquely theirs, they are also unable to meet the inner challenge of their instincts on their own but rely here, too, on outside example or approval, be it the neighbor's, the "expert's" or the psychiatrist's. While this holds true mainly for the sex drives, it is often true for aggressive tendencies too. In either case, the person ends up overpowered—not only by outside pressures, but also by instinctual tendencies he can neither control nor discharge in a truly autonomous and hence fully satisfying way.

If the sum of external controls becomes overpowering, not only the individual but society too ceases developing until finally society grows rigid. The best that control can ensure is equality of opportunity—and in a mass society, variety and an abundance of basically impersonal goods. Only personal autonomy permits their full enjoyment. Liberty demands not only equality of opportunity but a variety of them. It also means a tolerance for those who fail to conform to standards that may be culturally desirable but are not essential for society to continue. Present day society often fails to offer this tolerance.

Inner controls

One recent change affecting autonomy in a mass society is in the ways in which society exerts control. Once controls used to be introduced in the most personalized form, namely by other human beings—parents, teachers, priests. Intimate knowledge of these persons made it possible to identify with them as a transition before controls were internalized and really became part of the personality. The fact that others made personal efforts at convincing or controlling man gave him a sense of his own significance.[8]

Inner controls are built up only on the basis of direct personal relations, not by obeying society's demands. They are only internalized when we identify ourselves with people we love, respect, or admire; people who have made these demands their own just as we did, by identifying with persons they respected.[9] The more a person conforms to society's standards on a shallow level of convenience or fear, the less

---

[8] With these educational methods went other conditions we do not wish to revive, including restricted opportunities for education. But again, an impersonal system is not inherent in mass education, and in the long run, not cheaper. It lies with the body politic to decide, or allow to be decided for them, what proportions of the national income go to the military, the highways, the schools, etc., and whether for narrowly conceived economic advantages the personal touch must disappear in education. There is no necessity for high schools of five thousand or more students, where, to use a single example, an attendance office must deal with hundreds of students absent or tardy. No personal interest can be extended to the student who, by his irregular attendance, clearly indicates his need for it. In the mass society, often it is not only the funds available that set limits on the methods possible, but even more so the fetish of efficiency and the desire for, or adoration of bigness.

There is also no need to change teachers every few months and in this way prevent the educational process from acquiring the deeper meaning that comes only from intimate and prolonged association between a mature and a growing individual. Much has been achieved when a teacher has extended his teaching over several years, particularly at the grade school level, while teaching the same material year after year to the same age group is stultifying to even the best teacher. A major reason, though often unrecognized, for the change of teachers every few months is the wish to have the educational system akin to the factory or the machine, where one worker on the assembly line, or one part, can readily be exchanged for another.

[9] True, identification can also proceed on the basis of fear, but if so the consequences are destructive and will benefit neither society nor the individual.

he internalizes its mores, and the fewer of them will be internalized by his child.

The child develops the structure of his personality firstly by identifying with his parents (or equally important persons) and by internalizing their demands until they become what he demands of himself. Secondly, he does this by meeting the challenges of an environment that was chosen and made suitable by his parents and educators to allow him growth along these lines. If the parents have merely adopted various patterns externally, that is, without due regard to their inner consistency, and without changing their personalities accordingly, the child will internalize both the parents' true personality, and the superficial behavior which is alien to it or even contradictory.

The same is true for the environmental challenges. They have to be shaped by the inner convictions of whoever educates the child, not by advice from the experts which the educator does not really feel at home with. Otherwise contradictions will arise and prevent these challenges to growth from becoming a source of developing inner maturity. Then challenges from the environment, too, will be experienced as too confusing to be internalized in a consistent inner pattern, in line with one's talents, interests, and background.

An example of such contradictions is the child who cannot understand why parents claim that money is no basis for judging people, while at the same time catering to a wealthy person whom they despise for his lack of morality or culture. Such behavior may still make sense to the parent, who really does believe that money is no basis for judging people but who nevertheless feels obliged to humor a person on whom his job depends. Remorse helps such a parent retain some tenuous integration. But the child, unaware of his parent's remorse, tries to guide his own behavior by belief in the unimportance of money, and belief in the importance of catering to the rich. This is impossible. He gives up trying to develop independent values, inner controls of his own, and turns to society with the demand, direct or indirect, that he be told what to do.

The less succeeding generations have truly learned to evaluate and apply society's mores through successful identification with parents and teachers, the more control society must exercise so that both society and the individual can function. And here it is immaterial whether such control is exercised by command or seductive persuasion. This process of external control has now been going on for at least two generations, and society must use greater and greater pressure to insure the degree of cooperation it must have. This alone shows what dangers lie ahead unless we again find ways to understand, accept and make our own society's legitimate demands in a machine age, and to reject those unacceptable in any age.

Mass controls cannot carry their weight by an appeal to individuality. Although the managers of public opinion are very sensitive to this and go out of their way to stress concern for the individual, their actions do not bear them out. If individual behavior is modified by such control, it is not the result of a personal act of internalization and is therefore contrary to man's autonomy.

Those who dislike mass control (often without being able to resist its influence) usually recognize that it denies human uniqueness. We are less aware of how its uniform appeal robs us of the pleasure we find in other forms of control or influence involving personal contact. Therefore mass controls try to make up for their poverty by other devices.

In the absence of personal identity, the individual looks to something outside himself to provide it. In the last analysis, he must look to the state. Therefore, the state, the nation, must make a show of uniqueness to compensate him secondhand for his loss. But again, anonymity, though it offers some security, does away with personal identity and leaves the individual with a feeling of helplessness contrary to the security he bargained for. Feeling his inner weakness, he yearns for something strong and powerful to support him. So to be attractive a mass must be powerful, or at least make a show of power. A powerless mass is not only unattractive, it creates anxiety and depression.[10] That is why a mass society must always claim and often demonstrate that it is powerful, that its strength provides security; otherwise it would lose its hold over its subjects.

Typical devices used by the modern mass state for exerting control are the impersonal bureaucracy, impersonal tastemakers, and impersonal sources of information; all evade individual responsibility behind a screen of objectivity and service to the community. All exert persuasive control through the mass media which lead man to believe that he longs for and needs what the propaganda wishes him to need. Instead of looking for satisfactions more suited to his particular personality and circumstances, he accepts what he finds offered by those who manage the productive process, the mass media, or the masses. He can do that because he no longer has singleness of purpose. That comes only with inner integration, and with knowing what one needs and wants; after a personal solution has been found to the conflicts between one's inner and outer worlds. Instead, he has many vague desires which he thinks are so interchangeable that the satisfaction of one can be substituted by another one more readily available.

To put this differently, an age that offers so many chances for escaping personal identity because it offers so many comforts and distractions requires equal strengthening of the sense of identity. A time that offers so much seduction to letting machines provide what seem like the essentials of

---

[10] The reformer or saint who joins a powerless mass is an exception who can be understood on the basis of his guilt or the gratification he feels at being a savior.

living, needs, more than other societies, to understand clearly what are the essentials and what the accidentals of human living, an understanding little needed when so few accidentals were available.

Just as democracy requires a more educated and moral population than do more primitive forms of society, so modern man requires a more highly developed emotional sensitivity so as not to succumb to temptations inherent in a machine age. The more mechanized and fragmented the world around us, the more we must develop the humanity of human relations. The more we live in a mass society, the better we must know how to have intimate relations.

Up to now, the Hitler state has been the outstanding example of an oppressive mass state, and its weakening influence on personality structure has been widely recognized. Less note has been taken of how it managed to exist for more than a decade by giving men outlets for at least one of their instinctual tendencies, namely, hostility. But release for instinctual needs is something very different from satisfying man's longings. Release can only temporarily make up for lack of satisfaction.

The Hitler state also offered its followers a pseudo identity through identification with the unique German state, and pseudo self respect through its ideology of the superior German race. These pseudo satisfactions were necessary for the state to gain complete external control of the individual without bringing about his immediate and utter disintegration.

In societies where the level of technology is low, the relative strength of inner controls may be based on a relative absence of choices; the business of life is strictly regulated by tradition and carried down to the individual through his parents. Therefore, the individual is always sure of himself and of what he is doing; he also feels in accord with his parents and age mates, which increases his self respect. These societies also allow amply for instinctual gratifications, both of sex and aggression. Lack of freedom (in the modern sense) is made up for by spontaneous satisfaction in the family sphere. Moreover, the relatively backward technology may permit a man some autonomy in his work.

Theoretically, in the "good" mass state, individual freedom would neither be suppressed nor manipulated out of existence. Nor would it lead to explosive behavior and societal chaos, because there would be enough emotional satisfaction in the private sphere of the family, and in the rewards of achievement in wider domains; these would guarantee self respect, autonomy and an expanding consciousness of freedom despite the impact of mass society. The individual's personality would then be strong enough for inner controls to govern his asocial tendencies, and a minimum of outside controls would be needed for the well being of society.

But in the "mass" state as we now know it, both inner controls and deep inner satisfactions seem to weaken from generation to generation. If this should continue and is not just a temporary effect of the tremendous changes wrought by technology, as I believe it to be, it will have to be compensated by stronger and stronger outside controls. Otherwise, weakened and irresolute, man's inability to provide for his own emotional needs, including the need to respect himself, may lead to dangerous inertia, or to explosions of instinctual violence. The tendency of the mass state to provide release will never make up for lack of satisfaction. The release of vacations cannot make up for deep frustration at work. As a matter of fact, the reliance on vacations to accomplish that often destroys them; by expecting too much, one gets less from the holiday than otherwise. Only an emotionally satisfying life, even within a hardworking existence, is enriched by vacations which are then equally though differently satisfying.

Closing the gap

The potentially devastating nature of one type of mass state was demonstrated under Hitler. There, the subject was caught in a vicious circle once he submitted to state control and allowed himself to conform at the expense of his self respect and his personal independence. Much of what was considered the result of a steady move toward state control over the individual was due at least in part to a mutual process. Man's inability to regulate his own life encouraged the state to control him. This made him even less able to make decisions and required even broader control, which in turn added to failure at self regulation. Here again a vicious circle of disintegration was set in motion.

While the state made him dependent, the citizen of the Hitler state remained ungratified in his dependent wishes. But that made him even more anxious to be "taken care of," and led to still greater feelings of frustration. He came to rely on outside guidance for all of his life activities, even how to satisfy his instinctual demands until finally, for the party elite, the state even selected his marital partner. Thus, in its ultimate form, the Hitler state tried to limit the area of personal freedom to a choice of the time and conditions of death, so that his own destruction would be the only true act of self assertion. In the concentration camps even this freedom was outlawed, and in the extermination camps it was abolished.

In view of this tentative discussion, efforts to explain the Hitler state on the basis of so-called national characteristics or of Germany's particular history seem academic. Germany's economic recovery after World War I, and that it then became the first true mass state in modern times, suggests weakness of personality structure, but not an inherent weakness. Instead of striving for greater personal autonomy, all energy went toward building the mass state in spite of unfavorable economic and cultural conditions. This was more of a tour de force than a case of weakness. The personality disintegration that followed was the result of an almost sudden change to the mass state, and not its cause.

This change was so fast that the average person did not develop adequate ways to master it on his own. Moreover Germany, as well as Italy, Spain and Russia up to the advent of the modern tyranny, were semifeudal states in which industrialization with its rapid changes developed much later than in Western Europe. Citizens of these states had had even less chance to integrate into their personality structures the necessary adjustment to a new social order.

During the transition from the relative freedom of late capitalism to an oppressive mass state, the central problem is one of inducing citizens, if necessary of forcing them, into conformity. Once created, the existence of such a state depends on citizens who are willing to give up personal identity and individualized ways of life and let themselves be managed. The greatest hope of mankind, but also the greatest danger to this type of mass state lies in the existence of a sizable minority who resist such a fate. They must be eliminated or else made to conform whether or not they are supervised, because any other course would endanger the state if its controls should lapse. The only way to guarantee such conformity at all times is to make sure that subjects conform of their own free will. On the other hand, the paramount task of those who wish to safeguard individual freedom is to find ways to protect it despite the power of modern mass control and mass persuasion.

The system of terror that characterized the Hitler state becomes understandable only when this need to change individual freedom and spontaneous action into willing submission is recognized as its central purpose.

Throughout history, tyrants have murdered their enemies. A regime's desire to destroy opposition is rationally understandable, though humanly we do not condone it. For centuries, torture has been used to extract confessions or satisfy a desire for revenge. Not even the scale of murder and torture in the German concentration camps was new. Genghis Khan, with whom Hitler compared himself, may have surpassed him. What was genuinely novel was the use of these devices against a government's own subjects, and their deliberate use for destroying the integrity of human beings.

The Hitler state as it later developed could hardly have grown from preconceived plans. Modern technology with its efficiency and disregard for human values coincided with the nihilistic philosophy of National Socialism, anti-humanitarian and wanting power at all costs. Each re-enforced the other and was further aggravated by the technological demands of preparing for total war.

When the Hitler system came to power it was thus well prepared for creating an oppressive mass state, though it began in a small way. The appalling phenomenon is how little resistance the process met, once it started, and how it gained momentum politically, economically and psychologically.

The most interesting reaction to my initial interpretation of the concentration camps was the strange relief some readers felt, despite the depressive content of the paper. It seemed that even when dealing with the most gruesome aspects of an oppressive mass society, the intellectual defense through understanding was still the most effective assurance that one was not altogether helpless and might even safeguard one's personality in the face of extreme threat.

This reaction is in line with some findings described in the analysis that follows. It seems to justify the hypothesis developed there that while an integrated personality and strong inner convictions, nourished by satisfying personal relations, are one's best protection against oppressive controls, another cardinal defense is the intellectual mastery of events as they happen.

In closing this chapter I would like to stress that although much of this book deals with the oppressive mass state, I believe that the Hitler variety was a passing phenomenon. The more we learn to understand it the more certain we can feel that it was only that, and not an image of things to come. Despite temporary setbacks, including the fall of the antique world, every new development in man has soon challenged him to reach a higher integration and a deeper consciousness of freedom. These alone can change technical advances into truly human progress.

We must not be downhearted because we feel the challenge but have not wholly mastered it yet. Technological progress just moves faster than personality integration. That is why I chose to work in the latter field, not the former, though eventually we always catch up with ourselves. Or so we must steadfastly believe, though the future is always uncertain.

4

Behavior in Extreme Situations: Coercion

FROM THE SIDELINES I HAD STUDIED THE problem of the German concentration camps since they were first established, long before I knew I was to become an inmate. After that, my interest was intensified. The result was an analysis, mainly psychological, written shortly after I was liberated, in which I tried to sum up some of the theoretical conclusions I had derived from the experience.[1] What motivated me to write it was firstly, a then widespread ignorance about the camps, which were still viewed as nothing but an outgrowth of sadistic impulses without further purpose; and secondly, their as yet unrecognized impact on the personality of prisoners.

Further reflection convinced me that the use of this analysis for understanding both an oppressive mass society, and what it takes to remain autonomous in any mass society, was more far-reaching than I first expected. If having to live under certain conditions which I called "extreme" could modify personality to such an extent, then I felt we must understand better why and how this can be so; not only to

[1] "Individual and Mass Behavior in Extreme Situations," *Journal of Abnormal and Social Psychology*, 38, 1943, pp. 417-452.

know what extreme situations can do to man and why, but
because other environments, too, shape personality, though
in different directions and ways.

The German concentration camps, which were very much
a thing of the present in 1943 when my first report appeared,
are by now only one of the more discouraging episodes in
the history of man. But what they taught about the influence
of the environment on man remains a lesson we need to
comprehend.

In order to understand their role, any emphasis on
atrocities as such or on individual fates will not do. Their
social meaning is what makes them important as an example
of the very nature of the coercive mass state. They are specially suitable examples because, once imprisoned, there
was little chance to counteract the onslaught against personal
integration, and because cause and effect were so exaggerated.

Therefore I have no intention of recounting once more
the horror story of the concentration camps, since it is now
common knowledge that prisoners suffered extreme deprivation and were deliberately tortured.[2] Suffice it to review here
the minimum facts: prisoners were clothed, housed and fed
in total inadequacy; they were exposed to heat, rain, and
freezing temperatures for as long as seventeen hours a day,
seven days a week. Despite extreme malnutrition, they had
to perform hardest labor. Every single moment of their lives
was strictly regulated and supervised. They had no privacy
whatsoever, were never allowed to see a visitor, lawyer, or
minister. They were not entitled to medical care; sometimes
they got it, sometimes not, but if they did it was rarely
administered by medically trained persons. No prisoner was
told why he was imprisoned, and never for how long. All

[2] For the earliest official report on life in the camps, see: *Papers concerning the treatment of German nationals in Germany,* London: His
Majesty's Stationery Office, 1939. For the most complete official account,
see the records of the Nuremberg trials: *Nazi Conspiracy and Aggression,*
United States Government Printing Office, Washington, D. C., 1946 ff.

of which may explain why I speak of them as persons finding themselves in an "extreme" situation.

In 1943 I restricted myself to my own experiences. The present, considerably revised and much enlarged discussion, also draws on the observations of others which have become available in the meantime. Therefore my remarks are no longer based entirely on personal experience.[3]

For some time the inhuman treatment of prisoners by the SS so fully absorbed all interest, that the Gestapo found it easy to screen its real purposes in the camps. Partly this was because those persons who were anxious and best able to discuss the camps were former prisoners, who were obviously more interested in what had happened to them than why it happened.

Nevertheless, the Gestapo had several varied, though related purposes. One major goal was to break the prisoners as individuals, and to change them into a docile mass from which no individual or group act of resistance could arise. Another purpose was to spread terror among the rest of the population, using prisoners both as hostages and intimidating examples of what happened if you did try to resist.

In addition, the camps were a training ground for the SS. There they were taught to free themselves of their prior,

---

[3] In 1942, three years after my release, the policy of mass extermination was instituted and all camps were classified into three groups. Type I camps were basically forced labor camps where prisoners were deprived of mobility, and maximum work was extracted from them; otherwise these camps were fairly livable and the prisoners had considerable latitude in arranging their lives. Type II camps were more or less of the type in which I spent a year; both Dachau and Buchenwald became Type II camps when this classification went into effect. Type III camps were extermination camps where no effort was made to modify personality since their only purpose was to exterminate prisoners as efficiently as possible.

Thus most of what follows pertains to Dachau and Buchenwald at the time of my imprisonment (1938-39) when all camps were a combination of what were later separated into Type II and III camps. *"Muselmän-ner,"* for example, were present in the camps at that time and my discussion of their behavior is based on personal observation.

more humane emotions and attitudes, and learn the most effective ways of breaking resistance in a defenseless civilian population; the camps thus became an experimental laboratory in which to study the most effective means for doing that. They were also a testing ground for how to govern most "effectively"; that is, what were the minimum food, hygienic, and medical requirements needed to keep prisoners alive and fit for hard labor when the threat of punishment took the place of all normal incentives; and what was the influence on performance when no time was allowed for anything but hard labor, and the prisoners were separated from their families. This use of the camps as experimental laboratories was later extended to include the so called "medical" experiments, in which human beings were used in place of animals.

By now the German concentration camps belong to the past. We cannot be equally certain that the idea of changing personality to meet the needs of the state is equally a thing of the past. That is why my discussion centers on the concentration camp as a means of changing personality to produce subjects more useful to the total state.

These changes were produced by subjecting prisoners to conditions specially suited to the purpose. Their extreme character forced the prisoners to adapt themselves entirely and with the greatest speed. In order to analyze the process it may be broken down into several stages. The first stage centered around the initial shock of being imprisoned, the journey to the camp, and the prisoner's first experiences inside it. The second stage comprised the adaptation to the camp situation in a process that changed both the prisoner's personality and his outlook on life.

While the process was going on, it was very hard to recognize the magnitude of its impact, because after the first great change, all the rest happened small step by small step. So, to make things more obvious, I will compare two groups of prisoners: one in whom the process had only started, namely, the "new" prisoners; and a second group in whom the process was already far advanced, the group I call "old prisoners." The final stages of personality change were reached when a prisoner had adapted himself fully to life in the concentration camp. This last stage was characterized, among other features, by a radically changed attitude toward and evaluation of the SS, or at least of its values and the way of life they stood for.

Why I began to study the prisoners

When I first collected and examined my thoughts on the camps, to prepare them for publication, it was easy to say that I wished to publish them because they dealt with important problems which, to my knowledge, had never before come to public attention. But this was not my original motive. Inside the camps I did not study my behavior, nor did I study my fellow prisoners or question them because I intended to make a distinterested survey of a problem that had roused my scientific interest. Quite the contrary; not detached curiosity, but vital self interest induced me to study my own behavior and the behavior I noticed around me. To observe and try to make sense out of what I saw was a device that spontaneously suggested itself to me as a way of convincing myself that my own life was still of some value, that I had not yet lost all the interests that had once given me self respect. This, in turn, helped me to endure life in the camps.

I can still remember, after more than twenty years, the moment when it occurred to me to study other prisoners. Early one morning toward the end of my first month at Dachau I was deep in the middle of what was the favorite free time activity: exchanging tales of woe and swapping rumors about changes in the camp conditions or possible liberation. There were only minutes, but that did not rule out intense absorption in these conversations. As before on such occasions, I went through many severe mood swings from fervent hope to deepest despair, with the result that I was emotionally drained before the day even began, a day of seventeen long hours that would take all my energy to survive it. While swapping tales that morning, it suddenly flashed through my mind, "this is driving me crazy," and I felt that if I were to go on that way, I would in fact end up "crazy." That was when I decided that rather than be taken in by such rumors I would try to understand what was psychologically behind them.

I do not claim that from then on such tales were without interest to me. But at least I stopped getting so emotionally involved in their content, because I was also trying to understand what went on in those who listened to the rumors and in those who invented or spread them about. It was to prove to myself that I was not losing my mind (i.e., my old personality) that I studied these stories, as a defense against taking for the truth what were obviously delusional tales. Observing and speculating about what went on in prisoners as they spun these wishfulfilling or nightmarish fantasies brought so much emotional relief that it obviously seemed a good idea to extend my observations and speculation whenever chance allowed it.

Thus my interest in trying to understand what was going on psychologically is an example of a spontaneous defense against the impact of an extreme situation. It was individually conceived, was neither enforced by the SS nor suggested by other prisoners, and was based on my particular background and training. Although at first I was only dimly aware of this, it was meant to protect me from a disintegration of personality I dreaded. Like other types of private behavior that arose among prisoners, as distinct from responses common to all of them, it followed the path of least resistance; that is, it followed closely some of my former main interests.

Perhaps a different type of private behavior, adopted out of similar defensive needs, may further illustrate. Among my prisoner friends were some whose chief interest in life, outside of their families and occupations, was stamp collecting. Two of them in particular had built up notable collections and become experts in philately. Within days after imprisonment they found each other, and from then on, without consciously being aware of why or how, they tried to protect themselves from the impact of camp life by trying to be together whenever possible. In this way they could keep their hobby alive in talks that permitted them to escape their misery for moments.

Up to a point, this served its purpose, as did my interest in what it meant psychologically, to be in the camps. Since their "defense" existed only when they were together, they tried to stay together at work, even when that was not safe. At this point their private behavior ceased being a defense and became a danger.

As time passed, and there was no new information they could feed into their talks about stamps, these became less and less satisfying, while they felt the loss of their collections more and more sharply. They ended up deeply disgusted with each other and their old hobby, and then had little of their former interests left to keep them going. Discouraged in what had given so much meaning to their lives, their private defense collapsed and soon they were only shadows of their former selves.

Since my own is the only extensive example of a private behavior I can offer, and since much of this account is one long illustration of it, a few words on why and how it developed may be added. As related earlier, I had studied and become familiar with the pathological picture presented by certain types of abnormal behavior. Psychoanalysis had taught me to observe myself, and later others, with great care. Since then I had continued to do the first, particularly when I found myself in critical situations.

Almost from the moment I was imprisoned, and particularly during the transport to Dachau and my first days inside it, I was aware that I not only acted, but more important, often felt differently than I used to. At first I made myself believe this was only on the surface, changes that did not touch my personality. But soon I realized that what had happened to me—for instance, the split within me into one who observed and one to whom things happened—was a typical schizophrenic phenomenon. So I began to ask myself, "Am I going insane or am I already insane?"

When to this was added the self observation just described—that behavior I was practising without being forced to was "driving me crazy"—it became doubly urgent to find answers to my questions. With no one knowledgeable to consult, I could only compare myself with my fellow prisoners. This was little help because they, too, were behaving in peculiar ways, although I knew that some of them (and had every reason to assume so for the rest) had been perfectly normal persons before imprisonment. Now they appeared to be pathological liars, were unable to restrain themselves, unable to separate clearly between reality and their wishful or anxious daydreams. So to the old worries, a new one was added, namely, "How can I protect myself from becoming as they are?"

The solution was relatively simple in theory: it consisted of finding out what had happened in them, and to me. Since I worried most about myself, the first issue to be settled was whether I was going mad. If I did not change any more than all other formerly normal persons, then what happened in me and to me was a process of adaptation, not the setting in of insanity. So I set out to learn what changes had occurred and were occurring in other prisoners.

My interest in observing how other prisoners and I had

changed, now merged with my efforts to find out which prisoners invented rumors and why, and what that did to them. Soon I realized I had found a solution to my main problem: by occupying myself whenever possible with problems that interested me, by talking with my fellow prisoners and comparing impressions, I was able to feel I was doing something constructive and on my own. It also offered great relief during the hours without end when we were forced to perform exhausting labor that asked for no mental concentration. To forget for a time that I was in the camp, and to know that I was still interested in what had always held my interest before, seemed at first the greatest advantage of my efforts. As time went on, the renewed self respect I felt because I was managing to occupy myself in ways that were meaningful to me, became even more valuable than the pastime.

Memorizing the data

It was impossible to keep notes, because there was no time for it, and no place to keep them. Every prisoner was subject to frequent searching of his body or belongings, and for any kind of notes found in his possession, however innocuous, he was punished severely. It seemed purposeless to risk such punishment because there was no way to take notes out of the camp since the naked prisoners due for release were again searched most carefully.[4]

---

[4] This was true when I was in the camps. But during the disorganization of the last years of the war a very few prisoners who enjoyed special prerogatives managed to keep and hide notes on which, after liberation, they based accounts of their experiences. Even those notes could never have been taken out of the camps; they exist because the prisoners were still alive when liberated by the Allied forces. Only two such diaries have come to my attention: Odd Nansen's notes, on which he based *From Day To Day* (New York: L. P. Putnam's Sons, 1949) and the unpublished notes kept by Edgar Kupfer while in the camp, which he tentatively titled: *The Last Years of Dachau* (Microfilm, University of Chicago).

The only way to get around this handicap was to make special efforts to remember what happened. Here I was seriously hampered by extreme malnutrition and other factors that deteriorate the memory; most important of these was the ever present sense of "what's the use, you'll never leave the camp alive," which was daily re-enforced by the death of fellow prisoners. So I often doubted if I would be able to recall what I wanted to remember. Still, trying to make sure that I could was one of the few things that made sense to me, so I tried to concentrate on what I believed were characteristic or outstanding phenomena, repeated my thoughts to myself again and again—time was abundant and had to be killed anyway—made a habit, at work, of going over it all to impress it better in my memory. Much as I doubted this method, it turned out to work. Because when my health improved after leaving the camp, and much more so when emigration made me feel secure, much of what seemed (and temporarily was) forgotten, came back.

While some prisoners were reticent, most were more than willing to talk about themselves, because to find someone interested in them and their problems helped their badly shaken self esteem. Talking at work was not permitted; but since practically everything was forbidden and punished severely, and since the guards were so arbitrary that prisoners who never broke a rule fared no better than those who did, all rules were broken whenever there was some chance of getting away with it.

Every prisoner was confronted with the problem of how to endure degrading work for from twelve to eighteen hours a day. Just about the only relief was to talk, whenever the guards did not prevent it. Though much of the day one was far too exhausted or depressed to make conversation, there were times for it at work, though it was forbidden, or else during the short lunch period or after work in the barracks, when it was permitted. Most of this time had to be used for resting or sleeping, but those who had not given up all interest in living felt a need for some conversation.

Prisoners often had to change the labor group in which they worked, and quite often the barrack in which they slept, because the SS did not want prisoners becoming too intimate with one another. I, for example, though lucky in having relatively stable work assignments (sometimes through bribing the foremen) still worked in at least 20 different labor groups whose number varied from 20 to 30 all the way up to several hundred. I slept in five different barracks, each of them housing from 200 to 300 prisoners. In this way, like most other prisoners, I came into personal contact with at least 600 prisoners at Dachau (out of about 6000) and at least 900 at Buchenwald (out of about 8000). Only prisoners of the same category (criminals, politicals, homosexuals, etc.) lived together in the barracks, but the various categories were mixed at work; so if one was interested, one could get to talk to prisoners of all categories.

Bias in the listener

After I began to have definite impressions about what I believed was going on in the prisoners, psychologically, I tried to check my thinking with others. Unfortunately I found only two who were both capable and interested in sharing observations. They, too, had personal contact with several hundred prisoners though our contacts, of course, overlapped. Every day, particularly before and during the morning roll call and while waiting for assignment to our labor groups, we shared observations and engaged in often wild theories; scientific detachment about the prison experience was not to be found among inmates. But despite the strong emotional flavor of these conversations, the main purpose of which was more often than not to forget the conditions of our lives, they proved very helpful in rectifying one-sided viewpoints.[5]

Shortly after coming to this country, within a few weeks after my release, I began to put some of my memories down on paper. I hesitated for almost three years to interpret them, because I felt that my anger about the camp experience would interfere with objectivity. By then I thought I had reached as objective an attitude as I could ever expect to reach,[6] so I began to prepare the manuscript for publication.

The difficulty of observing and analyzing mass behavior when the reporter is part of the group seems obvious: so is the task of observing and analyzing oneself when there is nobody around to check and correct. It is still more difficult to remain objective when one discusses experiences which, by their very nature, arouse the strongest emotions. I hope that full awareness of these limitations has helped me to avoid at least the most obvious pitfalls.

[5] One of the participants was Alfred Fischer, M.D.; at the time my original paper appeared he was on duty in a military hospital somewhere in England. I have since lost track of him. The other, Ernst Federn, remained in Buchenwald until its liberation in 1945 and is now a social worker in the U.S. Some of his observations he reported in "Terror as a System: The Concentration Camp," *The Psychiatric Quarterly Supplements*, 22, 1948, pp. 52-86.

[6] Most helpful in reaching this state of objectivity was the certainty that within a short time the Gestapo as an institution would be destroyed. It is now of minor interest that from 1939 to 1942 I met disbelief and criticism when I spoke of the German concentration camps as serving important purposes for the Nazis. The notion of ascribing purpose or intelligent planning to the SS, of taking them seriously, was considered both unwise and unsafe. It was put down to a natural loss of perspective after imprisonment in a concentration camp. So uniform was this reaction that I spent two years wondering if I had correctly evaluated my experience and the meaning of the camps, or if my analysis of them was indeed the result of a prison neurosis. Finally I decided to submit it for publication.

The manuscript was rejected by some psychoanalytic journals in 1942 and 1943 for reasons such as noted above. I am indebted to Gordon Allport for its first publication. Owing to him, and to Dwight MacDonald who republished parts of it soon afterward, the wider meaning of the concentration camps became more generally known.

TRAUMATIZATION

The shock of imprisonment

Sudden personality changes are often the result of traumatic experiences. In discussing the impact of the camps on the prisoners, the initial shock of being torn away from one's family, friends and occupation and then deprived of one's civil rights and locked into a prison, may be separated from the trauma of subjection to extraordinary abuse. Most prisoners experienced these two shocks separately, because they usually spent several days in a local prison where they were relatively unharmed, before being transported to the camp.

Their "initiation" to the concentration camp, which took place while on transport, was often the first torture prisoners had ever experienced and was, for most of them, the worst torture they would be exposed to either physically or psychologically.

Whether and how much the initial shock was experienced as severe trauma depended on the individual personality. But if one wishes to generalize, the prisoners' reactions can be analyzed on the basis of their socio-economic class and their political sophistication. Obviously these categories overlap, and they, too, are separated only for the purposes of discussion. Another factor of importance was whether a prisoner had ever been in prison before, either as a criminal or for political activity.[7]

---

[7] During my stay in the camps the main categories, in order of their respective sizes, were: *Gentile political prisoners,* mostly Social Democrats and Communists (the majority of lower class origin, though some were middle class), also a few aristocrats who, as monarchists etc., had opposed Hitler (all of these, upper class). The *asocial* or *"work-shy"* groups, imprisoned because they had objected to working conditions, had no regular jobs, had complained about wages, etc. (lower class). *Jewish political prisoners* (mostly middle class). Former members of the *French Foreign Legion,* the *Jehovah's Witnesses (Bibelforscher)* and other conscientious objectors (mostly lower class). The so called

Non-political middle class prisoners (a minority group in the concentration camps) were those least able to withstand the initial shock. They were utterly unable to understand what had happened to them and why. More than ever they clung to what had given them self respect up to that moment. Even while being abused, they would assure the SS they had never opposed Nazism. They could not understand why they, who had always obeyed the law without question, were being persecuted. Even now, though unjustly imprisoned, they dared not oppose their oppressors even in thought, though it would have given them a self respect they were badly in need of. All they could do was plead, and many groveled. Since law and police had to remain beyond reproach, they accepted as just whatever the Gestapo did. Their only objection was that *they* had become objects of a persecution which in itself must be just, since the authorities imposed it. They rationalized their difficulty by insisting it was all a "mistake." The SS made fun of them, mistreated them badly, while at the same time enjoying scenes that emphasized their position of superiority. The group as a whole was especially anxious that their middle class status should be respected in some way. What upset them most was being treated "like ordinary criminals."

Their behavior showed how little the apolitical German middle class was able to hold its own against National Socialism. No consistent philosophy, either moral, political, or social, protected their integrity or gave them strength for an inner stand against Nazism. They had little or no resources to fall back on when subject to the shock of imprisonment. Their self esteem had rested on a status and respect

---

"*professional*" *criminals, Jewish work-shy* prisoners, and a few members of such Nazi formations as the followers of Roehm (entirely or predominately lower class). The following small groups included members of all classes: *race offenders,* i.e., Jews who had had sex relations with gentiles; *homosexuals;* and a few persons imprisoned to extract money, or because some Nazi bigwig wanted revenge.

that came with their positions, depended on their jobs, on being head of a family, or similar external factors.

Those familiar with the mores of this group will appreciate what a blow it was when raw privates in the SS addressed them not as *Herr Rat* (or some other titles of office) but with the degrading "thou"; even worse, they were forbidden to address one another with the titles of office that were their greatest pride, and were forced to use the much too familiar "thou" form when they spoke to each other. Up to then they had never realized just how much extraneous and superficial props had served them in place of self respect and inner strength. Then all of a sudden everything that had made them feel good about themselves for so long was knocked out from under them.

Eventually they could not help realizing their abysmal change in status. Since to them this was tantamount to a total loss of self respect, they disintegrated as autonomous persons. For them, imprisonment alone was often enough to start the process and carry it quite some length. For instance, the several suicides that took place in prison and during the transport were mostly confined to this group.

Nearly all of them lost their desirable middle class characteristics, such as their sense of propriety and self respect. They became shiftless, and developed to an exaggerated extent the undesirable characteristics of their group: pettiness, quarrelsomeness, self pity. Many became depressed in an agitated way and complained eternally. Others became chiselers and stole from other prisoners. (Stealing from, or cheating the SS was often considered as honorable as stealing from prisoners was thought despicable.) They seemed incapable of following a life pattern of their own any more, but copied those developed by other groups of prisoners. Some followed the behavior pattern set by the criminals. Only a very few adopted the ways of the political prisoners, usually the most desirable of all patterns, questionable as it was. Others tried to do in prison what they preferred to do outside of it, namely to submit without question to the ruling group. A few tried to attach themselves to the upper class prisoners and emulate their behavior. Many more tried to submit slavishly to the SS, some even turning spy in their service (which, apart from these few, only some criminals did). This was no help to them either, because the Gestapo liked the betrayal but despised the traitor.

Here the code of gang honor asserted itself which early National Socialists had to rely on. Spies were used and protected only as long as they provided new information, but sometimes not even that long, so deeply did the SS despise them. Moreover, to protect them for any length of time would have implied that a prisoner was more than just a number, more than a nonentity. This was so contrary to SS principles that no exception was made even for useful informers. Under no circumstances would they let a prisoner become a person through his own efforts, even if those efforts were useful to the SS. As soon as protection by the SS ceased, sometimes sooner, informers were killed by other prisoners as a warning, and for revenge.

For those *political* prisoners who had expected persecution by the SS, imprisonment was less of a shock because they were psychologically prepared for it. They resented their fate, but somehow accepted it as something that fit their understanding of the course of events. While understandably and correctly anxious about their future and what might happen to their families and friends, they certainly saw no reason to feel degraded by the fact of imprisonment, though they suffered under camp conditions as much as other prisoners.

As conscientious objectors, all *Jehovah's Witnesses* were sent to the camps. They were even less affected by imprisonment and kept their integrity thanks to rigid religious beliefs. Since their only crime in the eyes of the SS was a refusal to bear arms, they were frequently offered freedom in return for military service. They steadfastly refused.

Members of this group were generally narrow in outlook and experience, wanting to make converts, but on the other hand exemplary comrades, helpful, correct, dependable. They were argumentative, even quarrelsome only when someone questioned their religious beliefs. Because of their conscientious work habits, they were often selected as foremen. But once a foreman, and having accepted an order from the SS, they insisted that prisoners do the work well and in the time allotted. Even though they were the only group of prisoners who never abused or mistreated other prisoners (on the contrary, they were usually quite courteous to fellow prisoners), SS officers preferred them as orderlies because of their work habits, skills, and unassuming attitudes. Quite in contrast to the continuous internecine warfare among the other prisoner groups, the Jehovah's Witnesses never misused their closeness to SS officers to gain positions of privilege in the camp.

The *criminal* group were least affected by the shock of imprisonment. Much as they hated being in the camps, they showed open glee at finding themselves on equal terms with political and business leaders, with attorneys and judges, some of whom had once sent them to prison. Their resentment of those who had once been their "betters" explains in part why many of them became willing tools of the SS in policing the camps; when to this was added the chance of exploiting other prisoners economically, it became irresistibly attractive to them to serve the SS against the prisoners.

Initiation to the camps

Usually the standard initiation of prisoners took place during transit from the local prison to the camp. If the distance was short, the transport was often slowed down to allow enough time to break the prisoners. During their initial transport to the camp, prisoners were exposed to nearly constant torture. The nature of the abuse depended on the fantasy of the particular SS man in charge of a group of prisoners. Still, they all had a definite pattern. Physical punishment consisted of whipping, frequent kicking (abdomen or groin), slaps in the face, shooting, or wounding with the bayonet. These alternated with attempts to produce extreme exhaustion. For instance, prisoners were forced to stare for hours into glaring lights, to kneel for hours, and so on.

From time to time a prisoner got killed, but no prisoner was allowed to care for his or another's wounds. The guards also forced prisoners to hit one another and to defile what the SS considered the prisoners' most cherished values. They were forced to curse their God, to accuse themselves and one another of vile actions, and their wives of adultery and prostitution. I never met a prisoner who had escaped this kind of initiation, which lasted at least twelve hours and often much longer. Until it was over, any failure to obey an order, such as slapping another prisoner, or any help given a tortured prisoner was viewed as mutiny and swiftly punished by death.

The purpose of this massive initial abuse was to traumatize the prisoners and break their resistance; to change at least their behavior if not yet their personalities. This could be seen from the fact that tortures became less and less violent to the degree that prisoners stopped resisting and complied immediately with any SS order, even the most outrageous.

There is no doubt that the initiation was part of a coherent plan. Quite a few concentration camp prisoners had to travel to Gestapo headquarters for questioning, or to appear in court as witnesses. On the return to the camp they were hardly touched. Even when they were transported along with a group of new prisoners, they were left alone by the SS as soon as they made their status known as prisoners already initiated. When a thousand of us Austrian prisoners were arrested in Vienna and brought to Dachau, scores were killed or died on the transports, and many more were permanently injured; hardly one of us escaped without injuries of some sort. But when half a year later a similar number were transferred from Dachau to Buchenwald, a transport we dreaded would be like the first one, not one of us died in transit, and if anyone was severely injured I failed to learn about it. By and large, this second transport lasting about as long as the first, was not much worse than a day in the camps, except for our desperate anxiety.

It is hard to say just how much the process of personality change was speeded up by what prisoners experienced during the initiation. Most of them were soon totally exhausted; physically from abuse, loss of blood, thirst, etc.; psychologically from the need to control their anger and desperation before it could lead to a suicidal resistance. As a result they were only partly conscious of what happened. In general, they remembered details afterward and did not mind talking about them, but they did not like to talk about what they had thought or felt while being tortured. The few who volunteered information made vague statements that sounded like devious rationalizations to justify their having endured treatment so damaging to their self respect without trying to fight back. The few who did try to fight back could not tell about it; they were dead.

I can recall my own extreme weariness, partly from a slight bayonet wound received early in the transport and from a heavy blow on the head later on. Both led to a loss of blood that left me groggy. Nevertheless, I have a clear recollection of my thoughts and emotions during the transport. I wondered all the time why the SS did not kill us outright, and that man can endure so much without going insane or committing suicide, though some prisoners did, by jumping out of the train windows.

I wondered that the guards really tortured prisoners just as I had read about it in books on the concentration camps; that the SS was as simple-minded as they appeared to me; i.e., that they enjoyed forcing prisoners to defile themselves and expected to break their resistance in that way. I wondered that the SS were so lacking in fantasy in the means they chose for torturing prisoners; that what I took to be their sadism was without imagination.

What had most value for me in these reflections was that things happened according to expectation; that therefore my future in the camp was at least partly predictable from what I was already experiencing and from what I had read; that the individual SS was more stupid than I had expected, which eventually proved small satisfaction and not always true. Most of all, I felt pleased with myself because the tortures had not driven me out of my mind (as I may have feared) nor changed either my ability to think or my general point of view.

In retrospect these considerations seem futile, but they were important. Because if I should try to sum up in one sentence what my main problem was during the whole time I spent in the camps, it would be: to protect my inner self in such a way that if, by any good fortune, I should regain liberty, I would be approximately the same person I was when deprived of liberty.[8] So it seems that a split was soon

---

[8] I have several times referred to how much I learned from my concentration camp experience; so in reality I did not leave the camps the same person I was when I entered. But the notion that spending time in a concentration camp could be a growth experience did not occur to me until many months after I was gone from the camps, and even then it was at first dismissed as just a wishfulfilling daydream. It was not uncommon for prisoners to think they might change some part of their lives for the better if they survived, but since practically everybody doubted his survival, such notions were never taken seriously.

forced upon me, the split between the inner self that might be able to retain its integrity, and the rest of the personality that would have to submit and adjust for survival.

Initial adjustment

I have no doubt that I was able to endure the horrors of the transport and all that followed, because right from the beginning I became convinced that these dreadful and degrading experiences were somehow not happening to "me" as a subject, but only to "me" as an object. The prevalence of such an attitude was borne out by many statements of other prisoners, although none would go so far as to say definitely that it was clearly developed as early as the time of the transport. Usually they couched their feelings in more general terms such as, "The main problem is to remain alive and unchanged," without specifying what they meant by unchanged. From additional remarks it became apparent that what was to remain unchanged differed from person to person, but covered roughly that person's general attitudes and values. Unfortunately, staying alive and unchanged was very difficult, since every effort to assure remaining alive implied inner changes, while efforts to avoid change endangered survival.

All thoughts and feelings I had during the transport were extremely detached. It was as if I watched things happening in which I took part only vaguely. Later I learned that many prisoners developed this same feeling of detachment, as if what happened did not really matter to oneself. It was strongly mixed with a conviction that "This can't be true; such things just don't happen." Not only during the transport but for a long time to come, prisoners had to convince themselves that this was real and not just a nightmare. Some of them were never wholly successful.

In the same vein, many prisoners behaved as if their existence in camp had no connection with their "real" lives. They went so far as to insist that this was the correct attitude. Their evaluation of their own and other persons' behavior differed considerably from what they would have thought and said outside of camp. The separation of behavior patterns and values inside and outside of camp was so radical, and the feelings about it so strong that most prisoners avoided talking about it; it was one of many subjects that were "taboo." The prisoners' feelings could have been summed up as follows: "What I do here or what is happening to me doesn't count at all; here, everything is permissible as long and insofar as it contributes to helping me survive in the camp."[9]

This attitude of denying "reality" to events so extreme as to threaten the prisoner's integration was a first step toward developing new mechanisms for surviving in the camp. By denying reality to overwhelming situations, they were somehow made bearable; but at the same time it constituted a major change in experiencing the world. Thus while the attitude was a necessary adjustment, it also implied personality change. The denial of reality was most obvious during extreme experiences that the prisoner could not have managed in any other way.[10]

---

[9] One more observation: during the transport no prisoner fainted, though some got themselves killed as noted above. To faint meant to get killed. So in this particular situation fainting was no device to ward off intolerable pain and in this way facilitate life; on the contrary, it endangered a prisoner's existence because anyone unable to follow orders was killed. Later on, in the camp, prisoners fainted; but there it was not so customary to shoot prisoners for fainting.

[10] Prisoners' dreams were an indication that extreme experiences were not dealt with by the usual mechanisms. Many dreams combined aggression and wish fulfillment in such a way that the prisoner was able to revenge himself on the SS. Interestingly enough, the reasons for revenge—where a particular reason was given—was always some relatively minor abuse, never an extreme experience. I had had some previous experience with reactions to shock in dreams. Once in the camp, I expected my dreams to follow the same pattern: a repetition of the shock experience in dreams, the shock becoming less and less vivid and the dream finally disappearing. I was astonished to find that in my dreams the most shocking events never appeared. I asked many

Psychological reactions to events somewhat closer to the normal or familiar were distinctly different from reactions to extreme experiences. Prisoners seemed to deal with less extreme events just as if they had happened outside the camp. For example, if a prisoner's mistreatment was not of an unusual kind, he seemed ashamed of it or tried to deny it had ever happened. If a prisoner was slapped in the face it was more upsetting and embarrassing to him than a whipping. Prisoners hated guards who kicked, slapped or swore at them much more than guards who had wounded them seriously. For serious abuse, the prisoner hated the SS as such, but not so much the individual who inflicted the punishment. Obviously it was unreasonable to differentiate in this way but it seemed inescapable. Prisoners felt deeper and more violent anger against particular SS guards for minor acts of cruelty than they felt against guards who behaved much more viciously.

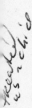

A tentative interpretation of this phenomenon is that those types of experiences that might have happened during a prisoner's "normal" life provoked what would have been "normal" reactions; for example, prisoners were particularly sensitive to being treated the way a harsh parent might act toward a helpless child. Punishing a child was within their "normal" frame of reference, but that they should be getting the punishment instead of giving it destroyed their adult frame of reference. So they reacted not in a mature, but a childish way—with embarrassment and shame, with impotent rage, directed not against the system (as would have been reasonable) but against the random person who inflicted the punishment. Like children, they were unable to accept the fact that their treatment was part of the Gestapo system: neither inflicted for any personal reasons, nor in-

---

prisoners if they had dreamed about what happened during the transport and could never find a single one who could remember having dreamed about it.

flicted on them as persons. Like children, they swore they were going to "get even" with the guard, knowing well how impossible that was.

It is also possible that prisoners resented minor abuses, in which they were dealt with as if they were silly children, more than extreme ones, because unconsciously they realized that the Gestapo was trying to reduce them to the status of children who have no rights and must obey blindly. Or it may have been that for severe punishment, the prisoner could expect to receive friendly support, which is some comfort. He could not reasonably expect it for being rapped on the knuckles with a ruler, or for a slap in the face. Moreover, if the suffering was great, he felt more like a man than a child, because children are not punished so brutally; or he may have felt a bit like a martyr suffering for a cause, and the martyr is supposed to accept his martyrdom, or at least to take it like a man.

Prisoners, in their group reactions, developed much the same attitude toward minor abuses. Not only did they not offer help, but would openly blame the prisoner for having brought trouble on himself by his own stupidity—by not having made the right reply, by having let himself get caught, by not having been careful enough. In short, they accused him of having behaved like a child. So the prisoner's degradation at being treated like a child took place not only in his own mind, but in the minds of his fellow prisoners too.

As time went on and the process of adjustment continued, most prisoners showed little difference in their reactions to major or minor sufferings. But by that time, most of them had reached a more advanced stage of personality distintegration, and all of them had come to feel somewhat like hapless children.

Besides traumatization, the Gestapo relied mainly on three other methods of destroying all personal autonomy. The first of these has just been touched on: that of forcing prisoners to adopt childlike behavior. The second was that of forcing them to give up individuality and merge themselves into an amorphous mass. The third consisted of destroying all capacity for self determination, all ability to predict the future and thus to prepare for it.

THE PROCESS OF CHANGE

Childlike behavior

To be filled with impotent rage is a situation frequent in childhood, but disastrous for one's mature integration. Therefore, the prisoners' aggressions had to be dealt with somehow, and one of the safest ways was to turn it against the self. This increased masochistic, passive-dependent, and childlike attitudes which were "safe" because they kept the prisoner out of conflict with the SS. But as a psychological mechanism inside the prisoner it coincided with SS efforts to produce childlike inadequacy and dependency.

It has been mentioned that prisoners were often mistreated in ways that a cruel and domineering father might use against helpless children. But just as even the cruelest parent threatens physical punishment much more often than he actually inflicts it, so childlike feelings of helplessness were created much more effectively by the constant threat of beatings than by actual torture. During a real beating one could, for example, take some pride in suffering manfully, in not giving the foreman or guard the satisfaction of groveling before him, etc. No such emotional protection was possible against the mere threat.

While there were many days for many a prisoner when he went unharmed, there was hardly an hour of the day when neither he nor some of his friends were not being threatened with a lashing. The vast majority of prisoners went through the camp without a public flogging, but the screamed threat that they were going to get twenty-five on the behind rang in their ears several times daily. To have to accept and make one's peace with the fact that one was constantly under threat of such infantile punishment made it much harder to retain one's self image as an adult than any actual beatings.

Threats like these, and also the curses thrown at prisoners by both the SS and prisoner foremen were almost exclusively connected with the anal sphere. "Shit" and "asshole" were so standard that it was rare when a prisoner was addressed otherwise. It was as if every effort were being made to reduce prisoners to the level they were at before toilet training was achieved.

For example, they were forced to wet and soil themselves. All elimination was strictly regulated in the camp and was an important daily event, discussed in detail. At Buchenwald it was repeatedly forbidden to defecate during the entire work day. But even when exceptions were made a prisoner who needed to eliminate had to get permission from a guard and then report to him when he was finished in ways that shattered his self respect.

The formula he had to use was the same one required in all cases of asking for something of the guards, such as a letter from home, etc. It was a formula that emphasized both an absence of personal identity, and abject dependence; for a Jewish prisoner it would go: "Jewish prisoner number 34567 most obediently prays to be permitted to (whatever the request was)." Some decent guards would wave a condescending okay. But many made degrading remarks or asked questions that could only be answered in a self degrading way; others would keep the prisoner waiting for a while, as if debating if he had been abject enough, or if his need was really urgent. If permission to eliminate was granted, the prisoner, having relieved himself, had to report back using the same formula, much as an infant might report on having done his "duty." Here too it was if the education to cleanliness were being repeated again.

The pleasure the guards seemed to find in having the power to grant or withhold permission to visit the latrines found its counterpart in the pleasure prisoners found in visiting them, because they could usually rest there for a moment, relatively safe from abuse. Actually they were not always so secure because sometimes enterprising guards enjoyed interfering with the prisoners even there.

Moreover, the latrines themselves were usually nothing but a trench with logs at either side on which prisoners had to balance. Any public elimination was extremely degrading to Germans, because in Germany utter privacy when eliminating was the absolute rule, except for infants and very small children. This is contrary to American custom which does not always insist on privacy in this respect. Therefore, enforced observation of and by others was a demoralizing experience.

Nor was this restricted to daytime, and the open latrines. In the barracks there were only rows of open toilets so that even in their living quarters they could never eliminate in privacy. Because of the small number of toilets, the brief time available and the large number of prisoners, they were also forced to form in long lines before each toilet. Those waiting, afraid they might not get a chance to use the toilet, nagged and swore at the prisoner using it to hurry up, to get done. Here the waiting prisoners treated the eliminating one as an impatient parent might urge his infant to get off the potty; another camp situation that pushed prisoners into treating each other as incompetent children.

In this context it may be repeated that all prisoners had to address each other in the familiar "thou" form, which in Germany is never used indiscriminately except among small children. On the other hand, they had to address the guards in the most obsequious manner, including the use of all their titles.

Another influence adding to regression into childhood behavior was the work prisoners were given to do. New prisoners in particular were given nonsensical tasks, such as carrying heavy rocks from one place to another, and after a while back to the place where they had picked them up. Or they were forced to dig holes in the ground with their bare hands although tools were available. They resented the senseless work, although it should have been immaterial to them whether their work was useful or not. They felt debased when they were forced to perform "childish" or stupid labor, and often preferred even harder work when it produced something that might be called useful. They felt even more debased when they were hitched like horses to heavy wagons and forced to gallop. By the same token, many prisoners hated singing rollicking songs by command of the SS more than being beaten by them. The less painful, the more nonsensical an activity was in itself, the more degrading it felt to have to perform it for the SS.

Frequently the SS assigned more meaningful tasks to old prisoners. This indicated that forcing nonsensical labor on the prisoners was a deliberate effort to speed their decline from self respecting adults to obedient children. There seems no doubt that the tasks they were given, as well as the mistreatment they had to endure, contributed to the disintegration of their self respect and made it impossible to see themselves and each other as fully adult persons any more.

Mass behavior

The difference between certain practices at Dachau (organized in 1933) and Buchenwald (in 1937), reflects the growing depersonalization of all procedures during that period.

At Dachau, for example, official punishment, as distinct from random abuse, was always directed at a particular individual. Beforehand he had a so-called hearing in the presence of a commissioned SS officer. According to Western legal standards these hearings were a farce, but compared to what later became standard procedure it showed great consideration for the individual because he was at least told what he was accused of and given a chance to refute the charges. If he knew what was good for him, he made no effort to defend himself. But he could add one or another detail and sometimes get off without punishment.

Before flogging, he was examined by the camp physician, another fairly empty procedure since the doctor rarely canceled the whipping, though he sometimes reduced the number of lashes. Even as late at 1939, prisoners at Dachau enjoyed some limited protection against too flagrant acts of injustice. When a guard shot or otherwise caused a prisoner's death he had to make a written report. That was all he had to do, but it was still something of a deterrent.

Such consideration of prisoners as individuals, though small enough, was out of the question at Buchenwald, which reflected a later phase of National Socialism. For example, prisoners who went insane—and there were quite a few of them—were no longer isolated, protected, or sent to mental institutions, but were ridiculed and chased about until they died.

But the greatest difference was that at Buchenwald it was nearly always the group that suffered, not the individual. At Dachau, a prisoner who tried to carry a small stone instead of a heavy one would have suffered for it; at Buchenwald the whole group including the foreman would have been punished.

It was almost impossible for prisoners not to cooperate with SS efforts to reduce them to passivity inside a deindividualized mass. Both the prisoner's self interest and SS pressure worked in the same direction. To remain independent implied dangers and many hardships; to comply with the SS seemed in the prisoner's own interest, because it automatically made life easier for him. Similar mechanisms were at work in the inhabitants of Germany outside the concentration camps, though not quite in such obvious form.

Whenever possible the prisoners were punished as a group so that the whole group suffered for and with the person who brought about the punishment. The Gestapo probably used this method because it was in line with its anti-individualistic philosophy and because they hoped that in this way the group would control the individual. It was in the group's interest to prevent anyone from endangering the group. As already noted, the fear of punishment was more frequent than the reality, which meant that the group asserted its power over the individual more often and more effectively than the SS. In many respects group pressure was practically permanent. Moreover, each prisoner was unusually dependent for survival on group cooperation. This added further to a situation where the group was constantly controlling the individual.

The following example may show how becoming part of a mass made life bearable even in a situation that would otherwise have been wholly insufferable. The example also shows that sometimes all the SS had to do to force prisoners into a mass was to increase the pressure of physical hardship.

Safety in the mass

On a terribly cold winter night when a snowstorm was blowing, all prisoners were forced to stand at attention without overcoats, after more than twelve hours of working in the open, and with almost no food in them. This was the procedure whenever attempts had been made to escape. The purpose was to motivate all inmates to prevent anyone from trying to escape since they knew they would have to suffer for it. Roll call did not end until the fugitives were found. In this particular instance the prisoners were threatened with having to stand all through the night.

After more than twenty prisoners had died of exposure the discipline broke down. Open resistance was impossible, as impossible as it was to do anything definite to safeguard oneself. Being exposed to the weather was a terrible torture; to see one's friends die without being able to help, and to stand a good chance of dying too, created a situation which obviously the prisoner as an individual could not meet successfully. Therefore, the individual as such had to disappear in the mass. Threats by the guards became ineffective because the mental attitude of most prisoners was now changed. Whereas before they had feared for themselves and tried to protect themselves as well as possible, they now became depersonalized. It was as if giving up individual existence and becoming part of a mass seemed in some way to offer better chances for survival, if not for the person, at least for the group.

Again it was as if what happened did not "really" happen to oneself. There was psychologically, and in experience, a split between the figure to whom things happened and the prisoner himself who did not care and was just vaguely interested, a detached observer. Unfortunate as the situation was, the prisoners then felt free from fear as individuals and powerful as a mass because "not even the Gestapo can kill us all tonight." Therefore, they were actually happier than at most other times of the camp experience. They did not care whether the guards shot them. They were indifferent to acts of torture. The guards no longer held authority, the spell of fear and death was broken. When this stage was reached, a quasi-orgiastic happiness spread among the prisoners who by forming a mass had defeated the Gestapo's effort to break them.

The extremeness of the situation kept the individual from protecting himself and forced him into mass formation; but there were other circumstances that helped create a deindividualized mass. Obviously it was easier to bear unpleasant experiences when everyone found themselves in "the same boat." Moreover, everybody was convinced that his chances for survival were very slim; therefore to preserve himself as an individual seemed pointless.

Before this change in attitude took place, before the prisoners gave up their individualities, they had been shocked and weakened by the inability to help dying comrades. Once they abandoned hope for their personal existence, it became easier for them to act heroically and help others. This helping and being helped raised the spirits. Another factor was that because they had become free of fear, the SS had actually lost its power, since the guards did seem reluctant to shoot all prisoners.

Because of this, or because by then more than fifty prisoners had died, the men were allowed to go back to the barracks. They were completely exhausted, but did not experience that feeling of happiness some of them had expected. They felt relieved that the torture was over, but at the same time felt they were no longer free of fear and could no longer rely strongly on mutual help. Each prisoner as an individual was now comparatively safer, but he had lost the safety that originates in belonging to a unified mass.

This event too was discussed freely in a detached way, and again the discussion was restricted to facts; prisoners' thoughts and emotions during that night were hardly ever mentioned. The event itself and its details were not forgotten, but no particular emotions were attached to them, nor did they appear in dreams.

The fate of the hero

In the example just given, the group was being punished for an individual's act of self defense (escape). But group pressure was no less effective when one prisoner made efforts to defend another.

In some ways, heroism can be the highest assertion of individuality. It was therefore contrary to Gestapo ideology to allow a prisoner to gain prominence by heroic action. Since all prisoners were exposed to severe mistreatment, those who died because of it, though perhaps martyrs to political or religious convictions, were not considered heroes by other prisoners. Only those who suffered for their efforts to protect other prisoners were accepted as heroes.

The SS was usually successful in preventing martyrs or heroes from being created, through its consistent suppression of all individual action or, if this was not possible, by changing it into a group phenomenon. If a prisoner tried to protect others and it came to a guard's attention, the prisoner was usually killed. But if his action came to the knowledge of the camp administration, the whole group was always punished severely. In this way, the group came to resent its protector because he brought them suffering. The protector was also kept from rekindling respect for the individual, or from inspiring an appreciation of independence. Moreover, he could never become a hero or a leader (if he survived) or a martyr (if he died) around whom group resistance might have formed.

Here a further example may illustrate. It concerns a labor command at Buchenwald in which men carried bricks to a building site, a "safe" command for which wealthy prisoners paid heavily with food, money, and cigarettes.[11]

---

[11] There were several ways of bribing fellow prisoners, prisoner foremen, and occasionally even guards. Easiest and most usual was to use money sent from home; money would buy cigarettes, extra food, etc. Those who received money regularly were the fortunate ones; many of those who never got any were glad to do favors in return for enough money to buy cigarettes, for example. Quite a few prisoners lost their lives by slowly deteriorating to the condition of *"Muselmänner"* (a group to be discussed later) because they craved cigarettes so much that they sold part of their food rations to get them, or enough money to buy some. With even less to eat than other prisoners,

The load they carried was not too heavy, and there was little beating by the heavily bribed kapo.[12] Commands of unskilled labor carrying reasonable loads on regular trips (carrier columns) were often preferred by prisoners who were in any position to choose. They had many reasons, which have bearing on this example. Walking in twos or fours as these carriers did, made conversation possible; the return trip was made without a load so that half the time was spent in easy walking except when the SS was in sight and prisoners had to run. Moreover, each trip divided the endless day which was otherwise insufferably long and unbroken. Here I might add a note:

Nobody had a watch. It is difficult to imagine what additional hardship it was not to be able to gauge how soon the horror of forced labor would end. One had to husband one's strength. If, driven by foremen or guards, one spent one's limited energy too soon, one might begin to slow down, be "noticed," and soon "finished off." To know, on the other hand, that each trip of the carrier column took half an hour meant that one knew exactly when the noon break would come with its half-hour rest, and when the work day would finally be over in the evening. Even when totally exhausted, to know that "this is the last trip for today" brought the strength to endure it. Feeling that one could not last much longer brought the impulse to give up; but not if one knew for sure that relief was in sight.

Thus the endless "anonymity" of time was another factor destructive to personality, while the ability to organize time was a strengthening influence. It permitted some initiative, some planning: for example, of the expenditure of one's energy.

Returning to the carrier column, its greatest advantage

and much less to eat than those who got money from home, they were less able to complete their work quotas or resist the rigors of camp life, were punished, and finally died.

[12] Prisoner foreman in charge of a labor command.

was that each prisoner carried the same load, marched in the same formation, was inconspicuous as an individual and almost never singled out to be "finished off." If the SS was dissatisfied the whole command might be punished, but group punishments were not usually so fatal to the individual.

One day, in October 1940, one such carrier column made up of Jewish prisoners[13] was "peacefully" returning after delivering its load. On the way they ran into the SS Sergeant Abraham who, as rumor had it, was particularly cruel to Jews because his fellow officers made jokes about his name. Noticing the group of prisoners walking without a load he ordered them to throw themselves down in the muddy road. He ordered them up and down again several times—a relatively harmless "sport."

In the column were two brothers from Vienna named Hamber. In throwing himself down, one of them lost his glasses which fell into a water-filled ditch beside the road. Using the correct formula, he asked the SS man's permission to leave the formation and recover his glasses. This was a request within reason, even for the camp situation, and was usually granted. But by asking permission to act outside the group he became conspicuous. He was no longer an anonymous member of a unit, but an individual.

Having gotten his permission, he dived into the water-filled ditch looking for his glasses. He came up without them, and dived again. Then he was ready to give up. But now the SS man forced him to dive again and again. He had asked for permission to look for his glasses and he was told to keep diving until he found them. This was the SS man's revenge for having granted a personal request. When Hamber was utterly exhausted and resisted further diving, the SS man forced him down into the water again and

---

[13] The category a prisoner belonged to was plainly visible from insignia worn on his uniform.

again until he died—either by drowning or of heart failure.

What happened afterward is not entirely clear, since the available reports are somewhat contradictory. This, incidentally, is typical of the immediate distortion of all stories about camp happenings. Among other reasons was the fact that survival in the camp required not only that one be inconspicuous, but "unobservant" as well. The account as given here is based on three independent reports of the event which agree on the essentials as they happened, if not on the motives of the SS.[14]

For reasons never quite verified, the camp commander felt that an investigation of Hamber's death had to be made—rumor had it because a German civilian witnessed the scene and reported it in disgust to some official. For whatever reason, the whole carrier group was brought before the commander of the camp that evening and asked to tell what they knew about the incident. Each of them stated he had seen nothing and could give no information, which was just what was expected of a prisoner, namely to see, hear, and say nothing of what took place in the camp. Only Hamber's brother felt obliged to do what he could to avenge his brother's killing. He stated that his brother died after being forced by the SS man to dive into the water beyond his endurance. When asked about witnesses, he stated that all prisoners of the command had seen the incident. With that the group was dismissed. It seemed to have been a routine interrogation with no consequences, such as often took place when a prisoner had been killed in front of civilian observers. The only difference was that this time a prisoner had claimed he could bear witness.

---

[14] I met the Hamber brothers in Buchenwald, but was released before this incident took place. In my judgment, their behavior on this occasion was consistent with the opinions I had previously formed of them. My description of the incident and its consequences follows closely what has been reported by Ernst Federn (private communication), Benedict Kautsky (*Teufel und Verdammte,* Zürich: 1946, pp. 106 ff), and Eugen Kogon (*Der SS-Staat,* Frankfurt: 1946, p. 81).

Later the same evening, Hamber was called to appear before the rapport leader.[15] By then he was in utter despair. It was clear that his courageous statement had not only endangered himself, but all his comrades in the labor group, including the kapo. They all feared the vengeance of the SS, but they also feared that their labor command might "explode," i.e., be dismissed and reformed with different prisoners. To lose a good command was disastrous. It was particularly disastrous for Jewish prisoners to whom most good commands were closed. Moreover, even if the command were to continue, it would be some time before it was a "good" one again, for it was now in the limelight and would be ridden by the SS. In addition, the kapo would certainly behave differently. However bribed, he would never forgive the fact that one of them had made his command conspicuous and thus endangered him as a kapo and a person.

Besides having lost a brother that day, Hamber now had to fear for his own life and for his labor command, and to face the reproaches of his comrades. These were the consequences for a prisoner who tried to behave as an individual and who put individual allegiance before personal safety and the safety of the group. Now Hamber realized the straits his emotional courage had led him to and was ready to recant. But in a hurried conference with his friends in the barracks, it was decided that he could not retract his original statement much as he now wished, because it would mean certain death for him as having falsely accused an SS man. It seemed better to stick to the truth.

When he presented himself for questioning, he was examined by the commander of the camp and other ranking SS officials. On his return to the barracks he reported that they had urged him to tell the truth, promising that nothing would happen to him if he did, but that he would suffer

---

[15] Senior SS officer, directly under the camp commander.

maximum punishment if he distorted it. He had therefore signed an affidavit giving a truthful account of what had happened.

It was late in the evening when he returned from this interview. In the middle of the same night he was taken out of his barrack and brought into the *Bunker* (the building for solitary confinement and special torture). It was ten days later before he was next seen there by chance. He did not then seem to be in bad shape, nor did he show signs of torture. But a few days later his corpse came into the morgue.

The official version was that he had hanged himself, but the towel he supposedly used, and which was brought in with the corpse, was far too short to strangulate a man. It was obvious he had been strangled in the *Bunker*. Nor was any of this unexpected. On the contrary, it was "quite in order." The SS always eliminated dangerous or inconvenient witnesses. The only unusual factor was that Hamber himself had brought about his death, and this was widely repeated as a warning to everyone to be even more careful not to see, hear, or talk.

Approximately eight days later, three prisoners of the command (all numbers had been taken down on the day of Hamber's killing) were ordered to appear for questioning. They never returned to the barracks, but three days later the first of them came into the morgue, followed by a second and third corpse. They had been killed by injection. A week later three more prisoners of the command were similarly "disposed" of. It took about three months before the command, and thus all possible witnesses, was eliminated. One can imagine the feelings of those who, after the second group was disposed of, knew their fate. Nevertheless, not one of them committed suicide.

Thus SS-imposed control by the group over the individual prisoner had its counterpart in the prisoner's self interest and made group control nearly inescapable. The treatment all prisoners suffered daily kept them explosive with justified rage. To give vent to it meant almost certain death. The group helped the individual to restrain himself.

SELF DETERMINATION

The will to live

The question arises as to why, in the concentration camp, although some prisoners survived and others got killed,[16] such a sizeable percentage simply died.

Reports about the mortality rate in the camps vary between 20% and 50%, but any overall figure is misleading.[17]

---

[16] These include prisoners sent to extermination camps, groups of prisoners ordered to be executed or "finished off," and those who died on the transports before reaching camp.

[17] The following data (reported in Kogon, *op. cit.*, pp. 118 ff) cover a six month period in 1942, the only period for which such figures were found after the war. These data probably held true for most concentration camps of Type II (i.e., camps neither for forced labor nor extermination).

At the beginning of the period there were an estimated 300,000 prisoners already in these camps. Doubling the figures available for the six months period, to arrive at yearly data, we can estimate that 220,000 new prisoners were sent to the camps in 1942, making an accumulated total of 520,000 for the year. During the same time about 9,500 prisoners were released, 18,500 were executed, and 140,000 died. When the total accumulated number of 520,000 is used, it appears that less than 2% were set free, 3½% were executed and 27% died, yielding a total mortality of a little over 30%. But these yearly statistical figures are, psychologically and factually, grossly misleading. Despite the 220,000 new prisoners added to the 300,000 already in the camps, there were only 52,000 more prisoners in the camps at the end of the year than there were at the beginning. Thus, the population of the camp varied little, comparing one random day of the year with another.

On the gross average this meant a daily population of about 325,000 prisoners. And this, not the 520,000, was the base figure from which deaths and liberations were reckoned by prisoners. Using their base

More significant is the fact that the vast majority of the thousands of prisoners who died at Buchenwald each year died soon. They simply died of exhaustion, both physical and psychological, due to a loss of desire to live.

After one had learned how to live in the camps, the chances for survival increased greatly. Except for rare occasions, such as the Hamber episode, large scale executions of old prisoners were rare. While one was never without fear for one's life, the fact that several thousands of the prisoners liberated in 1945 had spent five and even ten years in the camps suggests that the death rate for old prisoners was very different from what overall figures would suggest.

Since the only data we have is for a six month period in 1942, the following estimates are admittedly based on impressions. But I feel safe in assuming that the death rate of old prisoners (always excluding extermination, etc.) was rarely more than 10% a year, reckoned from the number of old prisoners present at any one time. On the other hand, the early death rate of new prisoners, particularly during their first months in the camp, may have been as high as 15% *a month*. This, of course, intensified the terror of new prisoners to an unbearable pitch and explains why many of them soon deteriorated into the deathlike state I will soon speak about.

In addition to their high mortality, this group also lived in the worst barracks, amid the worst overcrowding and least sanitation, all of which was soon considerably worsened by their own deterioration. They received the worst food, the least of it, and often no money or mail for months because it took a long time for money and mail to begin to arrive or be distributed.

---

figures, it appears that out of the average daily camp population 3% were set free during the year, nearly 6% were executed, and over 43% died. This may explain the divergent reports about mortality rates in the camps depending, it seems, on whether one used the total additions to the camps as the base figure, or the number imprisoned on any given day.

The unpredictable environment

What happened in the concentration camp suggests that under conditions of extreme deprivation, the influence of the environment over the individual can become total. Whether it does or not seems to depend a great deal on impact and timing; on how sudden the impact, and how little (or how much) the individual is prepared for it (because it is also destructive if someone has always expected something terrible to happen to him and it does). It depends even more on how long the condition prevails, how well integrated the person is whom it hits, and finally whether it remains unmitigated. Or to put the last point differently: whether the conviction is given that no matter what one does, no positive response can be drawn from the environment through efforts of one's own.

This was so much so, that whether or not one survived may have depended on one's ability to arrange to preserve some areas of independent action, to keep control of some important aspects of one's life, despite an environment that seemed overwhelming and total. To survive, not as a shadow of the SS but as a man, one had to find some life experience that mattered, over which one was still in command.

This was taught me by a German political prisoner, a communist worker who by then had been at Dachau for four years. I arrived there in a sorry condition because of experiences on the transport. I think that this man, by then an "old" prisoner, decided that, given my condition, the chances of my surviving without help were slim. So when he noticed that I could not swallow food because of physical pain and psychological revulsion, he spoke to me out of his rich experience: "Listen you, make up your mind: do you want to live or do you want to die? If you don't care, don't eat the stuff. But if you want to live, there's only one way: make up your mind to eat whenever and whatever you can, never mind how disgusting. Whenever you have a chance, defecate, so you'll be sure your body works. And whenever you have a minute, don't blabber, read by yourself, or flop down and sleep."

This advice, after a while, I made my own and none too soon for my survival. In my case, trying to find out what went on in the prisoners took the place of the activity he had had in mind when he suggested reading. Soon I became convinced of how sound his advice had been. But it took me years to fully grasp its psychological wisdom.

What was implied was the necessity, for survival, to carve out, against the greatest of odds, some areas of freedom of action and freedom of thought, however insignificant. The two freedoms, of activity and passivity, constitute our two most basic human attitudes, while intake and elimination, mental activity and rest, make up our most basic physiological activities. To have some small token experiences of being active and passive, each on one's own, and in mind as well as body—this, much more than the utility of any one such activity, was what enabled me and others like me to survive.[18]

By contrast, it was the senseless tasks, the lack of almost any time to oneself, the inability to plan ahead because of sudden changes in camp policies, that was so deeply destructive. By destroying man's ability to act on his own or to predict the outcome of his actions, they destroyed the feeling that his actions had any purpose, so many prisoners stopped acting. But when they stopped acting they soon stopped living. What seemed to make the critical difference was whether or not the environment—extreme as it was—permitted (or promised) some minimal choices, some lee-

[18] Maybe I should explain why I call it a self chosen act of freedom to force oneself to eat repellant food, etc. Given the initial decision—to stay alive—the forcing oneself to eat was self-imposed, not SS enforced, and unlike turning spy for survival it did not violate inner values or weaken self-respect. The patient who is critically ill likewise indicates an active desire to live when he swallows bitter medicine.

way, some positive rewards, insignificant as they seem now, when viewed objectively against the tremendous deprivation.

That may be why the SS vacillated between extreme repression and the easing of tension: the torture of prisoners, but occasional punishment of particularly inhuman guards; sudden respect and reward from the SS for some random prisoner who insisted on his dignity; sudden days of rest, etc. Without these, for example, no identification with the SS could have taken place, to mention only one outcome. Most prisoners who died, as opposed to those who got killed, were those who could no longer believe in, or take advantage of, those sudden remissions that happen in even the most extreme situations; in short those who had given up all will to live.

It was impressive to observe how skillfully the SS used this mechanism of destroying man's faith in his ability to predict the future. For want of evidence we cannot say if this was deliberate or unconscious but it worked with deadly effectiveness. If the SS wanted a group (Norwegians, political prisoners who were not Jewish, etc.) to adjust, survive, and serve in the camps, they would hold out the promise that their behavior had some influence on their fate. To those groups whom they wished to destroy (Eastern Jews, Poles, Ukrainians, etc.) they made it quite clear that no matter how hard they worked or tried to please their masters, it would make no difference whatsoever.)

Another means of destroying the prisoners' belief that they had some basis for hope, some influence over their fate, and therefore some reason for wanting to live, was to expose them to sudden radical changes in living conditions. At one camp, for example, a large group of Czech prisoners was utterly destroyed by giving them the promise that they were "honor" prisoners entitled to special privileges, letting them live in relative comfort without any work or hardship for a time, then suddenly throwing them into quarry work where labor conditions were worst and mortality highest, while at the same time reducing their food rations; then back again into good quarters and easy work, and after a few months back into the quarries with little food, etc. Soon they all died.

My own experience of three times being called up to be freed and each time being dressed in civilian clothes to be ready for release, is another example. Possibly it happened because I had provoked an SS official. The first time, nearly all other prisoners called up with me were released while I was sent back into the camp. The second time may have been chance, because quite a few besides myself were sent back, and rumor had it that the SS had run out of money and could not pay the sums due the prisoners for the trip home. In any case, when I was summoned the third time I refused to go and be put into civilian clothes because I was convinced it was just another effort of the SS official to break me. But this time the call was authentic.

The question is: why did I deliberately provoke an SS officer? I believe that in order not to collapse, I had to prove to myself that I had some power to influence my environment. I knew I could not do it positively, so I did it negatively. Nor was this reasoned out. I acted on the unconscious realization of what I needed most to survive.

The penalty for suicide

Since the main goal of the SS was to do away with independence of action and the ability to make personal decisions, even negative ways of achieving it were not neglected. The decision to remain alive or to die is probably a supreme example of self determination. Therefore the SS attitude toward suicide may be mentioned.

The stated principle was: the more prisoners to commit suicide, the better. But even there, the decision must not be the prisoner's. An SS man might provoke a prisoner to commit suicide by running against the electrically charged wire fence, and that was all right. But for those who took the initiative in killing themselves, the SS issued (in Dachau in 1933) a special order: prisoners who attempted suicide but did not succeed were to receive twenty-five lashes and prolonged solitary confinement. Supposedly this was to punish them for their failure to do away with themselves; but I am convinced it was much more to punish them for the act of self determination.

Also, since protecting life, either one's own or that of others, is a major act of self assertion, it too had to be inhibited. Therefore the same punishment was threatened to any prisoner who tried to prevent a suicide before it happened, or tried to bring back to life a prisoner who tried it. To my knowledge this punishment for attempted suicide or for helping a suicidal person was only once carried out; but it was not the punishment the SS was interested in, it was the threat of punishment and what that did to destroy self determination.[19]

MUSELMÄNNER: *The walking corpses*

Prisoners who came to believe the repeated statements of the guards—that there was no hope for them, that they would never leave the camp except as a corpse—who came to feel that their environment was one over which they could exercise no influence whatsoever, these prisoners were, in a literal sense, walking corpses. In the camps they were called "moslems" (*Muselmänner*) because of what was erroneously viewed as a fatalistic surrender to the environment, as Mohammedans are supposed to blandly accept their fate.

But these people had not, like real Mohammedans, made

---

[19] So when none of the doomed witnesses in the Hamber affair committed suicide, that too was "quite in order."

an act of decision and submitted to fate out of free will. On the contrary, they were people who were so deprived of affect, self esteem, and every form of stimulation, so totally exhausted, both physically and emotionally, that they had given the environment total power over them. They did this when they gave up trying to exercise any further influence over their life or environment.

That is, as long as a prisoner fought in any way for survival, for some self assertion within and against the overpowering environment, he could not become a "moslem." Once his own life and the environment were viewed as totally beyond his ability to influence them, the only logical conclusion was to pay no attention to them whatsoever. Only then, all conscious awareness of stimuli coming from the outside was blocked out, and with it all response to anything but inner stimuli.

But even the moslems, being organisms, could not help reacting somehow to their environment, and this they did by depriving it of the power to influence them as subjects in any way whatsoever. To achieve this, they had to give up responding to it at all, and become objects, but with this they gave up being persons. These walking shadows all died very soon. Or to put it differently, after a certain point of extreme deprivation, the environment can only move around empty shells, as the camp routine did with these moslems; they behaved as if they were not thinking, not feeling, unable to act or respond, moved only by things outside themselves.

One might even speculate as to whether these organisms had by-passed the reflex arc that once extended from external or internal stimulus via frontal lobes to feeling and action. First they had given up all action as being utterly pointless; then feeling, because all feeling was merely painful or dangerous or both. Eventually this somehow extended backwards to blocking out the stimulation itself.

These things could be readily observed in the deterioration of moslems. It began when they stopped acting on their own. And that was the moment when other prisoners recognized what was happening and separated themselves from these now "marked" men, because any further association with them could lead only to one's own destruction. At this point such men still obeyed orders, but only blindly or automatically; no longer selectively or with inner reservation or any hatred at being so abused. They still looked about, or at least moved their eyes around. The looking stopped much later, though even then they still moved their bodies when ordered, but never did anything on their own any more. Typically, this stopping of action began when they no longer lifted their legs as they walked, but only shuffled them. When finally even the looking about on their own stopped, they soon died.

Don't dare to notice

That the process was not accidental may be seen from the ban on daring to notice anything. Compared with the all pervasive order not to be conspicuous (noticeable), the prisoners were less frequently told the commensurate "don't dare to notice." But to look and observe for oneself what went on in the camp—while absolutely necessary for survival—was even more dangerous than being noticed. Often this passive compliance—not to see or not to know—was not enough; in order to survive one had to actively pretend not to observe, not to know what the SS required one not to know.[20]

Among the worst mistakes a prisoner could make was to

---

[20] Even trivial examples illustrate this: during some mistreatment on the transport my eyeglasses were broken. Since I can hardly see without them, I asked for permission, once I was at Dachau, to have new glasses sent to me from home. I had been warned in advance never to admit knowing of any mistreatment, including my own. So when asked why I needed glasses, I simply said that they got broken.

watch (to notice) another prisoner's mistreatment. There the SS seemed totally irrational, but only seemed so. For example, if an SS man was killing off a prisoner and other prisoners dared to look at what was going on in front of their eyes he would instantly go after them, too. But only seconds later the same SS would call the same prisoners' attention to what lay in store for anyone who dared to disobey, drawing their attention to the killing as a warning example. This was no contradiction, it was simply an impressive lesson that said: you may notice only what we wish you to notice, but you invite death if you notice things on your own volition. The issue was again the same; the prisoner was not to have a will of his own.

Many examples showed that all this happened for a reason and a purpose. An SS man might seem to have gone berserk about what he viewed as some resistance or disobedience, and in this state beat up or even kill a prisoner. But in the midst of it he might call out a friendly "well done" to a passing work column who, having stumbled on the scene, would fall into a gallop, heads averted, so as to pass by as fast as possible without "noticing." Obviously their sudden break into running and their averted heads showed clearly that they had "noticed"; but that did not matter as long as they also showed so clearly that they had accepted the command not to know what they were not supposed to know.

This all important enforced behavior was equally ap-

When the SS officer heard this he began to deliver a beating and screamed, "*What* did you say happened?" I corrected myself, saying I had broken them accidentally. At this he immediately said, "Okay, just remember that for the future," and matter-of-factly sat down to give me written permission to receive glasses. His reaction, incidentally, was swift but by no means spontaneous; on the contrary, it was deliberate and purposeful. No sadist bent on satisfying his desires will instantly stop mistreatment on getting a correct formula reply. Only a person simply after a specific goal will behave in that way.

parent when the SS was provoking a prisoner to commit suicide. If the unfortunate succeeded, anyone watching it was immediately punished. But as soon as the punishment for having observed on one's own was over, the same SS might warn: "See what happened to that man? That's what'll happen to you!"

To know only what those in authority allow one to know is, more or less, all the infant can do. To be able to make one's own observations and to draw pertinent conclusions from them is where independent existence begins. To forbid oneself to make observations, and take only the observations of others in their stead, is relegating to nonuse one's own powers of reasoning, and the even more basic power of perception. Not observing where it counts most, not knowing where one wants so much to know, all this is most destructive to the functioning of one's personality. So is finding oneself in a situation where what once gave security (the power to observe correctly and to draw on one's own the right inferences) not only ceases to offer security, but actually endangers one's life. Deliberate nonuse of one's power of observation, as opposed to temporary inattention, which is different, leads to a withering away of this power.

To make matters worse, while to observe was dangerous, to react emotionally to what one saw was frankly suicidal. That is, a prisoner who noticed mistreatment was punished, but only mildly when compared to what happened if his feelings carried him away to the point of trying to give help. Knowing that such an emotional reaction was tantamount to suicide, and being unable at times not to react emotionally when observing what went on, left only one way out: not to observe, so as not to react. So both powers, those of observation and of reaction, had to be blocked out voluntarily as an act of preservation. But if one gives up observing, reacting, and taking action, one gives up living one's own life. And this is exactly what the SS wanted to happen.

Thus the truly extreme environment first blocks self stimulated action (resisting or modifying the environment) and later also, response to any stimulus coming from the environment in terms of one's own personality (inner revulsion without overt action based on it). Finally, all this is replaced by no other than environment imposed action without even an inner personal response to it. This last situation leads first to a blotting out of responses, later to a blotting out even of perception; except that death then follows.

Prisoners entered the moslem stage when emotion could no longer be evoked in them. For a time they fought for food, but after a few weeks even that stopped. Despite their hunger, even the food stimulus no longer reached their brain clearly enough to lead to action. Nobody and nothing could now influence these persons or their characters, because nothing from inside or outside was reaching them any more. Other prisoners often tried to be nice to them when they could, to give them food and so forth, but they could no longer respond to the emotional attitude that was behind someone's giving them food. So food they took, up to the point where they had reached the final stage of disintegration, but it no longer replenished them emotionally; it just entered an always empty stomach.

As long as they still asked for food, followed someone to get it, stretched out a hand for it and ate what was given eagerly, they could still, with great effort, have been returned to "normal" prisoner status, deteriorated as they were. In the next stage of disintegration, receiving food unexpectedly still led to a momentary lighting up of the face and a grateful hangdog look, though hardly any verbal response. But when they no longer reached out for it spontaneously, no longer responded with thanks, an effort to smile, or a look at the giver, they were nearly always beyond help. Later they took food, sometimes ate it, sometimes not, but no longer had a feeling response. In the last, just before the terminal stage, they no longer ate it.

The last human freedom

Even those prisoners who did not become moslems, who somehow managed to remain in control of some small aspect of their lives, eventually had to come to longer range terms with their new environment. The mere fact of survival meant that in the matter of Caesar's dues, it was no longer a question of whether to render them or not, nor even, with rare exceptions, of how much to render. But to survive as a man not a walking corpse, as a debased and degraded but still human being, one had first and foremost to remain informed and aware of what made up one's personal point of no return, the point beyond which one would never, under any circumstances, give in to the oppressor, even if it meant risking and losing one's life. It meant being aware that if one survived at the price of overreaching this point one would be holding on to a life that had lost all its meaning. It would mean surviving—not with a lowered self respect, but without any.

This point of no return was different from person to person, and changed for each person as time passed. At the beginning of their imprisonment, most inmates would have felt it beyond their point of no return to serve the SS as foreman or block chief, or to like wearing a uniform that made them look like the SS. Later, after years in the camp, such relatively external matters gave way to much more essential convictions which then became the core of their resistance. But those convictions one had to hold on to with utter tenacity. About them, one had to keep oneself informed at all times, because only then could they serve as the mainstay of a radically reduced but still present humanity. Much of the tenacity and relentlessness of political prisoners in their factional warfare is thus explainable; for them, political loyalty to party was their point of no return.

Second in importance was keeping oneself informed of how one felt about complying when the ultimate decision as to where to stand firm was not called into question. While less radical, it was no less essential, because an awareness of one's attitude toward compliance was called for almost constantly. One had to comply with debasing and amoral commands if one wished to survive; but one had to remain cognizant that one's reason for complying was "to remain alive and unchanged as a person." Therefore, one had to decide, for any given action, whether it was truly necessary for one's safety or that of others, and whether committing it was good, neutral or bad. This keeping informed and aware of one's actions—though it could not alter the required act, save in extremities—this minimal distance from one's own behavior, and the freedom to feel differently about it depending on its character, this too was what permitted the prisoner to remain a human being. It was the giving up of all feelings, all inner reservations about one's actions, the letting go of a point at which one would hold fast no matter what, that changed prisoner into moslem.

Those prisoners who blocked out neither heart nor reason, neither feelings nor perception, but kept informed of their inner attitudes even when they could hardly ever afford to act on them, those prisoners survived and came to understand the conditions they lived under. They also came to realize what they had not perceived before; that they still retained the last, if not the greatest, of the human freedoms: to choose their own attitude in any given circumstance. Prisoners who understood this fully, came to know that this, and only this, formed the crucial difference between retaining one's humanity (and often life itself) and accepting death as a human being (or perhaps physical death):

whether one retained the freedom to choose autonomously
one's attitude to extreme conditions even when they seemed
totally beyond one's ability to influence them.[21]

ADJUSTMENT FOR SURVIVAL

Old and new prisoners

Perhaps the changes forced upon most survivors in the
concentration camp may best be illustrated by comparing
"new" prisoners, in whom the process of enforced self re-
education had barely started, with "old" prisoners, in whom
it was nearly finished. The term "new" prisoner is used for
those who had spent no more than one year in the camp;
"old" prisoners are those who had been there at least three

---

[21] Kogon *(op. cit.,* p. 62) reports one of many incidents bearing this
out: Once a command of Jewish prisoners was working alongside of
some Polish Gentile prisoners. The supervising SS, spying two Jewish
prisoners whom he thought to be slacking, ordered them to lie down in
the ditch and called on a Polish prisoner, named Strzaska, to bury them
alive. Strzaska, frozen in terror and anxiety, refused to obey. At this
the SS seized a spade and beat the Pole, who nevertheless still refused
to obey. Furiously, the SS now ordered the two Jews to get out of the
ditch, Strzaska to get in, and the two Jews to bury *him.* In mortal anxiety,
hoping to escape the fate themselves, they shoveled earth into the ditch
and onto their fellow prisoner. When only Strzaska's head was barely
visible the SS ordered them to stop, and unearth him. Once Strzaska
was on his feet, the two Jews were ordered back into the ditch, and this
time Strzaska obeyed the renewed command to bury them—possibly
because they had not resisted burying him, or perhaps expecting that
they too would be spared at the last minute. But this time there was no
reprieve, and when the ditch was filled the SS stamped down the earth
that still lay loosely over his victims. Five minutes later he called on two
other prisoners to unearth them, but though they worked frantically,
it was too late. One was already dead and the other dying, so the SS
ordered them both taken to the crematorium.

years. As far as old prisoners are concerned, I can offer only observations but no findings based on introspection.

There was, of course, considerable variation in the time it took prisoners to make their peace with the possibility of having to spend the rest of their lives in the camp. Some became part of camp life rather soon, some probably never, though they may have spent more than ten years in the camps. When a new prisoner arrived he was told, "If you survive the first three weeks, you have a good chance of surviving a year; if you survive three months you will survive the next three years.[22]

During the first month in camp (including casualties of the transport) the monthly death rate for newcomers actually was at least 10% and probably close to 15%. In the following month—if there were no special mass persecutions—this figure was usually cut in half; that is, the death rate among new prisoners during the second month might be somewhere around 7%. During the third month it might again be halved to about 3%. And from then on (again barring mass executions) the monthly death rate for the surviving 75% may have dropped to 1% or less, where it remained, by and large.

This reduction in the death rate was due largely to the fact that by that time all those who could not survive the rigors of camp life had been weeded out. Those with physical disabilities, such as heart conditions, were already dead. So were most of those with personalities too rigid to develop the necessary defenses and adjustments; they, too, succumbed in the first few weeks. The lowered death rate was thus a measure of both the survival of the fittest, and of the heightened chances for survival as one learned to adjust. By the same token the halt in deaths was a compelling reason for

---

[22] At the time this comment was made, the yearly death rate, in my estimation, was about 30%. The yearly death rate of 50% reported on p. 145 pertains to a later period of the camps.

prisoners to change, to do it on their own steam, and do it fast, if they meant to survive.[23]

The chief concerns of new prisoners were to remain physically intact and return to the outer world the same person who had left it. Therefore all efforts were directed toward these goals, and they tried to combat as much as possible any weakening of their maturity or self sufficiency. Old prisoners seemed mainly concerned with the problem of how to live as well as possible inside the camp. Therefore they tried to reorganize their personalities as well as they could to become more acceptable to the SS. Once they had embraced this attitude, everything that happened to them, even the worst atrocity, was "real." No longer was there a split between a figure to whom things happened and the prisoner who observed in detachment. The split in personality had disappeared, but at the price of the prisoner's personality no longer being integrated. It dropped to a different, lower level: one of resignation, dependency, submission, and passivity.

Old prisoners could accept this because they could scarcely believe they would ever return to the outer world which had grown strange to them. But once they had changed, there was every indication that they were afraid of returning. They did not admit it directly, but from their

[23]What I have explained here by statistics has been described by an "old" prisoner as an inner experience.

Kupfer, after two years at Dachau, reflected on what went on in him as he adjusted to life in the camp (my translation from page 1199 of the German original, *op. cit.*): "Now I am a 'Dachauer,' prisoner no. 24814. I think and feel as is fitting for a prisoner at Dachau. Slowly a process of acclimatization has taken place in me. I did not realize it then, but for life in the camp this is great progress, because whoever becomes a concentration camp prisoner through and through does not perish so soon, compared to the prisoner who remains a newcomer inside, and therefore one who externally and internally tries to remain outside of it all. I began in the very center of my inner life, but also in all externals, to act and feel like a true 'Dachauer,' ["old prisoner"—B. B.] though I did not realize this at all at the time."

talk it was clear that in their own minds, only a cataclysmic event—a world war or world revolution—could free them. They seemed aware of what had happened to them as they aged in the camp. They realized they had adapted to camp life and that this process had brought a basic change in their personalities.

The realization was given dramatic expression by those few prisoners who became convinced that no one could live in the camps longer than a certain number of years without changing his attitudes so radically that he could no longer be considered, or again become, the person he once was. Therefore they set a time limit for themselves beyond which, in their opinion, there was no point staying alive since from then on life would simply consist of being prisoners in a concentration camp. These were men who could not endure acquiring those attitudes and behaviors they saw developing in most old prisoners. They therefore set a fixed date for committing suicide. One of them set the sixth anniversary of his arrival in the camp because he felt that nobody there was worth saving after five years. His friends tried to watch him carefully on that day, but nevertheless he succeeded.[24]

One characteristic difference between old and new prisoners was that old prisoners could no longer evaluate correctly the outside, non-Gestapo controlled world. Whereas new prisoners tried to retain their attitude toward the world of the camp as being nonreal, to old prisoners it was the only reality. How long it took a prisoner to stop considering life outside the camp as real depended to a great extent on the strength of his emotional ties to his family and friends, the strength and richness of his personality and the degree to which he was able to preserve important aspects of his old interests and attitudes. The greater the area of his interests, and the more he contrived to take advantage of them

[24] I witnessed this suicide. A very similar suicide is described by Kautsky, *op. cit.*, p. 283.

in the camp situation, the better able he was to protect his personality against too early impoverishment.

Some indications of changes in attitude were: the tendency toward scheming to find a better place of work in the camp rather than trying to contact the outer world. New prisoners, for instance, would spend all their money on efforts to smuggle letters out of the camp or to get letters without having them censored. Old prisoners used their money to get "soft" jobs such as clerical work in the camp offices, or labor in the shops where they at least had protection from the weather. This change also found expression in their dominant thoughts and topics of conversation: new prisoners were most concerned with life outside of camp; old prisoners were interested only in camp life.

It so happened, for instance, that on one and the same day, news was received of a speech by President Roosevelt denouncing Hitler and Germany, and rumors spread that one SS officer was going to be replaced by another. New prisoners discussed the President's speech excitedly and paid scant attention to the rumors; old prisoners were indifferent to the speech, but devoted their conversation to the rumored change in camp officers.

When old prisoners were asked why they spoke so little about their futures outside the camp, they often admitted they could no longer visualize themselves living in a free world, making decisions, taking care of themselves and their families.

The attitude of the old prisoner toward his family had undergone a significant change. One reason for this was the total reversal of his status within the family. In line with the paternalistic structure of most German households, the family had been wholly dependent on the man for decisions, much more so than would be true in an American family. Now he was not only unable to influence his wife's or his children's decisions, but was utterly dependent on them for taking steps to secure his release and to send him the money that was so important to him in the camp.

As a matter of fact, although many families behaved decently toward prisoners, serious problems were created. During the first months they spent a great deal of energy, time, and money in their efforts to free the prisoners, quite often more than they could afford. Later on they ran out of money, while new demands were being made on their time and energy. To have lost the wage earner meant great hardship for the family. Also, it should not be overlooked that the wife had often objected to the husband's political activities as being too dangerous or too time consuming. Now as she pleaded with the Gestapo, an unpleasant task at best, they told her repeatedly that it was the prisoner's own fault that he was imprisoned. Wives had a hard time finding employment because a family member was suspect; they were excluded from public relief; their children had difficulties at school, etc. So it was natural that many came to resent having a family member in the camp.

Their friends showed them little compassion, because the German population at large developed its own defenses against the concentration camp, most important of which was denial. As discussed in the last chapter, they refused to believe that prisoners in the camps had not committed outrageous crimes to warrant such punishment.

Another subtle, but most effective device the SS used to alienate the family from the prisoners, was to tell the wife or other relatives (usually only closest relatives were permitted to plead the prisoner's case), that not only was it the prisoner's own fault that he was in the camp, but that he would have been released long ago had he behaved there as he should. This led to recriminations in letters; relatives pleaded with the prisoner to behave better, which often outraged him, considering the conditions of his camp existence.[25]

---

[25] The Gestapo had numerous devices to make pleading for the prisoner seem senseless, and make it easy for the family in self-

He, of course, could not answer such accusations. At the same time he was resentful because what probably enraged him most was the family's own ability to act and move about freely when he was so helplessly unable to act for himself. In any case it was one more experience separating the prisoner from his few remaining ties to the non-camp world.

These and similar attitudes were reflected in letters to and from home, but often mail for prisoners came irregularly or not at all. Naturally, letters contained hopes and promises of reunion, sometimes because the Gestapo had made promises to the family, sometimes because relatives were trying to cheer the prisoners up. But when promises did not materialize, they led to still greater disappointment, and added resentment toward home.

In another effort to cut prisoners off from all connection with the outer world, the SS forbade them to have pictures of their relatives; if they got hold of any pictures, they were taken away and the prisoners were punished for keeping them. So actually a slow alienation took place between the men and their families. But for the new prisoners, this process was only beginning. As recollections of the family grew dimmer, this strongest bond linking prisoners to the outside world grew weaker. The resentment of those who, rightly or wrongly, felt deserted by their families only reinforced it. The less emotional support they got from the ouside, the more they were forced to adjust to life in the camp.

Therefore, old prisoners did not like to be reminded of

preservation to separate itself from the prisoner. They would set a date for the prisoner's release, only to inform the relatives on that date that some new misdeed made freedom impossible. Often not even that much reason was given for misinformation. My mother was several times given a date for my release, each one untrue. Once she was told I was probably home already, waiting for her, and to hurry home. Another time she was encouraged to travel from Vienna to Weimar, the town closest to Buchenwald, either to receive me on my release, or at least have a visit with me. She presented herself in Weimar, where she was given a run-around for several days until in desperation she returned to Vienna.

their families and former friends. When they spoke about them, it was in a very detached way. They still liked to get letters, but it was not very important to them because they had lost touch with the events related in them. Also, they had come to hate all those living outside the camp, who "enjoyed life as if we were not rotting away." This outside world which continued to live as if nothing had happened was represented, in the minds of the prisoners, by those whom they used to know best, namely their relatives and friends. But even this hatred was very subdued in old prisoners. Just as they had forgotten how to love their kin, they seemed to have lost the ability to hate them. Showing little emotion either way, they seemed unable to feel strongly about anybody.

New prisoners, after an initial delay, were usually the ones who received most letters, money, and other signs of attention. But even newcomers consistently accused their families of not doing enough, of betraying them. At the same time they loved to speak of their families and friends even when they were complaining about them. Despite open ambivalence, they never doubted they were going to resume living with them just where they had left off.

Similarly they hoped to continue their professional lives just as before. Unlike old prisoners, they loved to talk about their positions in the outside world and of their hopes for the future. They spoke boastfully, and seemed to be trying to keep their pride alive by letting others know how important they had been, the implication being that they were still important people. Old prisoners seemed to have accepted their state of dejection; to compare it with their former splendor (and anything was magnificent compared to their present existence) was probably too depressing.

For such reasons it made a difference to prisoners, psychologically, whether the camp was enclosed by just a wire fence (which let them see the surrounding world) or whether a solid wall blocked their view. The wire fence was usually preferred by new prisoners who tried to deny their exclusion from the world, while those who preferred the additional wall sought protection from nostalgia. On labor assignments outside the camp, prisoners were always in contact with some segments of the outside world, but were also exposed to the sometimes curious but often hostile stare of the passerby. Here again, old prisoners detested the experience while newcomers enjoyed seeing civilians, particularly women and children.

Probably as a result of malnutrition, mental anguish, and ambivalence toward the outside world, prisoners tended to forget names, places and events of their past lives. Often they could not recall the names of their closest relatives, even while remembering insignificant details. It was as if their emotional ties to the past were breaking, as if the ordinary order of importance, of the connections of experiences, was no longer valid. Prisoners were quite upset about this loss of memory for things past, which added to their sense of frustration and incompetence. This too was a process which had only begun for new prisoners, and was nearly completed in most old prisoners.

All prisoners engaged in a great deal of daydreaming. Both individual and group daydreams were wildly wishful-filling and a favorite pastime if the general emotional climate was not too depressed. Nevertheless, there was a marked difference between the daydreams of new and old prisoners. In general, the longer the time a prisoner had spent in camp, the less specific, concrete and true to reality were his daydreams. This was in line with the expectation that only such an event as the end of the existing world order would liberate them.

They would vaguely daydream of some coming cataclysm. Out of this earth shaking event they felt sure of emerging as the new leaders of Germany, if not the world. This was the least to which their sufferings entitled them. Alongside of these grandiose expectations went a great vagueness about the nature of their leadership, or what ends it would serve; they were even more nebulous about how they were going to arrange their future private lives. In their daydreams they were certain to emerge as prominent leaders of the future, but they were less certain they would continue to live with their wives and children, or be able to resume their roles as husbands and fathers. Partly these fantasies were an effort to deny their utter dejection, and partly a confession of the feeling that only high public office could help them to regain standing within their families, or win back their own good opinion of themselves.

In the process of forcing prisoners to relinquish maturity, the group exercised a strong influence. The group did not interfere with a prisoner's private daydreams or his ambivalence toward his family, but it asserted its power over those who objected to childlike deviations from normal adult behavior. Those who objected to an absolute obedience to the guards were accused of risking the security of the group, an accusation that was not without foundation, since the SS punished the group for the individual misdeed. Therefore, regression into childlike behavior was more inescapable than other types of behavior imposed on the individual because it was triply enforced: by the SS, by the prisoner's inner psychological defenses, and by his fellow prisoners.

The result was that most prisoners developed types of behavior more usually characteristic of infancy or early youth. Some of these behaviors developed slowly, other were immediately imposed on the prisoners and increased only in intensity as time went on.

The prisoners, like children, sought their satisfactions in empty daydreams, or worse, in contradictory ones. If real satisfactions were available, they were the most primitive kind: eating, sleeping, resting. Like children, they lived only in the immediate present; they lost their feeling for the sequence of time, they became unable to plan for the future or to give up tiny immediate satisfactions to gain greater ones in the near future. They were unable to establish durable relations. Friendships developed as quickly as they broke up. Prisoners would, like children, fight one another tooth and nail, declare they would never look at one another or speak to one another, only to become fast friends within minutes. They were boastful, telling tales of what they had achieved in their former lives, or how they had contrived to cheat foremen or guards. Like children, they felt not at all set back or ashamed when it became known that they had lied about their prowess.

Final adjustment

The result of all these changes, by no means fully produced in all old prisoners, was a personality structure willing and able to accept SS values and behavior as its own. Of these, German nationalism and the Nazi race ideology seemed easiest to accept. It was notable how far even well-educated political prisoners went in this identification. At one time, for instance, American and English newspapers were full of stories about cruelties committed in the camps. The SS punished prisoners for the appearance of these stories, true to its policy of group punishment—for the stories must have originated in reports by former prisoners. In discussing this event old prisoners insisted that foreign newspapers had no business bothering with internal German institutions and expressed their hatred of the journalists who tried to help them.

When in 1938 I asked more than one hundred old political prisoners if they thought the story of the camp should be reported in foreign newspapers, many hesitated to agree that it was desirable. When asked if they would join a foreign power in a war to defeat National Socialism, only two made the unqualified statement that everyone escaping Germany ought to fight the Nazis to the best of his ability.

Nearly all non-Jewish prisoners believed in the superiority of the German race. Nearly all of them took great pride in the so-called achievements of the National Socialist state, particularly its policy of expansion through annexation. In line with their acceptance of the new ideology, most old prisoners took over Gestapo attitudes toward the so-called unfit prisoner. Even before an extermination policy went into effect, the Gestapo had been liquidating unfit persons. Prisoners, for reasons of their own, followed their example. They considered their actions justifiable; some even thought them to be correct.

Newcomers to the camp presented old prisoners with difficult problems. Their complaints about the misery of the camp situation added new strain to life in the barracks; so did their inability to adjust to it. Bad behavior in the labor gang or in the barrack endangered the whole group. To become conspicuous was always dangerous, and usually the group to which the conspicuous person belonged at the moment would also be singled out by the SS for special attention. So newcomers who did not stand up well under the strain tended to be a liability to others.

Moreover, weaklings were those most apt to turn traitor. Weaklings, it was reasoned, usually died in the first weeks anyway, so it seemed as well to get rid of them sooner. Therefore, old prisoners were sometimes instrumental in getting rid of so-called unfit new prisoners, thus patterning their own behavior after Gestapo ideology. They did it by giving newcomers dangerous assignments, or by denying them help that could have been given.

This was one of many situations in which old prisoners showed toughness, and modeled their way of treating fellow prisoners on examples set by the SS. That it was really a taking over of SS attitudes could be seen from their handling of traitors. Self protection asked for the elimination of traitors, but the way in which they were tortured for days and slowly killed was taken over from the Gestapo. Here the excuse was that it might deter others. Yet the rationalization did not apply when prisoners turned their hostility against one another, as they did continuously. New prisoners did it much as they would have done in the world outside the camp. But slowly most prisoners accepted terms of verbal aggression that definitely did not originate in their previous vocabulary, but were taken over from the very different vocabulary of the SS. Only attempts to emulate the SS can explain such behavior.

From copying SS verbal aggressions to copying their form of bodily aggression was one more step, but it took several years to reach that. It was not unusual, when prisoners were in charge of others, to find old prisoners (and not only former criminals) behaving worse than the SS. Sometimes they were trying to find favor with the guards, but more often it was because they considered it the best way to treat prisoners in the camp.

Old prisoners tended to identify with the SS not only in their goals and values, but even in appearance. They tried to arrogate to themselves old pieces of SS uniforms, and when that was not possible they tried to sew and mend their prison garb until it resembled the uniforms. The lengths prisoners would go to was sometimes hard to believe, particularly since they were sometimes punished for trying to look like the SS. When asked why they did it, they said it was because they wanted to look smart. To them looking smart meant to look like their enemies.

Old prisoners felt great satisfaction if, during the twice daily counting of prisoners, they really had stood well at attention or given a snappy salute. They prided themselves on being as tough, or tougher, than the SS. In their identification they went so far as to copy SS leisure time activities. One of the games played by the guards was to find out who could stand being hit the longest without uttering a complaint. This game was copied by old prisoners, as if they were not hit often enough without repeating the experience as a game.

Often an SS man would for a while enforce some nonsensical rule, originating in a whim of the moment. Usually it was quickly forgotten, but there were always some old prisoners who continued to observe it and tried to enforce it on others long after the SS had lost interest. Once, for example, an SS man was inspecting the prisoners' apparel and found that some of their shoes were dirty on the inside. He ordered all prisoners to wash their shoes inside and out with soap and water. Treated this way, the heavy shoes became hard as stone. The order was never repeated, and many prisoners did not even carry it out the first time, since the SS, as was often the case, gave the order, stood around for a few minutes, and then left. Until he was gone, every prisoner busied himself with carrying out the order, after which they promptly quit. Nevertheless there were some old prisoners who not only continued to wash the insides of their shoes every day but cursed all who failed to do so as being negligent and dirty. These prisoners believed firmly that all rules set down by the SS were desirable standards of behavior, at least in the camp.

Since old prisoners had accepted, or been forced to accept, a childlike dependency on the SS, many of them seemed to want to feel that at least some of the people they were accepting as all-powerful father images were just and kind. Therefore, strange as it may seem, they also had positive feelings toward the SS. They divided their positive and negative feelings in such a way that all positive emotions were concentrated on a few officers relatively far up in the hierarchy of the camp, but hardly ever on the commander himself. They insisted that behind a rough exterior these officers hid feelings of justice and propriety. They were alleged to be genuinely interested in the prisoners and even trying, in a small way, to help them. Since not much of these assumed feelings became apparent, it was explained that they had to be well hidden or there would be no way for them to help.

The eagerness of some prisoners to find reasons for such claims was sometimes pitiful. A whole legend was woven around the fact that of two SS inspecting a barrack, one had cleaned the mud off his shoes before entering. He probably did it automatically, but it was interpreted as a rebuff to the other, and a clear demonstration of how he felt about the concentration camp.

These examples, to which many could be added, suggest how, and to what degree, old prisoners came to identify with the enemy, and tried to justify it somehow in their own eyes. But was the SS really just an enemy any more? If so, the identification would be hard to understand. The SS was in fact the callous, unpredictable enemy, and remained so. But the longer prisoners survived in the camp—that is, the more they became old prisoners who had lost hope of any other life and tried to make a go of the camps—the more prisoners and SS found areas in common where cooperation was better for both of them than being at cross purposes. Having to live together, if one can call it that, led with necessity to such areas of common interest.

For example, one or several barracks were usually supervised by a noncommissioned SS officer, called a blockleader. Each blockleader wanted his barracks to be beyond reproach. It should not only be inconspicuous, but the one found in best order; this would keep him out of trouble with his superiors or even gain him a promotion. But the prisoners who lived there had the same interest: namely, that he should find it beyond reproach, and thus avoid severe penalty for themselves. In this sense they shared a common interest.

This was even more true of the workshops. The N.C.O. in charge of a production unit was vitally interested that everything in his workshop be in top shape when it was inspected by his superiors, that the output should be great, etc. The prisoners, for their own reasons, had identical interests. And the longer a prisoner had been in the camp, the more skilled his labor, or the more a particular SS came to rely on it for making his command show up well with his superiors, the greater the area of common interest.[26]

The fate of a Jewish command of bricklayers at Buchenwald is a telling example. While tens of thousands of Jewish prisoners were killed in the camp this group of some forty Jews survived with only a few losses of life. The group, made up of Jewish political prisoners, decided at the beginning of the war that with the shortage of steel, concrete, etc., the camp command would soon return to using bricks for its buildings. They managed to be assigned to the bricklayers' command, and since skilled bricklayers were scarce, they were considered unexpendable throughout the war. While nearly all other Jews were destroyed, most of this command was alive on the day of liberation. Had they served the SS poorly, they would have served themselves not at all. But had they taken professional pride in their bricklaying skill, without continuing to hate having to work for the SS, their inner resistance might have died, and they with it.

In closing this summary of the adjustments made by old prisoners, I wish to emphasize again that all these changes worked only within limitations, that there were great individual variations, that in reality the categories of old and new prisoners were always overlapping. Despite what I have said about the psychological reasons forcing old prisoners to conform and identify with the SS, it must be stressed that this was only part of the picture; there were also strong de-

---

[26] A parallel to this development may be found in the situation of the anti-Nazi German outside the camp. He could not help himself from taking advantage of certain features of the Nazi regime, such as acquiring a better home or livelihood from the expropriation of Jewish property, the exploitation of Polish slave labor, etc.

fenses within them that worked in the opposite direction. All prisoners, including those old prisoners who identified with the SS on many levels, at other times defied its rules. In doing so, a few occasionally showed extraordinary courage, and many more retained some of their decency and integrity all during their stay in the camps.

5

Behavior in Extreme Situations: Defenses

L̲IFE IN THE CONCENTRATION CAMP
was extremely complex. The pressure to obey, conform, submit to the SS, and change one's entire personality and behavior, was obvious and visible. The prisoners' counter efforts
at trying to change the camp, to ward off inner changes, to
forestall enforced adjustment, all these had to proceed in
secrecy.

While the Gestapo used mainly physical and psychological
pressure to achieve its goals, the prisoners tried to counteract with organizational defenses, and more subtle psychological ones. But often their efforts to defend themselves
found them deeper enmeshed in the system. Just as the SS'
desire for efficient workshops led to areas of common interest between SS and prisoners, so the prisoners' efforts to
defend themselves through prisoner organizations forced
them to cooperate with the SS. The resulting contradiction
was that the more effective the organization, the better it
also served the SS.[1]

For example, the largest growth of power among prisoner

---

[1] Here, then, is an interesting parallel to all organizational efforts
to resist the coercive mass society. For example, it is not unusual to
see a professional group trying to defend its independence and self
interest against encroachment by the state. But to be effective it must
often wage battle on two fronts, each one defeating the purpose of

foremen coincided with the beginning of human experimentation and the policy of extermination. Rousset,[2] in his report on the camps, points out that once prisoner kapos in the camp hospital were in a position to dispense typhoid serum, they could give it to those who needed it and thus preserve their lives; they could withhold it from those who needed it; and they could give lethal doses to those they wished to liquidate. A prisoner's position of power was always one of being able to protect *and* to kill—almost never of being able to protect or to kill—because without killing one's enemies, one did not retain power. This made the position and the policies of all members of the ruling prisoner group highly ambiguous.

But how did it come about that prisoners to a large degree ran the camps for the SS; that this gave rise to a complex prisoner hierarchy; that the class structure of this hierarchy made life miserable, if not literally intolerable, for those who could not lift themselves out of the lowest class of prisoner society; that prisoners who hoped to rise into the higher strata betrayed, took advantage of, even mistreated fellow prisoners; that the different groups (politicals, criminals, etc.) conspired against each other to win or hold on to their positions; and that in so doing they accepted as their own much of the values and behavior of the SS?

The prisoner elite

As early as 1936 some prisoner organization appeared in the concentration camps, when prisoners were put to use to

safeguarding freedom. In order to be effective it has to organize its members tightly, thus interfering with their freedom. In order to gain concessions from the state, it has to compromise, thus again cutting into the freedom of its members which the organization was designed to safeguard. To set power against power just will not lead to freedom; setting inner freedom against external power might.

[2] D. Rousset, "The Dotkins—Hessel—Pool Affair," *Politics,* IV, July-August 1947, p. 158.

erect and maintain the camps, and for other more complex assignments.

But labor asked for foremen. As a ruling elite, the SS shunned manual labor; they were a warrior caste, meant only to command the laboring masses. So it was easy for prisoners to volunteer as foremen. Here it must be borne in mind that certain work assignments offered what seemed like irresistible chances for power, safety and privilege. Classes were not based on economic services rendered to society and were therefore not anchored in significant functions. They rose or fell by whim of the SS.

For example, the division between skilled and unskilled labor which often meant the difference between life and death to a prisoner, was a division of "class" stratification inside the camp, not one of skill. "Middle class" prisoners were assigned to commands of skilled labor whether they had the skill or not. If they had it, good. If not, they acquired it in the camp; in this way prisoners became electricians or surgeons as needed. In the same way, by becoming "nearly middle class," the forty Jewish political prisoners just described became bricklayers. Kapos handed out labor assignments almost wholly on the basis of political interests or personal gains.

But assignments to skilled labor were the exception, and reserved for a favored minority. Unskilled labor, entailing the greatest danger and suffering, was the permanent fate of the majority of all prisoners, and of almost all prisoners at one time or another.

Since unskilled labor was easily shifted from one task to another because none of them called for any training, unskilled labor was always expendable. From this dreaded fate derived the original power of the prisoner elite.

In practice, the working of the prisoner hierarchy proved that a handful of SS men could actually rule tens of thousands of hostile prisoners, could even induce prisoners to work and control others for them without ever becoming dangerous. The very inception of classes, despite the fact that most leading prisoners were communists, and in theory committed to a classless society, indicates that even the most resistant groups of the population succumb to the pressure of the total mass society if it is strong enough. There were several reasons for this development.

As already indicated, prisoners in power could use their positions to give limited protection to prisoners, but in order to stay in "office" they had most of all to serve the SS. Self interest demanded that they retain power at all cost. Since they were often punished for what the SS considered short-comings in the barrack block or labor gang they were in charge of, they tried to protect themselves by anticipating any demand the SS might make so that often they ended up outdoing the SS. While this was true for the majority of the ruling prisoners, a few outstanding persons used their positions with daring and unselfishness to better the lot of common prisoners. There were a few super-kapos who suc-cessfully interfered with an SS private mistreating prisoners, but they were the exception, since their action called for extraordinary courage.

As the number of prisoners grew and they became more and more expendable, particularly with the onset of the extermination policy, having an in with some member of the prisoner aristocracy became the only way a prisoner could save his life. But even before that, just to find and keep a good labor command was always a matter of life and death, and so was getting a better food ration each day, or even once in a while.[3] As the institution of the camps grew

---

[3] Fights of life and death took place around the ladling of soup, the main fare of the day. It came into the barracks in huge containers from which the prisoner in charge of a barrack ladled it out. His friends got a full ladle, with the soup well stirred, so that some meat and vegetables swam in it. Those who had not bought or otherwise gained his favor might get only three-quarters of a ladle, skimmed from the

larger and more elaborate, they became more of a miniature mass society. With each step, more members of the prisoner aristocracy became more powerful, and more of them had to be befriended for survival.

Let me give an example. Earlier in this chapter I recounted how hundreds of prisoners died one winter night, or soon after, as a result of exposure on the parade grounds while the SS hunted two escaped prisoners. The escape had been discovered early in the afternoon. The SS called in the kapo of the labor gang the two escapees worked in, the chief of their barracks block, and the doyens of the camp (who held the very top positions in the prisoner aristocracy) to help them speculate on where the two might be hunted. Through them, other leading prisoners learned what lay in store for the whole camp, and rumors spread like wildfire.

Block chiefs who felt a responsibility to prisoners in their block, and who felt they could rely on them not to be betrayed, now informed them of the situation. Immediately frantic preparations began among those few who were able to, though they risked severe punishment if discovered. This was a chance many were willing to take. Very little time elapsed between the time the vast majority of prisoners returned from work and the time they had to report at the assembly grounds to begin standing at attention. The main problem was to provide oneself and others with some protection against exposure, and to ready things for prisoners returning from work so that they could prepare themselves for the ordeal in a few minutes.

Prisoners were forbidden to wear anything but their prison uniforms and one woolen sweater; only kapos, block chiefs, etc., were given and allowed to wear overcoats. Frequent inspections kept prisoners from owning any clothing except the scanty underwear issued, and the prison uniform.

---

top; this would mean only hot brew without any bits of solid food in it.

Any attempts to keep warm in other ways was punished. In view of what lay ahead, it seemed wiser to risk detection and punishment than to forego the extra protection. So with the connivance of kapos and foremen, and depending on the attitude of the latter and the prisoners' daring, some prisoners began to "organize" (in camp slang: to acquire by any means, mostly illegal) paper or other material that would give added warmth.

Prisoners at Buchenwald normally had their main meal, little nourishing as it was, after being counted on the assembly ground. If they were going to be kept at attention, they would miss it. This meant standing all night in a bitter frost without having eaten. Some prisoners kept small supplies of food on their shelves, but they were not supposed to enter the barracks between the end of work and the start of roll-call assembly. Nevertheless, some prisoners stole away from work in the early afternoon, collected whatever food and paper they could find, and pooled it so that every prisoner in their group could have at least a bite to eat and some paper to stuff under his uniform before the night watch began.

All this sounds quite simple; and it would have been, except for the utter scarcity conditions in the camp. There, collecting enough waste paper for one person's protection was a frightful task. Now, when each of the few who could and did risk leaving work had to provide a dozen or more with added protection, it asked for frantic activity and great ingenuity. Doors into SS store rooms had to be broken open, bags of cement emptied (the heavy paper of these bags was the best insulation available), the cement disposed of so that the theft would not be noticed immediately, etc. When the time for assembly came, most political prisoners and Jehovah's Witnesses had had something to eat and acquired some extra protection against the cold. This they owed to the greater helpfulness of their groups. But it would still have been impossible without the connivance of block chiefs, of the kapos who did not report them for leaving work, and smaller fry in the prisoner hierarchy, such as room chiefs, and store keepers.

On such occasions, when their own status and safety was not in danger, many ruling political prisoners helped others as well as they could. This was less true for nonpolitical foremen, and not at all true for the thousands of asocial prisoners whose block chiefs felt little sympathy for them, put no trust in them to keep their help a secret and thus offered no help. So that night they suffered considerably more than most other prisoner groups.

On this occasion the fact that prominent prisoners were "in the know" was an advantage to some prisoners. But there were many other occasions when their greater power led to questionable practices.

Ambiguous power

All ruling prisoners were responsible for the destruction of some prisoners, to save themselves, their friends, or other members of their group. But everything was deemed necessary, including the extermination of whole groups of prisoners, when it was a question of staying in power. So it came about that some of the political groups formed to protect fellow prisoners ended up giving full, if heavy-hearted cooperation to the extermination of thousands of prisoners in order to save some of their own group.

The ambiguous attitude of the prisoner elite toward other prisoners went beyond motives of safety, or economic and social advantages. Often equally attractive was the psychological appeal of power.

Firstly, all prisoners, including those forming the ruling group, were so devoid of true autonomy and self respect that they craved it to an unheard degree. So those who could, clung tenaciously to such chances for exerting power as passed for genuine independence of action. Power and influence—power at any price, and influence for no matter what purpose—were extremely appealing in an environment whose sole purpose was to emasculate the individual. No prisoner felt really free, but he felt the lack of freedom less if he had absolute power to make others jump.

Secondly, looking down upon lower class prisoners was an important psychological defense against one's own fears. Like my fellow prisoners, I was deeply shocked when we entered Buchenwald and saw the large numbers of work-shy prisoners who looked like walking skeletons; the distintegration of their bodies and personalities showed so obviously. We were also repelled to see them eat refuse. The prisoner group we belonged to had entered the camps well fed, our health well taken care of, in short with a reserve of strength built up during years of good living. The asocial prisoners, coming mostly from submarginal strata of society, had no such reserves on which to draw.

Seeing them made every prisoner afraid he might become like them. The easiest way to quiet such anxiety was to believe one was made of "different stuff" and could never fall so low. Fear of sinking into that subhuman stratum of prison society—the asocials, the "moslems"—was a powerful incentive to fighting a class war against them. It could be rationalized because they were actually dangerous—as carriers of disease, because their desperate conditions led them to steal (and even a middle class prisoner had so little that the loss of a sweater or a loaf of bread could mean life or death), and because their desperation and nihilism were contagious. It was difficult to keep up one's own morale, and one hated them because one feared their example.

This may explain the behavior of the prisoner elite, communist or not. As with most ruling classes, and particularly those groups newly come to power, they lost all empathy with the fate, the feelings and suffering of these lower class prisoners. They no longer understood what it did to them to be exposed to the worst miseries of the camp, to hard labor, bad weather, lack of rest, and the inability to care for their bodily needs. The fact was that they could not afford to understand it because any softening of attitude toward common prisoners would soon have been noted by the SS and they would swiftly have fallen from power. So their own survival depended on becoming and remaining insensitive. In self protection they sought and found reasons for standing off from these lower class prisoners. They criticized them for a lack of restraint that threatened the camp with contamination and epidemics. They disparaged them for drinking contaminated water at a time when nothing but boiled water should have been used.

What they could not afford to recognize was that privileged prisoners were reasonably well supplied with food and boiled water and hence had an easier time restraining themselves, while most others were suffering such hunger and thirst that considerations of health, their own or anyone else's, were feeble compared to the overwhelming pressure of their need.

A typical example was the attitude of block and room chiefs toward those starving prisoners who scavenged for potato peelings in the refuse containers. Strong in their normal weight of some 170 pounds, they whipped (for their own good) these miserable shadows who were down to some 90 pounds for transgressing the camp rule against eating refuse. True, many prisoners acquired serious stomach disorders after eating food scraps that were often in a state of decay. Nevertheless, such attitudes of righteousness on the part of well fed prisoners seemed outrageous to those who were starving.

For all this, the prisoner elite, except for some of the criminals, were rarely without a sense of guilt over the advantages they enjoyed. But given their striving for survival the most this usually came to was a greater need to justify themselves. This they did as members of ruling classes for centuries have done—by pointing to their greater value to society because of their power to influence, their education, their cultural refinement.

Kogon's attitudes are fairly representative. For example, he took pride that in the stillness of the night he enjoyed reading Plato or Galsworthy, while in an adjacent room the air reeked of common prisoners, while they snored unpleasantly. He seemed unable to realize that only his privileged position, based on participation in human experiments, gave him the leisure to enjoy culture, an enjoyment he then used to justify his privileged position. He was able to read at night because he was neither shivering, nor stupid with exhaustion, nor starved. The attitude of superiority felt by privileged prisoners is apparent in some of his comments on the psychology of the prisoners: "Psychological complications of importance existed only in those who were of higher value as individuals, groups, or classes," he wrote. The educated classes, he added, were, after all, not prepared for life in the concentration camps.[4] The inference seems to be that ordinary prisoners were suited to life in the camps, or did not suffer any psychological complications.

These remarks are no indictment of Kogon, who was obviously one of the more concerned and conscientious members of the ruling group, deeply disturbed by camp conditions. But his own life depended on keeping his position of privilege and to that end he had to find means to justify it. No man who is basically decent and sensitive can do otherwise.

This then, is another example of the truth of an often repeated comment: that in the camps, not the SS but the prisoner was the prisoner's worst enemy.[5] The SS, sure of

---

[4] Kogon, *op. cit.*, p. 302 ff.
[5] Kogon, *op. cit.*, p. 311.

its superiority, had less need to demonstrate and prove it than the prisoner elite who could never feel secure about it. The SS descended on prisoners like a destructive tornado that struck several times a day, and one lived in constant dread of them; but there were hours of respite in between. Prisoner foremen exerted pressure without letup; one felt it continuously—during the day at work, and all night in the barracks.

Individuals who played leading roles in factional warfare and who belonged to the prisoner aristocracy sometimes admitted with resignation that prisoners could have done much more for one another, and the SS would have permitted it, condoned it, or been unable to prevent it, if the terrible internecine class war among prisoners had not constantly interfered with such efforts.

Basically then, only the SS benefitted from the inner warfare among prisoners for survival and positions of power. In the fully developed oppressive mass state even the victim's efforts to organize in self defense seem to work toward personality disintegration.

It is relatively easy to show why this had to happen when a single overwhelming organization, the SS, was pitted against a very weak one whose members felt they could only succeed by cooperating with the powerful opponent. It may be harder to realize that the same held true for the individual prisoner's psychological defenses.

PSYCHOLOGICAL DEFENSES

Early rationalizations

Even sooner than any recourse to organization, each prisoner mustered his own psychological defenses to protect him from the impact of the concentration camp. Mention has been made of how members of different social and economic groups reacted differently to the shock of imprisonment. Understandably, they first fell back on those psychological mechanisms which had given them security in the past. And here at the very start many prisoners, particularly those of the middle class, came to grief. They tried to impress the guards with the important positions they had held or the contributions they had made to society. But every effort of this kind only provoked the guards to further abuse.

The SS was, after all, serious in its wish to create a different society. Their deep dissatisfaction with pre-Hitler society was part of why they joined the SS in the first place. To tell them that one had been a pillar of this hated society, and to ask for respect on that account was not only misguided effort, but aroused great animosity in the average SS. Some middle class prisoners needed repeated experiences before they learned this lesson. At first they clung to the belief that it was just a particular SS who failed to see that they deserved better treatment or more respect for what they had been or done.

Even a cursory consideration of the SS attitude to pre-Hitler society should have taught them that none of this counted for anything any more. For the SS, the society that had once assigned them such a low status was dead. Many prisoners had a hard time learning that lesson because they were unable to see the SS as they really were. Another reason was the need to hold on to their belief in old sources of security, a belief they clung to the harder as they saw no way of acquiring any new form of security in the camp.

Politically conscious prisoners, on the other hand, found some support for their self-esteem in the fact that the Gestapo had singled them out as important enough to take revenge on. Members of the various parties relied on similar types of rationalization. Radical leftists found proof, in the fact of their imprisonment, of how dangerous their activities had been for the Nazis. Former members of liberal groups argued that it was clear now how unjustly they had been accused of a middle of the road policy, since their imprisonment showed that it was just such a policy that the Nazis feared most.

The same kind of reasoning supported the badly shaken self esteem of small upper class groups such as monarchists, who felt their imprisonment just as strongly as the middle classes. But the high esteem they had enjoyed before imprisonment carried over for some time and they were treated as exceptions by many prisoners, if not by the SS, which enabled them to view themselves as exceptions. (I am reminded here, for example, of the former Lord Mayor of Vienna.) This enabled them to deny, for some limited time, the "reality" of what was happening to them. They were still convinced they were special and felt there was no need to adjust to the camp; that they would soon be released due to their importance to society. This was particularly true for members of the high aristocracy, for some prisoners who had held very high political positions, and a few extremely wealthy prisoners, the multimillionaires.

Their conviction of superiority, and the respect accorded them by other prisoners, brought some middle class prisoners into a dependency on them. The middle class prisoners hoped that their patrons, after release, would help them too, to gain liberty, and once free, would make provisions for them and their future. One result was that upper class prisoners did not form a group; most of them remained more or less isolated, each one surrounded by his group of middle class "clients." But this superior position was held only as long as there was some reason to believe in a speedy release and as long as they could dispense money freely. When time passed and experience convinced them (and their clients) that they were no closer to release than any other prisoner, their special status collapsed and there was no further difference between them and other prisoners.

This was not equally true for the very few upper-upper-class prisoners, the formerly "anointed." They were chiefly members of former royal families, and their number was too small to permit many generalizations. But they did not collect "clients," did not readily use money to buy favors of other prisoners, did not discuss their hopes of release. They looked down on most other prisoners nearly as much as they despised the SS. In order to endure life in the camp, they seemed to develop such a feeling of superiority that nothing touched them. Thus, from the outset they acquired a feeling of detachment, a denial of the "reality" of the situation in which they found themselves, that came to most other prisoners only after excruciating experiences. How well they stood up was quite remarkable, but like the Jehovah's Witnesses, they were a special case. While the SS treated all other prisoners as numbers, the attitude was more pretended than real toward members of former royalty.

It would be interesting to ask where, exactly, the SS drew the line without wishing to, and probably without knowing it. At one time I worked alongside of a count, the scion of one of the most aristocratic families of Germany, and he felt and was treated like all other prisoners. But when, for example, a Duke of Hohenberg, grandnephew of the Austrian Emperor, was cruelly mistreated and humiliated, it was done very much with the attitude, often verbalized in just those words: "I'll show you you're no different from any other prisoner." So these upper-upper-class prisoners really were singled out, if only to make a point of the SS' contempt for them. Their abuse was special since they were treated for the persons they were; they were not interchangeable with all other prisoners. It is possible that for this reason their self esteem never suffered so radical a destruction as did other prisoners'. By remaining special, even if only in the way they were abused, they remained individuals.

While the various political groups blamed one another for the success of National Socialism, many prisoners, particularly those who were politically oriented, blamed themselves for not having stemmed the tide by fighting it more courageously and effectively. This guilt feeling was apparently relieved, and their pride redeemed in some measure, by the same rationalization that helped ease the shock of imprisonment itself: the fact that the Gestapo found them dangerous enough to send them to a concentration camp.

Atoning for others

One of the ways in which some prisoners tried to protect their integration was to feel newly important because their suffering protected others. After all, concentration camp prisoners had been singled out for punishment by the SS as representative of all the dissatisfied elements.[6]

This having to suffer for others was used by many prisoners to pacify inner guilt over their antisocial behavior in the camps, while the actually unbearable living conditions were used to rationalize such behavior toward others. Indications of this were to be found whenever one prisoner called another one to task for misbehavior. If a prisoner was reprimanded for taking advantage of another prisoner or for beating him, for obscene talk, dirtiness, or some other negligence, the typical response was: "I can't be normal when I have to live in such circumstances."

By a parallel reasoning they felt they had atoned for any shortcomings in the past, whether in themselves or in their relations to family and friends, as well as any future changes they might still undergo. They felt free to deny responsibility or guilt on a number of scores, felt free to hate other people, including their own families, even where

---

[6] Though prisoners were never told exactly why they were imprisoned, those imprisoned as representatives of a group came to know it. So they rightly felt that they were atoning for the rest of the group, even if outsiders could not see it that way.

the shortcomings were obviously their own. The form this took is illustrated by the attitude of one prisoner who was reminded of some past neglect in his duties. He replied that this counted for nothing now because those he had wronged were enjoying liberty while he suffered in the camp. That proved that he was the wronged one, not they.

Such defenses, aimed at retaining self respect by denying all guilt, actually weakened the prisoners' personalities; by blaming outside forces for their actions, they not only denied having personal control of their lives, but also that what they did was of any consequence. Blaming others, or outside conditions for one's own misbehavior may be the child's privilege; if an adult denies responsibility for his actions, it is another step toward personality disintegration.

Emotional detachment

It has been mentioned that one of the safeguards against giving up the will to live was the ties binding a prisoner to his family. But since the prisoner could do nothing to make them stronger, he lived in constant fear that those ties might be broken. The fear was intensified by stories of wives divorcing their prisoner husbands, a decision encouraged by the SS, and by the more frequent rumors of faithlessness, etc. Anxiety and ambivalence was transparent whenever there were letters from home.

Prisoners would weep over a letter telling of efforts to liberate them, but curse in the next moment as they read that some of their property had been sold without their permission, even when the purpose was to buy them their freedom. They would swear at their families who "obviously" thought them "already dead," since their possessions were being disposed of without their consent. Even the smallest change in their former private world assumed tremendous importance. They might have forgotten the names of some of their best friends, but on learning that a friend had moved or gotten married, they were terribly upset and nothing could console them.

Over the years, it is not surprising that some of the news they got was extremely upsetting, though it was nothing but the outcome of life on the outside going on. For example, one prisoner learned that his daughter, whom he carried in his memory as a little teenager, had just been married to a man whose name meant nothing to him. With such events taking place outside, and themselves in such an abject state, how could they believe they would ever again fit in? All too often, the long awaited letter turned out to contain information that failed to support their self love or their sense of being loved, but on the contrary showed how little they counted for, or at least they read it so.[7]

Many aspects of the prisoners' ambivalence about the outside world seemed to hinge on a desire to return home exactly the same person who had left it. The desire was so great that they dreaded any change, however trifling, in the situation they had left. Their worldly possessions had to remain secure and untouched, although they were of no use to the prisoner where he was. Even harder for their families to comply with, was seeing that nothing in the structure of

---

[7] I recall a personal instance of how easy it was to misinterpret the intentions of a letter, though on other levels one was quite aware of its nature. One day my mother wrote me that one of my colleagues had presented a paper, using some of my ideas, and that it was very well received. Reading the letter on one level, I knew that both my colleague and my mother hoped that the acceptance of my ideas would please me, which is why I was told about it. Nevertheless, on a much more important level it sent me into a cold fury to think that my colleague was enjoying success with my ideas while I lived in such misery. The net result was not the hoped for lift in morale, but on the contrary, greater feelings of misery; a small bit of pleasure against massive anger. The first I could have done without; the latter was utterly destructive to me in a situation where I could do nothing with my anger but internalize it.

the family changed, and this over years, with the bread-winner absent.

It is hard to say if the prisoners wanted everything to remain the same because they realized how hard it might be to adjust to an entirely different home situation, or because of some sort of magical thinking that went roughly as follows: If all remains as it was, in the world I used to live in, then I remain the same too. In this way they may have been trying to counteract the feeling that they were changing, and how much. The violent reaction against any change in their families was then a counterpart of the realization of how much they were changing themselves.

What outraged the prisoners even more than the fact of changes taking place at home, was the change all this implied in their own status within the family. As noted earlier, their role in the family was now reversed; now it was the family which made decisions and the prisoner who was dependent. So not only did the SS degrade them, even their own families were destroying their badly wounded self esteem by deposing them as heads of their families. It was simply wrong not to be able to exercise one's function as the head of the family. So they felt doubly wronged: by the SS which kept them from presiding over their families, and by their families, when circumstances forced them to act on their own. And on one level the prisoner realized this. But on another level, and much more acutely felt, the family seemed to be treating him no differently than the SS.[8]

---

[8] In this respect their situation cannot be compared with that of ordinary prisoners in jail, because the latter enjoyed legal protection so that they usually knew the date of their release—nor with soldiers during a war, because soldiers are heroes to their families. Most concentration camp prisoners could not be heroes to their families because if fighting National Socialism was heroism, it would have implied that the family, too, had an obligation to fight it. This was unlikely because of the danger to themselves, and because the Gestapo made it clear that any subversive action on their part would endanger the life of their imprisoned relative.

So there was hardly a letter that did not at once cause elation and depression; elation because they were not yet wholly forgotten, and depression because decisions had been made that only the head of the family would normally have made. All these emotions in the wake of each letter were an added strain. They not only aroused impotent rage against the beloved (one of the most, if not the most, debilitating of all emotional experiences) but guilt, because one knew that the rage was unjustified.

The psychological defense against all this was to withdraw one's emotional attachment where it only led to pain. To avoid so much guilt, frustration and pain, one withdrew emotionally from one's family and those aspects of the outer world one was still strongly attached to. But while these emotional ties made life in the camp more painful, the alternative of denying, repressing, and loosening them all robbed the prisoner of what might have been his greatest source of strength.

As in many other situations, his emotional withdrawal was not only an inner defense but an outcome of how the SS handled messages arriving from the outside. Firstly, prisoners were only allowed to get two letters a month, and they had to be very short. Very often, as punishment, all writing and receiving of letters was stopped for months at a time. But even when letters were allowed, they were handed out amid so many degrading circumstances that often they made the letter seem not worth receiving. After a while it began to seem preferable not to pay too much attention to news from home, because the circumstances surrounding it were too painful.

One day, for example, the SS block leader arrived with a large packet of mail and read the names of the prisoners he had letters for. Finished with that, he said, "Now you pigs know you received mail," with which he burned the entire packet. Or again: one day an SS officer told a prisoner

—without showing him the wire conveying the message—that news had arrived of his brother's death. The prisoner humbly asked which of his brothers had died, since he had several. The answer was: "You can choose which one it should have been"; and this was all the information he ever received during his imprisonment.

Despite the gradual withering of old emotional ties, no new ones were apt to be formed in the camps to replace them. Emotional energy was continuously being drained because of the vital energy needed for mere survival. It could not be replenished by friendships with other prisoners because there was almost no emotion free to offer in support of others, and far too many occasions for friction, if not active hatred. Thus the various defensive efforts of the prisoner to ward off disappointments originating in his family removed almost his sole remaining source of emotional strength. From within and without, from the SS, from the struggle between prisoners for survival, from his own inner reaction, came the steady pressures toward emotional isolation.

Selective amnesia

As noted earlier, many prisoners showed a tendency to forget names and places because of ambivalence toward important events of their previous lives, and the people in it. Forgetting things of this kind created anxiety, because the prisoners began to fear they were losing their memories, even their intellectual capacities. This fear was aggravated by the knowledge that they could no longer reason objectively. They knew they were constantly being swayed by emotions, particularly anxieties. So they began to make conscious efforts to retain their memories and prove to themselves they were not losing their intelligence. For example, they tried to remember what they had learned in school.

Interestingly enough, they were best able to recall things they had learned by rote, facts with no bearing on their present life situation. To show the strength of their memories they tried to repeat the names of the German emperors, their dates of ascension, the names of the popes, and like facts they had memorized in class years ago. Thus their efforts to display and retain their memories led to further regression into childhood situations, into doing things automatically instead of spontaneously.

Being able to remember data that were of no importance at the moment, but unable to remember facts that would permit conclusions and then decisions in the urgent present was an experience that shook them. Even one's mind seemed to function in ways that no longer offered protection, but only along lines and at tasks formerly set down by persons in authority. One remembered facts one had been told to learn, not those one had wished to acquire for oneself.

Psychologically this mechanism is easily understood. Anything that had to do with present hardships was so distressing that one wished to repress it, to forget it. Only what was unrelated to present suffering was emotionally neutral and could hence be remembered. But to the prisoner, it was just one more experience of being able to function only where it did not count, of preserving old achievements only where they had no importance.[9]

For the prisoner to see his mind functioning about mat-

---

[9] Similar observations on remembering sets of data, etc., have been made by prisoners who spent stretches of time in solitary confinement, other than in concentration camps. They too tried to keep going by rehearsing neutral and emotionally unimportant facts. But their situation was entirely different. They had no influence over their fate; it made no difference whether they were able to pay close attention to what went on around them, because nothing did. So anything that occupied their minds was to the good and assured them they were still alive and functioning. The concentration camp prisoner, on the other hand, had to pay unflagging attention to make the right decisions. Any lapse could be fatal.

ters of no import to camp life, and going blank on issues of life and death—such as forgetting the address of an important relative who might be of help in getting him released—was a devastating experience. It proved once more how far one had deteriorated. Worse, it proved that one's efforts to remain intact (one's memory) proved that the opposite was happening (one's deterioration, where it counted).

This incidentally, and similar experiences teach a significant lesson: that what supports self esteem and true independence is not fixed and unchanging, but depends on the vagaries of the environment. Each environment requires different mechanisms for safeguarding autonomy, those that are germane to success in living, according to one's values in the particular environment. Doing well at rote learning supported self esteem and was a sign of adequacy in the school environment the prisoners knew as youngsters; it was not that in their present environment.

Sexual potency

As might have been expected, the prisoners' dread of losing their competence and integration found openest expression in fears for their potency. It has already been noted that the SS forced prisoners to regress to immature desires and interests. Here we are concerned with their efforts to ward off regression, and the effects of these defenses on their personal integration.

Virtually every prisoner was afraid of becoming impotent, and was tempted by the anxiety to verify his potency. That meant either homosexual practices or masturbation. Prisoners indulged in both: a minority in the first, an overwhelming majority in the second, but only rarely, and then less for enjoyment than to be sure they had not yet grown impotent. Still, in terms of their upbringing and adult standards, either practice meant a return to preadult behavior with a new increase in guilt feeling. So again an effort to protect the personality through reassuring experiences ended in lowered self respect.

The dread of becoming impotent was closely related to infantile castration anxiety, a fear revived by SS threats of castration. In reality, sterilizations were rare up to the time of the war; before 1940, only real or supposed sex offenders were sterilized. But the threat of sterilization, even of castration, was used frequently, and not only by the SS but by old prisoners who echoed it. In this case, the use of such threats by old prisoners was probably less a matter of identifying with the SS than a defense against their own anxieties.

For example, newcomers were occasionally told that all prisoners were emasculated on the day after arrival in the camp. After their experiences on the transport, they were ready to believe almost anything. Old prisoners realized the state of mind most newcomers were in. Therefore, the use of such a threat seems to have grown out of a strong psychological need on their part. Ordinarily they did not make it aggressively. They emphasized that they, too, had undergone the mutilation, survived it, and after all were not faring so badly. They told their stories so convincingly that some new prisoners asked the SS where they were supposed to report for the operation.

Old prisoners envied the newcomers' virility, and the fact that newcomers had recently enjoyed sexual experiences they themselves had been deprived of for years. That the SS emasculated prisoners was symbolically true, if not literally so. The threat of emasculation was probably the response of old prisoners to the anticipated question of the newcomer: How can a man permit himself to live under such degrading conditions? By telling newcomers that all prisoners in the camp are emasculated they answered this by implying that just as they had lost their virility and become impotent to revolt, so would the newcomer.

In general, if old prisoners used their greater camp experience for cowing new prisoners, it was to relieve their state of impotence by having the power to intimidate others for a change. But this defense too worked in favor of the SS, because it weakened the ability of new prisoners to resist, without strengthening that of old prisoners.

Daydreaming

The tendency among old prisoners toward megalomanic daydreams has already been mentioned. Here it may be added that prisoners daydreamed almost continuously in their efforts to escape a depressing reality. The trouble was that soon they were no longer sure what was daydream and what was real. There were always new rumors of improvements in the camp situation or of speedy release. The content of these rumors depended largely on the individual prisoner's frame of mind. But despite the differences, almost all prisoners enjoyed discussing rumors which in many cases had the character of common daydreams, or of *folies à deux, trois, quatre,* or more.

The credulity of most prisoners went far beyond reason and can only be explained by a need to raise their own and each other's morale with favorable rumors, believed against their better judgment. Conversely, when in a depressive state of mind, which was more usual, it seemed to bring temporary relief if one could justify with unfavorable rumors one's own utter dejection.

Certain rumors reappeared with regularity though they never came true. One was that of a general amnesty because of the fifth, seventh, or tenth anniversary of the Third Reich, because of Hitler's birthday,[10] because of victory in the West, etc. Other rumors were that the Department of Justice was going to take over the camps, that it was going to

[10] Sometimes there was just a shred of truth to these rumors. On Hitler's 50th birthday about 10% of the prisoners at Buchenwald were released.

review the reasons for everyone's confinement, that the dissolution of all camps was approaching, etc. On the negative side there were rumors that all prisoners, or a given group of them, were going to be exterminated at the beginning of the war, at the end of the war, on some occasion close at hand, and so forth.

Prisoners believed these irrealistic fantasies for some time and enjoyed the happy ones, only to feel more depressed when the rumors collapsed. Although created to offer relief, they actually weakened the men's ability to evaluate situations correctly. To a large degree they were just part of a broader tendency to deny validity to the environment. This they wished so ardently that often they simply daydreamed not living in it.

Their daydreams would have been harmless enough had they been prisoners in a jail, even in solitary confinement. They could have been a useful pastime. But many prisoners engaged in them to a dangerous degree. They behaved as if their old environment simply had not disappeared. They fantasied themselves in their old situations. This offered some temporary emotional relief, but it also hampered them from dealing adequately with the reality of the camps. More insidiously, it was another way of not looking around, not observing reality on one's own, "not noticing." Again, inner defenses coincided with external pressures to reduce prisoners to a dangerous passivity.

As for those who invented rumors, some prisoners did it to gain prestige because other prisoners were anxious to listen. Their own grip on reality was so weakened, and their need for emotional satisfaction so great, that often they did not clearly know they were even inventing stories, or why. Also because they had so little (or no) access to facts, each insignificant detail, because it had to stand for the unavailable important fact, was taken for it. This need to know, though no knowledge could be had, combined with the need to feel important even for moments, to stand in the center of attention, to be listened to instead of pushed around, led to the invention of rumors. But the inventors of rumors bore an emotional deficit; they had to pay a great price in rejection, even harsh abuse, from disappointed prisoners who had swallowed their stories.

Another demoralizing aspect of the prisoners' daydreams was their often contradictory nature. All prisoners hated the Nazi regime, even if and when, without knowing it, they had taken some of its values for their own. The end of the Nazi regime would mean the end of the concentration camps. So their hatred for the regime and their wish for liberation made them hope for the destruction of the regime. But the end of the regime would also mean the end of Germany. This was a price many German prisoners were hesitant to accept. There was also the possibility that before the SS was wiped out they would kill off all prisoners. It was generally assumed this would be the case.

Jewish prisoners were in still a different dilemma. As late as 1940 many of them were being released if they could immediately emigrate. It also became obvious that they were only released when the Nazi regime felt relatively strong, but were killed in large numbers when the regime felt itself threatened. So there were the Jewish prisoners: wishing ardently for the destruction of the enemy; wishing in the same breath (up to 1940) that it would remain strong until they could emigrate, or (later on) remain safe forever to ward off their own mass destruction and the slaughter of their families.

To be unable to solve a dilemma so crucial to one's life can easily destroy psychological well being; so can wishing for an event that means death for oneself and one's friends. The contradictory nature of such wishing and dreaming, as they replaced a more accurate evaluation of reality, was one more step toward childlike behavior forced on the prisoners by the strange reality they lived in.

Bread and values

The purpose of all defenses, psychological or otherwise, was first and foremost to safeguard one's life. Despite the foregoing discussion of defenses designed to protect status, self-esteem, independence of action, maturity, etc., psychological efforts of this kind were comparatively rarefied. In reality, the prisoners' lives were in such extreme danger that little energy or interest was left over. Most of the time concern for personal integration and integrity had to be sacrificed to preserve life. Nor was it always easy to decide when a psychological defense was meant to safeguard the one at the expense of the other, or which of the two was being protected.

For example, nothing but betrayal to the SS was more ruthlessly punished by prisoners themselves than the stealing of bread, and for good reasons, since it could mean life or death to an already starving man. Bread was so generally accepted as the basic food that the attitude toward bread stealing was in a class apart from all other theft. Even the emotional attitude toward bread was different from the attitude toward other foods. While there was constant griping about all other prison fare, complaints about the quality of bread were rare. Prisoners only regretted there was not more of it.

The stealing of bread was punished by the SS in ways that men rarely survived; also, the prisoner code ruled out informing on a prisoner. So transgressions were handled by the prisoners themselves, usually with severe beatings plus a social ostracism that was near "killing" in view of the utter dependence of prisoners on each other.

Once, a relatively new prisoner chanced to mention that his bread had been stolen, and that he had a fair notion of who took it. It was not yet a thing of critical importance to him, because he was still getting money from home for extras at the camp store. But his room chief overheard the conversation. As an old-timer, he was outraged, and demanded that the prisoner say who took it. The new prisoner refused, arguing that the thief must have been hungrier than he was, that he wasn't going to compound his misery with punishment so out of proportion to the crime. He was so stubborn about it that the block chief was called in, the man next higher up in the prisoner hierarchy. With mixed feelings, he threatened harsh penalty if the prisoner refused to inform; but in spite of beatings the prisoner kept his mouth shut. Finally, the chiefs lost patience and threatened to report him to the SS. Carrying out their threat, they started toward the gate (where the SS offices were located), alternating beatings with persuasion along the way. Yet at the last moment the two prisoner officials dropped the matter, half in shame and half in anger, and nothing more was said about it.

While this was an unusual instance of individual courage on the part of a still well integrated prisoner, it shows the very practical grounds on which prisoners waged the continuous struggle to hang on to their self respect and still manage to survive. In this case, a new prisoner reacted first as he would normally have done outside of the camp situation. But once challenged, it became a test of his ability to resist the pressures of terror and force, and particularly their power to alter his individual pattern of morals. To be tolerant of bread stealing was fatal, but so was doing violence to the values one lived by. It was inner or outer starvation, and in the end most prisoners chose to be sure of their bread rather than their self esteem.

Work

It was particularly hard to make fine distinctions about inner and outer survival where defensive systems were built around the work situation. Moreover, it was not always possible to say when a work attitude was a psychological defense against personality disintegration or an inner acceptance of SS values.

It has been mentioned that prisoners resented being forced into nonsensical labor, that it contributed to their personality disintegration. Here the reverse may be discussed. In order to gain self respect, some prisoners tried to work well. They did not usually admit it but would rationalize their behavior somehow, as by saying that what prisoners produced served all German citizens and not just the SS.

For instance, prisoners collected scrap in the camp because Germany was low on raw materials. When it was pointed out that this helped the Nazis and the war effort, they rationalized that by saving scrap, Germany's working classes, too, became richer.

When erecting buildings for the Gestapo, controversies would begin over whether one should build well. New prisoners were for sabotaging, a majority of the old prisoners for building well. Again it was rationalized that the new Germany would have use for these buildings. They also rationalized that regardless of who might finally enjoy the product of their labor, it was important to work well "in order to feel like a man"; or else they retired to the general statement that one ought to do well any job one had to do.

The majority of old prisoners realized that they could not keep working for the SS unless they could convince themselves that all this was so. Some even asserted that working hard and well would show the SS that prisoners were not the scum of the earth, as the SS insisted. Prisoners making the last type of statement came dangerously close to identifying with the SS, since they looked to them for prestige. But the psychological reasons for such an attitude were manifold. By working well, a prisoner may actually have saved his life through avoiding the more "killing" labor commands, as in the command of Jewish bricklayers.

The choice of hard physical labor as a major punishment in the concentration camp was not accidental. Behind it lay the general accusation which the German working classes, influenced by Socialist, Communist, and finally Nazi slogans, had long directed against the middle classes; namely that its members could not do an "honest" piece of hard work, and thought it degrading to labor with their hands.[11] But it still made a difference if the prisoner's labor resulted in products that were of interest to the SS. In such cases there was far less interference with the prisoners at work because too severe punishment lowered their output.

When prisoners were made to drag heavy carts instead of moving them by tractor, the arrangement was illogical from the point of view of productivity, but there was still some interest in the end product. Or the SS might order

---

[11] The SA and SS hated most those prisoners who came from the professional or otherwise well-educated middle classes. They hated them more than their Socialist or Communist labor class opponents, because political enmity toward professional people was aggravated by class resentment. Communists and Socialists had actually fought the SS and SA, which implied they had taken the Nazis seriously as valid opponents in a fight among equals. The intelligentsia, on the other hand (and not only the German intelligentsia), had chosen derision rather than fighting the Nazis face to face. For a long time these attitudes were reflected in the fact that to enter the camp with hornrimmed glasses was tantamount to a death warrant. They became the fatal insignia of the intelligentsia, and while external differences between working class and middle class prisoners soon disappeared, the hornrimmed glasses gave the middle class prisoner away and led to continued persecution by the SS. He was called *Brillenschlange* (verbatim: eyeglass-snake; actually: cobra), was given the hardest, most exhausting labor, and was constantly beaten until he managed to change his glasses for less conspicuous ones.

prisoners loading a cart with sand to throw their shovels away and load it with their hands. This was meant to degrade them below the use of tools, to punish them by making their work more difficult and themselves look ridiculous. Still, the cart had to be filled sometime, and transported to where the sand was needed. Therefore, after a sufficient show of their ability to degrade, and a proper submission, the SS would order shovels to be taken up once more.

No such consideration was shown prisoners ordered to do "sport" or senseless tasks. There all activity was planned as punishment. On dark foggy mornings when visibility was so poor that the SS dared not let the prisoners leave the fenced-in area, all commands working in the open might be ordered to do sport until visibility improved. Sport might include push-ups, crawling on hands and feet through the mud, rolling in the mud, snow or ice, and so on. At one time great heaps of gravel lay on the parade grounds of Buchenwald. Prisoners were forced to roll down them until their bodies were cut by the sharp edges of the stones. An hour of such sport usually did more damage than a whole day at hard labor.[12] Activities like these were not required of the minority of prisoners who worked in the shops because work there could proceed by artificial light.

For such reasons, prisoners often tried to work well on the chance of being assigned to a command where SS interest in the labor product could mean fewer hazards for the prisoner. To this there were two exceptions. The first was any command where the tempo of work depended on the speed of machines; the second was doing work against a deadline. These were always the most dreaded commands. As discussed early in this volume it is one of the contradictions of modern technology that the machines invented to improve man's condition have often become his master. In the camps this tendency was unchecked by human con-

---

[12] Kupfer, *op. cit.*, p. 1223.

siderations or the tendency to preserve human life, and therefore stood out more nakedly.

Quarry work, for example, was a command most prisoners shrank from because the speed with which stones had to be broken and brought to the machine, and the gravel carried away, was set by the pace of the stone breaking machinery. These were truly man-eating machines. At Dachau the SS was alleged to have thrown prisoners into the concrete mixing machine, and this may quite possibly have happened. What really mattered was that prisoners who fed stone into the machine believed it, and the SS frequently reminded them they might come to a similar end if they were too slow in bringing up supplies.

Working against deadlines was similarly dreaded. A typical example was a railroad track that Himmler ordered to be built in 1943 between Buchenwald and the city of Weimar; they were approximately eight miles apart, with a difference in altitude of three hundred yards. He specified that the first trial run was to take place within three months. The SS officer put in charge of the project declared that an impossible time limit. So he was replaced, and the rail construction was entrusted to another officer who had achieved the reputation of being a slave driver at Sachsenhausen. He instituted two twelve hour shifts in which constant beatings were the rule. He also set SS bloodhounds on to prisoners who seemed to be slacking.

The command devoured prisoners. Serious work accidents (no attention was paid to lesser ones) numbered in the dozens each day, and the track was finished on schedule. But as soon as the first heavy engine rolled over the rails, it sagged in. Part repairs proved insufficient and virtually the whole track had to be rebuilt, which took six months.[13] So much for the efficiency of slave labor.

---

[13] For a detailed account of this incident, see Kogon, *op. cit.,* pp. 221-222.

In spite of the foregoing discussion it should be stressed that the nature of work in the camps would be misunderstood if it were assumed that the labor required of prisoners was in itself always beyond endurance. On the contrary, it was more rare than usual for the SS or kapos to ask for the impossible, either in order to "finish off" a prisoner or to meet deadlines or the speed of machines. Nor was the work itself a prime cause of the great number of deaths in the camps.

In general, labor was insufferable most of all because of the physical and psychological exhaustion of the prisoners. Their state of malnutrition, insufficient rest, etc., made even a feasible work load a killing one. Labor was also insufferable because rewards that come in even the most mechanized factories were lacking—namely, wages to be spent with some freedom of choice, and the anticipation of advancement; it was contrary to one's desires and values because it helped one's tormentors; it was purposeless, extraneously enforced, without reward, repetitious and utterly boring—the more so because its results could never be enjoyed or provide recognition.

Thus when prisoners tried to work well there were numerous motives: they might increase their odds for survival; they might be given work that felt less degrading; they might enjoy some fleeting sense of self respect. Unfortunately this solution threw them into the conflict of having to serve the enemy well in order to enjoy a sense of adequacy. This, in turn, was even worse for their self respect; it meant not only having to serve well those they despised, and who also despised them, it meant that their self respect depended on the opinion of a mortal enemy.

Anonymity

Effacing oneself was a defense which, more than any other, helped to produce the kind of childishly submissive, easily manipulated person the SS wanted. To remain inconspicuous, and therefore unnoticed, was one of the best means of surviving in the camp (as typified by the fate of the Hambers).

True compliance with all commands and prohibitions was impossible if one wanted to live. So the real necessity was to just not get caught. That this was not simply a solution worked out by prisoners, but one intended by the SS, was made very clear to everyone. Again and again every SS, from the camp commander down, warned: "Don't dare to be noticeable," or "Don't dare to come to my attention." To the once traditional qualities of the "good" child, that he should be seen and not heard (never talk back or express an opinion) was now added the further injunction that the prisoner should be even more child than the good one: in addition to not being heard he should also be unseen. That meant he had to be so much a part of the mass, so devoid of individuality, that at no time could he be distinguished from all others.

The occasions proving the usefulness of this total disappearance in the mass were legion. For example, during morning roll call a fight of one against all often began for the least visible positions in the parade ground formation. The reason was that the bad humor of block and room chiefs, or worse, of the SS, was directed at those most accessible. If prisoners could not stand rigidly at attention, the ones most likely to get the blows or kicks were those who could be reached without breaking up the formation. Flaws in the cleaning of shoes or uniforms were also easier to see and punish in the first, last, and side rows of the formation. One was more likely to escape harm when protected on all sides by other prisoners.

Nor was that the only reason for avoiding positions of exposure. Standing up front, one could not help but see what went on all over the parade ground. Here, there, and everywhere, one saw prisoner officials abusing and beating those who moved, fidgeted or were not perfectly in line; the SS following with the same or worse. For reasons already discussed it was not only safer if one just didn't see, it protected one against the helpless fury that welled up at having to watch the mistreatment.

Still another reason was that sometimes one had to remain on the parade grounds for hours: if the roll call was not correct, if winter darkness or dense fog kept the prisoners from going to work and they were forced to stand rigidly at attention. Those inside the formation were hard to check; they could afford to stand at ease, and even while away the time by talking.

There were also the terrors of being "noticed" in the daily slave market. Every morning, after roll call, unassigned prisoners ran fearfully across the parade grounds to join some larger group without a labor command on that day. Speed was imperative, because a tired prisoner shuffling along was sure to attract attention. On the assumption that he had been dropped from his previous command as an undesirable, he would be placed in the least desirable work gang. Since he was unfit and tired, he was "expendable," a "drag" on the camp, and might as well be "finished off." Chances of escaping such a fate were better if one could quickly disappear in the mass.

Invisibility was thus a primary rule of defense whatever the situation might be. The need to feel invisible reduced men to the behavior of animals who also do their best to remain unseen, or of children who screen their faces or try to shrink away when confronted with danger. Adopting this enforced anonymity was a successful defense against the real dangers of the camp. But it meant making deliberate efforts to give up individuality and initiative, qualities much needed for the constantly changing emergencies of the camp situation.

Truly making such attitudes one's own had still other advantages. Not having a will of one's own removed the chances for having to go against one's own desires, or else having to repress or deny them. Not having a distinct personality meant not having to hide it, not having to fear that at any moment it might assert itself and bring on destruction. Anonymity meant relative safety, but it also meant giving up one's own personality, though the body walked about for some time, and more safely. But let the situation arise needing vision, independence of action, decision-making, and the ones who had given up personality to safeguard the body were least able to preserve the body they had safeguarded at such loss to their humanity.

Rude awakening

Another important strain on integration was the problem of what to do with one's hostility. Psychologically this problem was far more complex than dealing with the hostility of others. Prisoners found themselves in an impossible state of severe irritation, if only because of a steady interference, by guards or other prisoners, with anything they may have wished to do. The result was a steady accumulation of great amounts of aggression. Even getting up in the morning may illustrate these relentless pressures toward destroying each man as a self-respecting person.

Out of their slumber each morning, prisoners were rudely awakened long before they were rested. At Dachau the morning sirens sounded as early as 3:15 in summer; in winter somewhat later. Then there was roughly 45 minutes for chores. This would seem adequate time, but the actuality of the concentration camp made it otherwise. From the moment the siren sounded, a mad scramble began, with prisoners fighting to get all personal and official tasks done within the time allotted.

This was one of many occasions when friendly cooperation between prisoners and help from block and room chiefs
might have made all the difference in the world. Cooperation
between a few friends, which existed in most units, was in-
effectual against the ferocious disorder that reigned among
the majority. In these frantic moments, newcomers were
always in the way of old-timers, as were individuals who
could not fit themselves into a rigid discipline.

Very few blocks managed to get through the morning
period in an orderly fashion without tension, anxiety, fighting, beatings, all kinds of mutual aggravation. Relative peace
reigned only in the blocks housing prisoners who had been
inmates for years, and where rule was by decent block and
room chiefs. The reason was that finishing all required tasks
in the time allowed asked for great experience and skill in
each prisoner; even a few slow or clumsy ones threw the
whole process out of gear. That kind of skill was acquired
only after hundreds of performances, and only by prisoners
in good health. But no such conditions prevailed in the
majority of the barracks.

The first experience of the new day was one that forcefully impressed on each prisoner that they existed to obey,
that the rules laid down from above took precedence over
all natural desire to care for their bodily needs. It was an
experience that set prisoner against prisoner, making life
unbearable, and all this without the SS having uttered a
word. The SS achieved it by their insistence on a senseless
order and cleanliness. The enforcement of absolute and
irrational orderliness and cleanliness in the barracks was one
of the worst tortures of camp life, partly because all prisoners
were in constant dread of punishment if even one of their
number proved deficient.

The two major tasks in the morning were to "build"
one's bed (if any) and to clean one's locker. The first was
such a difficult task that prisoners sometimes preferred to

sleep on the floor sooner than risk destroying their well built beds by sleeping in them and then being unable to rebuild them in the morning. For this they risked discovery and punishment for violation of rules. But it took even a skillful and experienced prisoner ten to fifteen minutes to build his bed. Some prisoners never learned to do it, particularly some of the older ones who could not balance well standing on the edge of the lower bunk while building the upper one.

As soon as the siren sounded (before then no light could be turned on and therefore no beds could be built) the prisoners jumped out of bed and those sleeping in the top row began. They were pestered by those who slept below them not to deface their mattresses, though it was almost impossible to build the top bed without messing up the one below. Then they were urged to hurry so that the prisoner below might begin his own bed. This often led to long feuds between those who slept above and those below. The same was true for two adjacent beds, since a well built bed might easily be defaced by the person building the one next to it.

To build a bed correctly, the straw mattresses had to be so restuffed and fixed that they were flat as a table, while the sides had to form an absolute rectangle. Pillows, if any, had to be placed on top of the mattress and also fixed so as to form an absolute cube. Both the pillow cube and the mattress had to be covered with a blue and white checked coverlet. These checks were quite small but the cover had to be so placed that the checks were in perfect alignment, horizontally and vertically. To make things more difficult, not only had every single bed to be perfectly built, but the whole row of beds and mattresses had to be in perfect alignment. Some SS checked with yardsticks and levels to make sure that the beds were built correctly and the rectangles perfect; others shot their gun across the beds to see that they were absolutely flat.

If one prisoner's bed was not built to perfection, he was punished severely; if several beds in a barrack were found wanting, the entire unit suffered severely. Always to one's own fear of punishment was added the pressure of others who feared punishment if anyone else's bed or locker was imperfect. Thus, the building of beds was one more fear haunting the prisoner, because whether at work or at rest, he could never be sure that during the day somebody might not inadvertently or maliciously touch his bed so that a piece of dust would fall on it, or a row of squares be out of place and thus render him liable to punishment. Or he may have seen another prisoner build his bed poorly and been in fear that the unit might suffer.

Many a prisoner who never learned to build his bed had to pay every day with money, labor or food to those who were willing to make his bed in addition to their own. In general, because of the haste in performing all chores, prisoners in units not extremely well organized were always having to make choices as to which activities they were willing to skip or neglect.

This sort of pressure was just one more device forcing men to work with gearlike precision, like automatons, running one another with speed and efficiency. It permitted no thoughts of one's own, nor could one do things in the tempo and sequence of one's own volition. All activities were externally regulated to prevent any autonomy on the part of the prisoner.

To take a few minutes longer at washing usually meant losing the chance to brush one's teeth, drink the morning coffee, or use the latrine. Having to rebuild one's bed because one had failed at the first attempt nearly always meant going without washing and coffee.

No prisoner could use the toilet or washroom after the first half hour in the morning, nor was he usually permitted to use the latrines till hours later. So it was absolutely necessary to eliminate before leaving the barracks. An average of six to eight open toilets had to serve anywhere from 100 to 300 men, nearly all suffering from digestive ailments because of the camp fare. So prisoners who had just finished fighting one another over the building of beds, now exploded at those who seemed to be leisurely about sitting on the toilet. Nor did having to watch others eliminate increase their good will toward one another. And so began the new day.

Before the sun had risen, a fight of one against all had already taken place with its tensions, degradations, and depression. It was forced upon prisoners even before a guard had entered the camp in the morning. The distant, still invisible SS had already ground them into a mass of people, unable to act upon their anger, frustrated in their impotence.

Targets for fury

It was tantamount to suicide to direct any of this anger where it belonged: against the SS or prominent prisoners. It could only be diverted. Some prisoners turned their aggressions toward the outside world. But this gave little relief because they could not reach an outside world that was physically distant and emotionally remote.

When it was directed against other prisoners it only created new aggressions because of the limited circle the prisoners lived in. In most cases it also led to guilt, because everyone knew that other prisoners suffered almost as much as oneself. Every time hostility was directed at someone, new aggressions were created in him; these had to be discharged somehow or he would be forced to turn them against himself. There was no energy available for sublimating, or for integrating all this hostility. It could be repressed, and some prisoners tried that. But repression asked for too much emotional energy and determination. Even when these were available at times, they were soon spent in the onslaught of fresh anger, fury and exasperation that accumulated without end in each prisoner.

This growing need to discharge aggression may explain part of the violence of prisoners toward each other: the warfare within the camp among the various prisoner factions, the cruelty against spies, and the mistreatment of prisoners by prisoner officials at work and in the barracks.

Only one outlet was more or less open: aggression toward minority groups. At first this meant only Jewish prisoners, but later foreign nationals were added. The advantage was that these groups could not return aggression with counter-aggression. But German prisoners had to justify their behavior to themselves. They could not face the true reason: that minority groups could not retaliate, being far worse off than German prisoners. So they rationalized by accepting SS attitudes on the racial question.

Projection ⌢ minorities)

Aggression toward minorities was not an outlet open to all prisoners, since some belonged to minorities themselves, while others could not accept it either in the SS or themselves. For them an alternative outlet was to extrapolate it and project it into the SS man. This relieved them of some of their hostility and at the same time protected them from aggression toward the enemy, whose overpowering strength they had to stress. It was a most ineffective system of defense, and may be compared with delusional efforts to master inner pressures by externalizing them.

Psychologically, reality-testing might have destroyed the fiction of the all-powerful SS which they needed for restraining themselves; but reality-testing had to be avoided at all cost. Any attempt to test the actual dangerousness of the SS would have endangered survival.

Thus the combination and interaction of an imaginary system with reality made it hard for such prisoners to escape the psychotic tendencies many of them were forced to develop. The imaginary system was built up out of infantile fears and the prisoner's rage reactions at being forced into infantile patterns; these he projected into the fictitious SS man. The reality interacting with it was the actually overpowering might of the SS. Real helplessness, the need to block every revengeful tendency, and the need to hang on to some narcissism were all motives for creating this fictional image of the persecutor.[14]

Many students of discrimination are aware that the victim often reacts in ways as undesirable as the actions of the aggressor. Less attention is paid to this because it is easier to excuse a defendant than an offender, and because they assume that once the aggression stops the victim's reactions will stop too. But I doubt if this is of real service to the persecuted. His main interest is that the persecution cease. But that is less apt to happen if he lacks a real understanding of the phenomenon of persecution, in which victim and persecutor are inseparably interlocked.

Let me illustrate with the following example: in the winter of 1938 a Polish Jew murdered the German attaché in Paris, vom Rath. The Gestapo used the event to step up anti-Semitic actions, and in the camp new hardships were inflicted on Jewish prisoners. One of these was an order barring them from the medical clinic unless the need for treatment had originated in a work accident.

Nearly all prisoners suffered from frostbite which often led to gangrene and then amputation. Whether or not a Jewish prisoner was admitted to the clinic to prevent such a fate depended on the whim of an SS private. On reaching

[14] Much of this discussion of persecution appeared in an earlier publication, "The Dynamics of Anti-Semitism in Gentile and Jew," *Journal of Abnormal and Social Psychology*, 42: 2, 1947, pp. 153-168.

the clinic entrance, the prisoner explained the nature of his ailment to the SS man, who then decided if he should get treatment or not.

I too suffered from frostbite. At first I was discouraged from trying to get medical care by the fate of Jewish prisoners whose attempts had ended up in no treatment, only abuse. Finally things got worse and I was afraid that waiting longer would mean amputation. So I decided to make the effort.

When I got to the clinic, there were many prisoners lined up as usual, a score of them Jews suffering from severe frostbite. The main topic of discussion was one's chances of being admitted to the clinic. Most Jews had planned their procedure in detail. Some thought it best to stress their service in the German army during World War I: wounds received or decorations won. Others planned to stress the severity of their frostbite. A few decided it was best to tell some "tall story," such as that an SS officer had ordered them to report at the clinic.

Most of them seemed convinced that the SS man on duty would not see through their schemes. Eventually they asked me about my plans. Having no definite ones, I said I would go by the way the SS man dealt with other Jewish prisoners who had frostbite like me, and proceed accordingly. I doubted how wise it was to follow a preconceived plan, because it was hard to anticipate the reactions of a person you didn't know.

The prisoners reacted as they had at other times when I had voiced similar ideas on how to deal with the SS. They insisted that one SS man was like another, all equally vicious and stupid. As usual, any frustration was immediately discharged against the person who caused it, or was nearest at hand. So in abusive terms they accused me of not wanting to share my plan with them, or of intending to use one of theirs; it angered them that I was ready to meet the enemy unprepared.

No Jewish prisoner ahead of me in line was admitted to the clinic. The more a prisoner pleaded, the more annoyed and violent the SS became. Expressions of pain amused him; stories of previous services rendered to Germany outraged him. He proudly remarked that *he* could not be taken in by Jews, that fortunately the time had passed when Jews could reach their goal by lamentations.

When my turn came he asked me in a screeching voice if I knew that work accidents were the only reason for admitting Jews to the clinic, and if I came because of such an accident. I replied that I knew the rules, but that I couldn't work unless my hands were freed of the dead flesh. Since prisoners were not allowed to have knives, I asked to have the dead flesh cut away. I tried to be matter-of-fact, avoiding pleading, deference, or arrogance. He replied: "If that's all you want, I'll tear the flesh off myself." And he started to pull at the festering skin. Because it did not come off as easily as he may have expected, or for some other reason, he waved me into the clinic.

Inside, he gave me a malevolent look and pushed me into the treatment room. There he told the prisoner orderly to attend to the wound. While this was being done, the guard watched me closely for signs of pain but I was able to suppress them. As soon as the cutting was over, I started to leave. He showed surprise and asked why I didn't wait for further treatment. I said I had gotten the service I asked for, at which he told the orderly to make an exception and treat my hand. After I had left the room, he called me back and gave me a card entitling me to further treatment, and admittance to the clinic without inspection at the entrance.

The victim

This incident may serve as a starting point for discussing certain aspects of minority discrimination as a psychological defense, since it was so widespread in the camps.

There is, of course, a significant difference between aggressor and victim in the origin of this particular defense. As many have observed, the aggressor defends himself mainly against dangers that originate in himself. The victim, in his counterreaction, defends himself mainly against dangers originating in the environment; namely, the threat of persecution. But as time goes on, both defensive reactions become more a function of inner motive than outer pressure, although the individual keeps thinking they come only from without. Since both sides are now responding more to inner drives than outside reality, it becomes understandable that their reactions have significant features in common.

For example, both Jews and SS behaved as if psychological mechanisms comparable to paranoid delusions were at work in them. Both believed that members of the other group were sadistic, uninhibited, unintelligent, of an inferior race, and addicted to sexual perversions. Both groups accused each other of caring only for material goods and of having no respect for ideals, or for moral and intellectual values. In each group there may have been individual justification for some of these beliefs. But the strange similarity indicates that both groups were availing themselves of analogous mechanisms of defense. Moreover, each group thought of the other in terms of a stereotype and was thus prevented from realistically evaluating any member of the other group and thus its own situation. Unfortunately members of minority groups, in my example the Jews, were much more in need of being able to reason clearly.

During my camp experience I was impressed by the unwillingness of most prisoners to accept the fact that the enemy consisted of individuals, not just so many replicas of one and the same type. Yet they had had enough close experience with some SS to know of great individual variations. Jews realized that the SS had formed a nonsensical stereotyped picture of *the* Jew and assumed that all Jews were alike. They knew how untrue the picture was, yet they oversimplified in exactly the same way when they thought of *the* SS.

This raises the question of why prisoners could not accept the idea of individual differences among the SS. If, at the clinic entrance, they overlooked the soldier's individuality in forming their plans, some psychological mechanism prevented it. Their violent reaction to my lack of preparedness offers the necessary clue.

Prisoners seemed to derive some security and emotional relief from their preconceived, more or less elaborate, fixed plans. But these plans were based on the assumption that one SS reacted like another. Any attitude throwing their stereotyped picture of *the* SS into question aroused fears that their plans might not succeed. Without plans they would have had to face a dangerous situation without armor, with only miserable anxiety about the unknown. They were neither willing nor able to suffer such anxiety, so they assured themselves they could predict the SS man's reaction and hence plan accordingly. My insistence on approaching the SS as an individual threatened their delusional security, and their violent anger against me becomes understandable as a reaction to the threat.

Overcoming anxiety was by no means the only reason prisoners thought in stereotype of the SS. Other important functions were also fulfilled. For instance, the stereotyped picture contained, among other features, the idea that every SS man was of low intelligence, little education, low social and cultural status. These characteristics, though true for some, were ascribed to all, because otherwise their contempt for the prisoners could not be dismissed so easily. What a stupid or a depraved person thinks can be disregarded. But if those who think badly of us are intelligent and honest, then our self respect is threatened. So whatever the reality, the aggressor had to be thought stupid so that the prisoner could preserve at least a minimal self esteem.

Unfortunately, the prisoners were at the mercy of the SS. It is damaging enough to one's self respect to have to humble oneself. Even worse is having to grovel before a person of undesirable character. The prisoners therefore faced a dilemma. Either the SS were at least their equals, for instance, in intelligence, and their charges against the prisoners carried weight as the opinion of discerning men; or else the SS were stupid, and their charges could be dismissed. But in that case the prisoners had to see themselves as submissive to vastly inferior persons. For their own inner status they could not do that, particularly since many SS demands were unreasonable and amoral. The very fact that they had to obey SS orders made the SS their superiors in what they themselves lacked most, namely, actual power.

The prisoners solved this conflict by thinking of the SS as superior in some other way, though vastly inferior intellectually and morally. They thought of them as all-powerful adversaries and pretended they were not even humans. As they invested the SS with inhuman characteristics, it became possible to submit to them without being degraded. They could admit, without losing self respect, that they were unable to fight against inhuman brutality or an all-powerful conspiracy.

Inside the camps the personal contacts of prisoners with SS were frequent, but not of such a nature as to permit a real understanding of what went on in the minds of the guards. In order to understand SS behavior the prisoners had to fall back on their own experiences. The only way they could explain and understand the actions of the SS was by imputing to them motives they were familiar with. Thus they projected into the stereotype of *the* SS most, if not all, of those undesirable motives and characteristics they knew best, namely, their own. By projecting into the SS everything they considered evil, the SS became still more powerful and threatening. But the process of projection kept them from using to advantage any chance of viewing the SS man as a real person; it forced them to see him only as an *alter ego* of pure evil.

Therefore the SS was always more cruel, bloodthirsty, and dangerous than any one person can possibly be. Many of them were quite dangerous, some were cruel, but only a small minority were actually perverted, stupid, bloodthirsty or homicidal. True, they were willing to kill and injure when so ordered, or when they thought their superiors expected it of them. But the fictitious SS was always, and under all circumstances, a bloodthirsty killer.

There resulted from this attitude a fear of the SS which on many occasions was actually unjustified and unnecessary. Most prisoners avoided contact with them at any price and, by doing so, often ran greater risks. For instance, some prisoners were so terrified that they went into hiding when ordered to present themselves to an SS. For running away they were always severely punished, frequently shot. When they did present themselves, their punishment was never as bad as if they had also run away.

A strange effect of the prisoners' attitude was that even those who committed suicide did not first try to kill a guard. Partly this was because they, like prisoners in the extermination camps, got caught by their own stereotype of the SS, as I shall discuss in Chapter 6. But mainly, since they had given up all interest in life, lost all strength for living, they lacked even enough strength to take revenge.

Psychic economy demands that tendencies toward compensation and defense find expression in a single psychological structure instead of several coordinated structures. For this purpose the powerful figure of the fictitious SS lent itself well. The stereotype made submitting to him less damaging to the prisoner's narcissism and allowed him to identify submissively with the great power of the SS. The prisoner could then enjoy the limited security that comes with utter submission, and could also share the power of the SS in a devious way.

Borrowing this power through psychotic-like introjection allowed the prisoners to gratify some narcissistic needs in a shaky and temporary way. On the other hand, the vital energy used up by the psychotic mechanisms drained the prisoners of a great deal of their total store of energy, just when they needed it most for mastering reality or fighting the enemy.

The persecutor

To the persecutor too, the victim appears much more dangerous than he really is. The SS, by externalizing their own undesirable tendencies and projecting them into the stereotyped picture of, for example, the Jew, tried to shake off their own inner conflicts. The anti-Semite is not afraid of the comparatively insignificant Jewish individual, but of his stereotype of *the* Jew, who is invested with all that is evil in himself. How dangerous his undesirable inner drives are, and how powerful, he knows only too well. An enumeration of the qualities which the SS, for instance, imputed to *the* Jew is some index of the qualities they tried to deny in themselves. Instead of fighting these qualities in themselves, they fought them by persecuting the Jews.

The strength of these unacceptable drives accounts for the violence of the persecution. The balance between the two mechanisms is a tenuous one: every step in projection threatens to undo the work of repression. The anti-Semitic SS had to see the Jew as a very dangerous person and in doing so applied psychological mechanisms much like the ones that accounted for the prisoners' distorted picture of the SS.

The SS could not see themselves waging a war of extermination on a helpless minority. In order to justify their treatment of prisoners they had to believe in a powerful and threatening conspiracy of the imprisoned groups against the Hitler state, including the SS. Their self justification took the form of accusations which, in their mildest form, involved a widespread belief in the racial inferiority of minority groups who were thought apt to contaminate the persecutors. Their most exaggerated form was the SS' conviction of an international conspiracy of Jewish plutocracy waging war against Germany.

The SS could not rely on any tangible proof of the existence of this powerful organization, since the Jews had no army and no fleet, nor were they in leadership positions in great nations. Therefore, the existence of a secret organization had to be postulated. And this is exactly what they did. Here again the delusional mechanisms shaping this kind of persecution become obvious. In his claim of a secret conspiracy, the anti-Semite's thinking may be compared with how the paranoid patient rationalizes. The patient offers the fact that nobody else recognizes the existence of his enemies as proof of their cunning.

The more violent the persecutor's actions, the more he must justify them by believing in the dangerousness of the victim's power. The greater he believes that power to be, the greater his anxiety becomes, which then spurs him to even more violent actions. Thus the persecutor, too, is caught in the vicious circle of his delusional system. It may be one of the reasons why persecution, once it becomes rampant, proceeds with self perpetuating vigor.

There were still other reasons making Jewish prisoners particularly fit objects on whom to project repressed desires. Projection is the result of an inner conflict. Desires that are unsuccessfully repressed and have to be projected are an "inner enemy" of the personality. For this the Jew was much better suited than any external enemy. He was the enemy living inside the structure of a society where he was not fully integrated. The parallel between this precarious position and those instinctual drives which, although part of a subject's personality, are consciously disapproved of, seems striking.

Some of the characteristics that anti-Semites (and not only the SS) often ascribe to Jews and use to justify disliking them are quite revealing. They claim that Jews are sneaky, sly, underhanded, and pushing. These traits may well be applied to how the instinctual drives try to overcome the forces of repression. In their desire for satisfaction, they first "push" against the individual's conscience, trying to force it not to block them. If conscience or self respect forbids their satisfaction in a direct way, the asocial or consciously disapproved drives may still be satisfied by devious means; for instance, by "outwitting" the conscience at off guard moments as in cases of apraxia. Some of the ways in which consciously rejected tendencies find satisfaction may well be called underhanded, or sneaky.

Now the example of the SS guard in front of the clinic may be used again, this time to clarify why he treated me differently. Firsthand knowledge of the psychological mechanisms at work in him is not available. Nevertheless, one may assume that whenever Jews approached him on the basis of their stereotyped picture of the SS, he dealt with them on the basis of his stereotyped picture of the Jew. He had been led to believe that all Jews were cowards and cheats who took advantage of Gentiles by deceitfulness. He knew that these prisoners wanted to enter the clinic and were trying to persuade him to let them in despite orders to the contrary. Their efforts to persuade him by telling implausible stories conformed to his expectations. He expected that Jews would cry and complain and, while asking for help, secretly contrive to make him break the rules. To approach him with a story that was obviously well prepared meant conforming to this expectation.

The stereotype of the "cunning Jew" is a creation of the anti-Semite. If a Jew acting in conformity with the anti-Semite's stereotype were to outwit the SS, it would mean, psychologically, that the SS was outwitted by his own creation. But the purpose of projecting one's evil tendencies is to get rid of them and feel more secure. A projection that gets the better of its creator adds to his helplessness instead of bringing more security. That is why the SS reacted so violently to all efforts to talk him into letting Jews enter the clinic.

Moreover, the SS probably knew he was less intelligent than some of the prisoners; therefore, the cleverness of their stories outraged him. Their intelligence was a threat to his pride, so he had to prove to himself that greater intellect did not work. When Jewish prisoners appealed to his compassion, the threat to his character structure was even greater. In order to conform to the SS ideal, he had to suppress all humanitarian feelings. Anyone who tried to arouse his compassion was threatening to destroy him as an SS soldier.

This too was just what he expected of them: that they would endanger his status as an SS. Only those who have seen the violent reaction of a person who is suddenly asked to yield to a suppressed desire can fully understand the anxiety such a demand would create in the SS who felt any compassion for his victims. His anxiety could be inferred from the degree of aggression he often directed at persons who tried to move him to compassion. The violence, more than anything else, revealed that deep within him more humane feelings were aroused which he tried to repress and deny through overt cruelty.

Perhaps a general observation on SS cruelty may be in point here. The truly sadistic SS either enjoyed inflicting pain or at least the active proof of his power to inflict it, and appeals to his compassion added greatly to this enjoyment. But since he enjoyed the prisoner's response there was no reason to be harder on him; all the SS wanted was that the prisoner should continue to gratify him, so he continued mistreating him. But when an SS was just doing what he considered his duty and was then exposed to appeals that aroused his compassion, he became furious. It enraged him to be thrown into inner turmoil by the prisoner, to be projected into a conflict between the wish to do his duty and his feeling that it was wrong to mistreat. This conflict made him angry. By growing more cruel he tried to deny the conflict, and at the same time to discharge his anger. The more such a prisoner managed to touch the SS, the angrier he got, and the more his anger exploded in violent abuse.

By not trying to arouse compassion I did not force the SS in front of the clinic into inner conflict. Since I made no effort to outwit him with intellectual superiority I did not conform to expectation. By admitting my awareness of the rules I made it clear there was no effort to deceive him. The absence of an elaborate story credited him with not being gullible. A matter-of-fact statement was the kind that was acceptable to an SS soldier. To reject a prisoner who behaved this way would have meant rejecting his own scheme of values, his own way of acting and thinking. This he either could not do or felt no need to.

Because my behavior did not correspond to what he expected of Jewish prisoners on the basis of his projection, he could not use his prepared defenses against being touched by the prisoner's plight. Since I did not act as the dangerous Jew was expected to, I did not activate the anxieties that went with his stereotype. Still he did not altogether trust me, so he continued to watch while I received treatment.

Throughout these dealings, the SS felt uneasy with me, though he did not unload on me the annoyance his uneasiness aroused. Perhaps he watched me closely because he expected that sooner or later I would slip up and behave the way his projected image of the Jew was expected to act. This would have meant that his delusional creation had become real.

To act in line with his delusional expectations of the Jew meant threatening him with the panic we all experience when our magical thinking suddenly materializes. He would then have been forced to defend himself against the terrible power he originally projected into that figure. Nothing is more threatening than a delusional figure that suddenly assumes body, appears in reality. For it must be remembered that the SS projection contained not only the cowardly and cunning Jew but also the overpowering international Jewish conspiracy bent on destroying him, and people like him.

To summarize then, most one-to-one interactions between prisoner and SS resulted only in a clashing of stereotypes. This was most exaggerated when the SS interacted with prisoners who were not even their own countrymen, but Jewish or Russian, etc. But pitting one delusional system against its delusional counterpart precluded any real inter-action as between real persons, and the odds were always heavily against the prisoners.

The only other outlet for prisoners' aggression, as noted earlier, was to direct it against the self. This was suggested by the camp situation in general and by innumerable SS devices all leading toward passive-masochistic attitudes. But directing aggressions against the self weakened the prisoner's personality to such a degree that he was forced to borrow strength from figures of prestige. The only persons who met the description were the SS. Hence another reason why old prisoners came to identify with them. Like the child who identifies with the parent, this identification helped prisoners to know intuitively what the SS expected of them. Such knowledge, and the behavior based on it, may often have saved a prisoner's life. The price they paid for it as a psychological defense was having to alter their personalities, of their own volition, toward becoming the type of persons the SS was trying to produce.

Only such identification enabled prisoners to keep their self respect and pseudointegration in a devious way when, for example, they watched prisoners being mistreated and killed and refrained from interfering. It also enabled some prisoners to help in the human medical experiments, and the extermination of prisoners. At the same time, these attitudes were another reason for avoiding too many or too great attachments to other prisoners although real friendship was badly needed for combatting emotional isolation.

Friendship

It was interesting that very few prisoners, and only those relatively new at camp, tried to work with their friends or with those living in their barracks. Most of them seemed to want as much variety of association as possible to avoid getting too emotionally involved. Basically, most prisoners lived a rather solitary life, or else moved within a small circle. Within his own barracks room every prisoner who hoped to survive had anywhere from three to five "comrades." These were not real friends; they were companions at work, and more often in misery. But while misery loves company, it does not make for friendship. Genuine attachments just do not grow in a barren field of experience nourished only by emotions of frustration and despair. Other than these comrades, the rest were just acquaintances.

In order to safeguard even comradeship, it was wisest not to tax it too much. With the best of intentions it was unavoidably endangered by the frustrations discharged against those nearest at hand, often explosively. It helped if a man could unload the annoyance experienced at work by relating it to his comrades in the barracks, who would then retaliate in kind. They would have been unwilling to listen to his tough luck at work if they had just shared the experience themselves.

After an evening, night, and morning in the barracks, he was relieved to meet a fresh set of faces and another group of people willing to listen to his complaints about barrack chiefs and the lack of comradeship among the men he lived with. Again the men were willing to listen if he would hear them out in turn.

What was true for associations in the barracks was thus equally true for those at work. There, too, slight irritations led easily to explosions. At any rate, after ten or more hours of strain at work, everyone was happy not to have to see the same faces, hear the same jokes, listen to the same obscenities and commiserate with the same gripes. Once more it was a relief to see another set of familiar faces, to hear voices other than those which had nauseated one at work, and to enter an atmosphere that seemed not quite so tense as in the labor gang.

Generally speaking, nothing was worse than to be in with a group of pessimists, because it was hard for the prisoner to keep up his own morale unless he spent his days and nights with people making the same effort. It was also depressing to have to hear men who limited their complaints to petty gripes, showing an utter incomprehension of what the camp was really about.

The layers of courtesy and kindness which made even negative attitudes sufferable outside the camp were nearly always absent. There was rarely a "No, thank you" either in tone or in words; responses were always in their harshest forms. One heard nothing but, "Idiot!" "Go to hell!" "Shit!" or worse; and no provoking was needed to get this in answer to a neutral question. Men lay in wait for any opening to spit out their pent-up frustration and anger. Also, the chance to express vehemence was an added relief. If one could feel, one was still alive, had not yet given in to everybody and everything; one was not yet a moslem. Even hurting someone's feelings was a satisfaction. It proved there was still somebody or something one mattered to, had an effect on, even if it was a painful effect. But in the process one came a step closer to the SS way of meeting life and its problems.

Conversation

When conversation was possible, it was nearly as important in making life bearable or unbearable as any other feature of camp life. Topics of conversation were as varied as the prisoners: there was always the talk of release (new prisoners) and details about camp affairs (old prisoners). But the most frequent topic of conversation among all prisoners, old and new, was food—recollections of good food they had enjoyed before imprisonment and daydreams about what they would eat after liberation. Hours of speculation were wasted on what the day's fare would be and what might be available in the camp store. Hopes and rumors of better food were just as earnestly discussed. Such conversations, though repetitious, were almost always prevalent. It was as if the mirage of food might set the prisoner's stomach at rest, and still its gnawing emptiness.[15]

These improbable and infantile daydreams added to the prisoner's disorganization. Men who had taken special pride in their wide interests felt their self respect shaken to find themselves so preoccupied with food. They tried to fight it and at the same time to escape boredom by forcing themselves into intelligent conversation. But the absence of outside stimulation and the hopeless and depressive nature of

---

[15] A crude indication of the continuous fear of starvation among most prisoners was their readiness to pick up crumbs of bread that had fallen in the mud, and to swallow them after the most perfunctory cleaning. The motive was at least as often fear of starvation as actual malnutrition. Prisoners were obsessed with food and hunger beyond all reason. To a large degree, this too can be explained by their reverting to infantile attitudes which made them turn to food as the most available and basic symbol of security.

their total situation soon exhausted their intellectual resources.

There were labor commands in which men told each other exactly the same story over and over again, aggravating the listener, or dulling his intellect to numbness. Even in very safe commands, such as that of the sock menders, where prisoners were seated rather comfortably at tables and worked quietly at a very easy task, it was a good day if two prisoners talked about anything of genuine interest to account for even a few hours.

Men who had formerly acquired a tremendous store of knowledge and followed a broad range of inquiry soon tired of talking to other prisoners, and so did their listeners when a discussion of medicine or history was interrupted with the rumor that sardines or apples were in the camp store. After a man had had that kind of experience several times, he recognized that food seemed much more important to everybody (and tacitly he had to admit, to himself too) than his life's work, and he gradually stopped talking about it.

Because of such experiences as well as the depressive atmosphere, most intelligent topics of conversation became exhausted and boring after two or three weeks spent among the same people. Then they became depressing in themselves because what had held the prisoner's interest for years suddenly seemed drab and unimportant. Sometimes a man would feel the need to talk about his wife and children but was suddenly and viciously told to shut up because his talk was evoking an unbearable nostalgia in one of his listeners. All this and many other factors narrowed the prospects of conversation, and prisoners knew how quickly it ceased being a defense against boredom and depression to become one more disintegrating experience. Still, it remained the most satisfying pastime in the camps.

The power balance

And yet the story of the prisoners' defenses against the concentration camp was not entirely a story of deliberate efforts to protect themselves being perverted into their opposites. Some friendships were formed despite conditions extremely adverse to their development. Prisoners tried to encourage one another to read, to exchange views and to teach one another in efforts to safeguard their old self respect.

The effort to protect friends by organizing prisoners and by collaborating with the SS were presented in their negative aspects. Here it should be said that for all their self defeating character, these organizations probably saved some prisoners by sacrificing others. Unfortunately, the power position was such that a tiny advantage for some prisoners had to be paid for by many services furthering the interests of the SS.

Typical of this was the experimentation with human beings. Prisoners who took part in the experiments helped to kill hundreds of men; but they could, on occasion, hide an endangered prisoner in the experimental station for a few days, or save a friend who was slated for experiment by putting another prisoner in his place. Thus they did not save a life; they saved a friend, but only by lending a hand in the murder of many men.

Within so tight a system as the concentration camp any defense that stayed within the frame of reference of the system promoted the goals of the system, not those of the defense. It seems that an institution like the concentration camp permits of no really successful defense—the only way not to submit to it in some measure would have been to destroy it.

6
The Fluctuating Price of Life

IN AN EARLIER CHAPTER I SPOKE OF HOW all life is a compromise between opposing tendencies, while the "good life" consists of achieving a successful concordance of these opposite strivings. This is so, regardless of what name is assigned to concordance by custom or fashion; in this volume my favored names for it are "personal autonomy" and "integration."

If no viable compromise is possible between environmental pressure and personal strivings, if either the person's idiosyncrasies or the power of society reigns supreme, then both personal life and society, as we know them, eventually cease to exist. Often this is not clearly recognized, because life can go well under a variety of social structures, while a still greater variety of personality structures are viable. On the other hand, how fast both life and society disintegrate, if no chance for mutual compromise exists, depends on many other circumstances. Mainly it depends on how rigidly either society or the individual refuses to budge.

If a total state enforces its dominion so powerfully that not even a margin is left for compromising with the individual's basic needs, then the individual can only survive by destroying (or changing) his society, as suggested in the preceding chapter. To this there is the corollary that if the state achieves total dominance over the individual, the perfect success of its goals amounts to the destruction of the individual. That the Hitler state did not destroy all of its subjects, but only several millions of them, is due to the fact that it fell short of that goal. Only because it had to temporarily compromise with a majority of its subjects did it continue to exist. But the compromises were temporary; they were not part of, but contrary to the basic, longer-range principles of the system.

Even many of its most dedicated followers, with whom the state was most apt to compromise, were nevertheless destroyed as persons in our sense, as may be seen from the fate of Roehm (see p. 277 n.), and the story of Hoess, commander of Auschwitz. Hoess, because of the total dominance which the state imposed on him and to which, true Nazi that he was, he expected himself to submit without question, so laid aside his personal existence that he ended a mere executor of official demands. While his physical death came later, he became a living corpse from the time he assumed command of Auschwitz. That he never became a "moslem" was because he continued to be well fed and well clothed. But he had to divest himself so entirely of self respect and self love, of feeling and personality, that for all practical purposes he was little more than a machine functioning only as his superiors flicked the buttons of command.

The leader principle on which this total state was based allowed only one person, the leader, to be alive, to make decisions. Because willing helpers were needed, particularly at the beginning, this principle could not be applied as rigorously as intended, or all at once. But that should not obscure its nature. The farther up in the hierarchy a man stood, not the more, but the less influence did he have on shaping decisions, and the more he lived only by the leader's will. Hitler's high command were his puppets. Many of his followers accepted the total state to such a degree that they lived only through their leader. The final result was that many no longer knew how to live, only how to die.

The Nazi state ruled over millions of Germans whose personalities were shaped in a very different society. This the hierarchy considered its greatest obstacle to success, but actually it was what kept the state going as long as it did. These "little" Germans insisted on their margin for compromise, much against the logic of the system. They were needed until such time as a new generation, bred by the system, had grown up. Then it was expected that the true total state would come into its own, no longer hampered by the need to allow for small compromises even among its own loyal subjects.

I believe, quite the contrary, that only the large number of persons with whom the system had to compromise enabled it to remain in existence. A total state in which all subjects have totally submitted to the leadership principle results in all of them being well fed, well clothed, well functioning corpses, knowing only how to die, not to live. But then subjects and state soon collapse.

The goal of this system was depersonalization, with the extermination policy only one of its logical consequences. But that policy was at once the worst abomination and the truest expression of its spirit. From documents found after the war it is possible to trace the dehumanizing process that culminated in the death camps, though there too, the larger part of the story is now common knowledge, and I mean only to comment on a few selected phenomena.

Some of the racial and eugenic notions of the Hitler ideology began to make their appearance in the camps as early as 1937. At that time not more than a dozen prisoners, most of them sex offenders or homosexuals, were sterilized. Later, sterilizations intended to improve the race were slowly implemented by the extermination of persons who were supposed to carry undesirable genes.

But practices that began on a small scale gained momentum, as repercussions failed to materialize, either from within Germany or from the outside world, and added courage was taken to proceed more openly. As time passed and the regime became more and more secure, its ideology was no longer restrained by any freely formed public opinion. Then the total state proceeded to realize its principles through an unlimited range of dehumanizing practices.

In the concentration camps, which threw all tendencies of the state into bolder relief, it became clearer each year how the theoretical nonexistence of the individual was being applied. In tyrannies of the past, the torture of an individual supposedly had something to do with him as a person. In the concentration camps, even torture and death stopped having much connection with personal history or concrete event.

Once, for example, a prisoner was to have gotten a flogging but was discharged before it happened. A newcomer was given his prison number and a few days later the punishment was administered to him, since the whole transaction was recorded under a number.

The punisher had no interest in knowing why the punishment was inflicted, or on whom. The unit beaten was just "a prisoner." Certainly punishment as such had purposes: to increase output, to debase prisoners, to increase the Gestapo's sense of power, to intimidate the prisoners and the population at large. But for such purposes any prisoner would do as well as any other. So even his supreme suffering now had nothing to do with the individual as such. He died because Jews had become superfluous, because there were too many Poles, or because civilians outside the camps had to be taught a lesson.

It was not easy for prisoners to understand all the implications of the dehumanizing process, and it took no small effort for SS men to embrace it themselves. For example, during my stay in the camps I often wondered about what seemed to me a particularly stupid piece of behavior by the guards. Almost daily one guard or another, tinkering with his gun, would tell a prisoner that he would shoot him down except that a bullet cost three pfennig, and that was too much of Germany's money to spend on him.

The identical statement was repeated too often, by too many different guards of various units, to be dismissed as free of meaning or purpose. But having heard the remark, I could only wonder why the guards thought I would feel particularly degraded by it. Only later did it dawn on me that this, like many other remarks and types of behavior, while meant to impress the prisoner, had their only really serious purpose in the education of the guards.

They repeated their statement so often because they had been told it so often in their indoctrination and must have been struck by its unusualness. Hard as it was to accept, it probably made such a deep impression on them that they believed it would impress prisoners as deeply; but prisoners by and large only found it silly. It was quite difficult for the average SS man to degrade human life to a thing of no value. He was impressed that his superiors could set the value of a human being below the trifling cost of a bullet. In his astonishment and disbelief he had to try it out again and again to convince himself.

Many such efforts were needed before the guards could finally believe it. At the same time they became overawed by the power of a state that so easily dispensed with a human being. Only after this attitude to persons had become their own—always with some hesitation, except for a few "killer boys"—could they disregard the person in the prisoner; only then could they treat prisoners as numbers, not individuals.

In defense of human beings it should be said that some of them never quite succeeded. Kautsky,[1] observing humanity in even a few SS men, came to understand this. He refers to one of them who never made anti-Semitic remarks, never hit prisoners, or reported them to be punished. There were

---

[1] *Op. cit.*, pp. 119-121.

others who risked their lives by smuggling letters out for prisoners, without expecting any reward. Certainly they constituted a small minority, but so did the decent prisoners. Most SS men never wasted a minute of their free time in mistreating prisoners; their laziness was one of the prisoners' best protections. Such behavior is alien to sadists who enjoy mistreating others.

Functional decisions

With the war against Russia, all remaining official concern for the human being disappeared, and the way was opened for the destruction of millions of persons. Because of the manpower urgently needed for waging total war, a change in policy was announced toward persons in and out of the camps who seemed of no value to the state. All undesirables who were able-bodied were to be worked to death[2] and the rest to be killed outright. The result was a decision to kill the Jews of Europe, as well as all those whose labor seemed valueless such as the cripples, the insane and so forth.

Thus the last years of the camps (1942 until liberation) was also one of total control over a mass labor force numbering millions, and theoretically aimed at comprising everyone but a small ruling class. It was the final apotheosis of the mass state, composed of few depersonalized managers and millions of dehumanized slaves, all under thrall to one charismatic leader, the only "person," the only one truly alive.

In a way, the use of prisoners for slave labor made more sense from a strictly "functional" point of view, than their continued mistreatment without economic purpose. For the same reason it constituted a major step toward dehumanization. When the Hitler state wished to alter prisoners' personalities to suit its own purpose, the state was still, to some small degree, considering prisoners as individuals worth

[2] *Nazi Conspiracy and Aggression,* vol. I, p. 949.

"saving." Theoretically, up to that point, the only prisoners to be killed were the ones who were not "educable."

The new slave labor and extermination policy did away with all considerations for the value of a life, even in terms of a slave society. In earlier societies of an analogous character, slaves were rarely less than investments. To be sure their labor was exploited without much thought for their humanity. But in the Hitler state slaves lost even their investment value. That was the great difference between exploitation by private capitalists and exploitation by a state answering only to itself.[3]

The first group selected for total extermination was the gypsies. All gypsies at Buchenwald were killed by injection in 1941.[4] But even then the mass murder was not yet centrally planned or executed in "factory" style on the basis of a master plan. This last step was inaugurated when the extermination camps were set up in 1942, as large numbers of Russians and Poles were added to the death lists.

Man as a commodity

Both the concentration camps and the death camps, and what happened in them, were an application beyond reason of the concept of labor as a commodity. In the camps not only human labor but the total person became commodity. People were "handled" as if they were made to order. They were used and changed according to the desires of the customer, in this case the state. When no longer useful, they were discarded, but with care so that no salvable material was wasted. To accomplish this they were processed by modern factory methods specially developed for the purpose.

[3] Athenian prisoners of war were "worked to death" too, in the quarries of Syracuse. But there again it was a state that exploited slave labor, not private capitalists. Nevertheless, the analogy between the quarries of Mauthausen and Syracuse, separated by more than 2000 years, is appalling.

[4] Kautsky, *op. cit.*, p. 118.

Yet the notion of man as a product for use was present in the ideology of the German mass state long before this; witness the terminology of the SS. If guards killed prisoners or planned to do so, they used the expression *fertig machen* which only rarely meant "to finish" (or "to finish off") but usually meant "to make ready" or "to prepare." On the other hand, *fertig machen* was an expression frequently used in industry to signify the final processing before a product was delivered to the customer. It was an expression not common in German parlance or slang to designate killing a person. The comparison with factory methods may be carried even further.

When the policy of mass extermination was decided upon and the man to head it was appointed, he went to work in a businesslike fashion. Like a competent manager, he made an inspection tour of existing plants to investigate all the newest and best methods and equipment before erecting a new plant.

Up to 1940, each concentration camp was more or less one organic "factory," receiving its raw material, the prisoners, classifying them, using their workpower, and disposing of them by death or discharge. Later, specialization set in. Separate "plants" were erected for each of the processes. There were receiving and distribution camps in which the prisoners were classified and sent to the various work or extermination camps. Thus "production" was carried on by at least three separate units: receiving camps, labor camps, and extermination camps. Like all modern factories, each of them had its own "research department," carrying on investigations of various kinds. Significantly, they all had one feature in common; every item of "research material" was looked upon as a mass product with all units freely interchangeable.

Since the Hitler state considered human beings mere

objects, it was often more practical to correct mistakes on humans instead of in the files. If errors were made in the counting of new arrests they were rectified by adding or liquidating enough of them to make up the difference. Errors in bookkeeping were corrected on the objects of bureaucratic transactions, not on the books.

Even their packaging was not overlooked. All prisoners were clothed in the same striped prison uniforms with shaven heads to make them look more identical. Cloth insignia were added to the uniforms, using specific colors for each group and also the subgroups. Thus the individuals were made alike, but the groups differentiated. Each prisoner also wore a number, and when speaking of himself to camp officials, he gave only his number, group and subgroup, never his name.

Inherent in any mass state is the tendency to organize and reorganize until each member is correctly placed in his category. If in addition, it is a class state then it wishes to insure that each person will be fixed in his class as permanently as possible, so that he will not threaten the ruling elite by trying to advance in status. The SS would have liked to classify each prisoner for eternity, and the first steps toward this end were the multicolored insignia and the numbers. Next the prisoner's category was inscribed on his body with indelible ink. In the extermination camps, it was finally tattooed into his skin so that units of the state were now permanently branded.

Here again the camps showed only in their full development what was still just a tendency in the German mass state. The Nazi ideal was to have each citizen labeled according to his status. The elite wore the insignia of the SS, the party members the party emblem, the Jews the yellow star. Efforts were also made to have foreign civilian workers wear some distinctive emblem but they resisted, and the effort was dropped. Nevertheless, a victorious Germany might well have forced everyone to wear the symbol of his own group as they already did in the concentration camp.

Characteristically, many of the SS including camp administrators, did not like their work, assignments which they accepted out of a sense of duty. Hoess, who eventually headed the largest of the extermination camps, had formerly been a member of the semi-mystical *Artamanen;* this was a group that took seriously the back-to-the-land movement to save German boys and girls from "corruption" in cities and factories, and to settle them down to a simple life on the farms, close to the soil and to nature. But once he entered the SS he laid aside all personal convictions and inclinations. He made himself stop being a person, and became a well functioning wheel in the total state.

When it became his task to rule Auschwitz, he wished to do it effectively, to run a clean and efficient factory; its function merely happened to be the destruction of human beings. To Hoess the perfect running of the factory mattered very much; that it "processed" human beings and not steel or aluminum had ceased to be his concern. An Allied journalist who observed him at the Nuremberg trials has described him as follows:

"Hoess, without the quiver of an eyelash, reported concisely and factually on his 'processing' some two to three million Jews and other victims through gas chambers, crematoria, and concentration camps. Hoess's appearance and manner were those of a man who would everywhere be considered, in government and business, an unusually competent and reliable administrator, thorough if unimaginative. The painfully correct witness never uttered a word that might offend; he spoke of mass murder in the terms of a technician, without any gruesome details, without any of the eloquence of the moralist or of the sadist . . . A fanatical believer in hard work, efficiency, order, discipline, and cleanliness, Hoess was constantly shocked by the failure of the Third Reich to provide adequate transportation, food, medical and sanitation supplies, and supervisory personnel for its victims ... He was always bothering his Berlin superiors for more supplies, for less corrupt and brutal personnel, above all for a slowdown in the shipments of new arrivals so as to allow him to build a more efficient processing machine: gas chambers and crematoria for the unemployable, and amenities for the employable in his work camps."[5]

Thus the business correspondence of Auschwitz reads

---

[5]E. Roditi, "The Criminal as Public Servant," *Commentary*, 28, November 1959, pp. 431 ff.

By contrast is the following glimpse of Hoess from his autobiography (R. Hoess, *Kommandant in Auschwitz*, Deutsche Verlagsanstalt, Stuttgart, 1958, p. 71, my translation) when he was only part way toward dehumanization and still displaying some human compassion. "One case touched me particularly deeply. An SS sergeant with whom I had a lot of dealings, since he frequently accompanied important prisoners and brought me important secret reports, was suddenly brought to me one night to be executed immediately. Just the day before we had been sitting together in our mess hall and had also discussed the recent executions. And now it was his own turn, and I had to obey orders. This was too much even for my Commanding Officer. After the execution we took a long, silent walk to get hold of ourselves. From the officers who had accompanied him, we learned that this SS sergeant had been ordered to arrest a former communist party member and bring him into the camp. From supervising him [in civilian life] he had gotten to know well the person now to be imprisoned. He had always behaved well, obeying all rules and regulations. So, out of kindness, he permitted him to stop at his home to change, and say goodbye to his wife. While the sergeant and another police officer talked with the man's wife in the living room, the person to be imprisoned escaped through another room. When the SS sergeant reported the escape, he was immediately imprisoned and within an hour a court martial had sentenced him to death. The policeman who had accompanied him (but who had not been in charge of the arrest) was sentenced to many years in prison.... The executed [SS] man had been a fine citizen, in his middle thirties, married and had three children; he had always been extremely conscientious and loyal in his service, and now he had to pay with his life for his kindness and trust. He went composed and quietly to his execution."

The moral of this story is clear enough. So if the case touched Hoess "particularly deeply" it was probably because of its renewed warning that allowing oneself any human emotion was a fatal error, leading to certain destruction.

like that of any other factory, as in the following excerpt from a correspondence between Auschwitz and the I. G. Farben chemical trust:

§ "In contemplation of experiments with a new soporific drug, we would appreciate your procuring for us a number of women."

§ "We received your answer but consider the price of 200 marks a woman excessive. We propose to pay not more than 170 marks a head. If agreeable, we will take possession of the women. We need approximately 150."

§ "We acknowledge your accord. Prepare for us 150 women in the best possible health conditions, and as soon as you advise us you are ready, we will take charge of them."

§ "Received the order of 150 women. Despite their emaciated condition, they were found satisfactory. We shall keep you posted on developments concerning this experiment."

§ "The tests were made. All subjects died. We shall contact you shortly on the subject of a new load."[6]

Behavior in extermination camps

The analysis of behavior inside the extermination camps, while more horrid, offers less of psychological interest, since prisoners there had no time or occasion to change much psychologically.

The only psychological phenomenon that seems pertinent in this report is the fact that these prisoners knew they were destined to die and still made almost no effort to revolt. The few exceptions, less than a handful among millions, I shall ignore for the moment, since they represent the behavior of such a tiny minority.

On occasions, only one or two German guards would be escorting up to four hundred prisoners toward the exter-

---

[6] *Time*, L. 21, November 24, 1947, p. 33.

mination camps over lonesome roads. There was every chance that the four hundred could have overpowered their armed guards.[7] Even if some prisoners had been killed in the process, the majority would have been free to join partisan groups. At the very least they could have enjoyed a temporary revenge without loss to themselves, since they were slated for death anyway.

A nonpsychological analysis of the behavior of these prisoners does not seem adequate for explaining such docility. In order to understand the phenomenon of men not fighting back, although certain death awaited them,[8] it must be realized that the most active individuals had long ago made their efforts to fight National Socialism and were now either dead or exhausted. The Polish and Jewish prisoners who formed a majority in the extermination camps were mostly persons who for some reason had failed to escape and were not fighting back.

Their feeling of defeat does not imply they felt no strong hostility toward their oppressors. Weakness and submission are often charged with greater hostility than open counter-aggression. In counter aggression, as for instance in the partisan or resistance movements, the opponents of German fascism found outlets for some of their hostilities through offensive action. But within the oppressed person who did not resist lay accumulating hostilities he was unable to discharge in action. Not even the mild relief of verbal aggression was open to him, because even that, he was afraid, would bring destruction by the SS.

The more hostility accumulated, the more terrified the prisoner became that it might break through in an explosive act spelling destruction for him. To prevent this, he felt he

[7] Even Hoess, in his memoirs, wondered why the prisoners did not revolt, since they could often have done it with ease, given their vast numbers.

[8] This knowledge of certain death made their case different from those other prisoners who could still hope for eventual liberation.

must at all times remain convinced of the extremely danger-ous character of the aggressor; in that way his own fear would restrain him more effectively. So for his own protection he invested the SS with those features most threatening to himself. These, in turn, increased his anxiety, frustration, and hostility, and to keep them all under control, the SS had to be seen as even more murderous.[9]

The twin process of repressing all hostility and inflating the terrible image of the SS devoured almost all his emotional energy. If anything was left, it was soon used up by the fight against depression due to loss of status, separation from family, exhaustion due to malnutrition and disease, and the absolute hopelessness of the situation.

In the concentration camps some hostility could be discharged in the fight among prisoner factions. While the battles lasted the hope still lived that one's own party might win, bringing better conditions for oneself. "Moslems" of course no longer fought, did not belong to factions, did not discharge hostility but turned it against the self, like the prisoners in the extermination camps. And like them, they died. In the extermination camps the prisoners were also deprived of anything that might have restored self respect or the will to live, while the pent-up hostility grew un-interruptedly.

All this may explain the docility of prisoners who walked to the gas chambers or who dug their own graves and then lined up before them so that, shot down, they would fall into the graves. It may be assumed that most of these prisoners were by then suicidal. Walking to the gas chamber was committing suicide in a way that asked for none of the energy usually needed for deciding and planning to kill oneself. Psychologically speaking, most prisoners in the

---

[9] This mechanism differs only in degree from the widespread use of projection as a psychological defense in the "ordinary" concentration camps.

extermination camps committed suicide by submitting to death without resistance.

If this speculation is correct, then one may say that in the extermination camps the goals of the SS found their ultimate realization. Through the use of terror the SS succeeded in forcing its opponents to do, out of their own will, what it wished them to do. Millions of people submitted to extermination because SS methods had forced them to see it not as a way out, but as the only way to put an end to conditions in which they could no longer live as human beings.

Since these remarks may seem farfetched, it should be added that the process just described is similar to what can be observed in some psychotic patients. The assumption that these prisoners developed states of mind similar to those observed in psychotic persons seems borne out by the behavior of former prisoners of extermination camps after their liberation. Their symptoms depended, of course, on initial personality assets and what the individual experienced after liberation. In some persons the symptoms appeared more severe, in others less so; some showed that their symptoms were reversible, others not.

Immediately after liberation nearly all prisoners engaged in asocial behavior that could only be explained by far reaching disintegration of their former personality structures. A few former inmates of extermination camps have been studied. Their grip on reality was extremely tenuous. Some were still suffering from delusions of persecution, others suffered from delusions of grandeur. The latter were the counterpart of guilt feelings for having been spared while parents or siblings had all perished. They were trying to justify and explain their own survival by delusionally inflating their importance. It also enabled them to compensate for the extreme damage done to their narcissism by the experience they had undergone.

Business as usual

A few words about the world's reaction to the concentration camps: the terrors committed in them were experienced as uncanny by most civilized persons. It came as a shock to their pride that supposedly civilized nations could stoop to such inhuman acts. The implication that modern man has such inadequate control over his cruelty was felt as a threat. Three different psychological mechanisms were most frequently used for dealing with the phenomenon of the concentration camp: (a) its applicability to man in general was denied by asserting (contrary to available evidence) that the acts of torture were committed by a small group of insane or perverted persons; (b) the truth of the reports was denied by ascribing them to deliberate propaganda. This method was favored by the German government which called all reports on terror in the camps horror propaganda *(Greuelpropaganda)*; (c) the reports were believed, but the knowledge of the terror was repressed as soon as possible.

All three mechanisms could be seen at work after liberation. At first, after the "discovery" of the camps, a wave of extreme outrage swept the Allied nations. It was soon followed by a general repression of the discovery. It may be that this reaction of the general public was due to something more than the shock dealt their narcissism by the fact that cruelty is still rampant among men. It may also be that the memory of the tortures was repressed out of some dim realization that the modern state now has available the means for changing personality. To have to accept that one's personality may be changed against one's will is the greatest threat to one's self respect. It must therefore be dealt with by action, or by repression.

The universal success of the *Diary of Anne Frank* suggests how much the tendency to deny is still with us, while her story itself demonstrates how such denial can hasten our own destruction. It is an onerous task to take apart such a humane and moving story, arousing so much compassion for gentle Anne Frank. But I believe that its world-wide acclaim cannot be explained unless we recognize our wish to forget the gas chambers and to glorify attitudes of extreme privatization, of continuing to hold on to attitudes as usual even in a holocaust. Exactly because their going on with private life as usual brought destruction did it have to be glorified; in that way we could overlook the essential fact of how destructive it can be under extreme social circumstances.

While the Franks were making their preparations for going passively into hiding, thousands of other Jews in Holland and elsewhere in Europe were trying to escape to the free world, the better to survive or to be able to fight their executioners. Others who could not do so went underground—not simply to hide from the SS, waiting passively, without preparation for fight, for the day when they would be caught—but to fight the Germans, and with it for humanity. All the Franks wanted was to go on with life as nearly as possible in the usual fashion.

Little Anne, too, wanted only to go on with life as usual, and nobody can blame her. But hers was certainly not a necessary fate, much less a heroic one; it was a senseless fate. The Franks could have faced the facts and survived, as did many Jews living in Holland. Anne could have had a good chance to survive, as did many Jewish children in Holland. But for that she would have had to be separated from her parents and gone to live with a Dutch family as their own child.

Everybody who recognized the obvious knew that the hardest way to go underground was to do it as a family; that to hide as a family made detection by the SS most likely.

The Franks, with their excellent connections among gentile Dutch families should have had an easy time hiding out singly, each with a different family. But instead of planning for this, the main principle of their planning was to continue as much as possible with the kind of family life they were accustomed to. Any other course would have meant not merely giving up the beloved family life, but also accepting as reality man's inhumanity to man. Most of all it would have forced them to accept that going on with life as usual was not an absolute value, but can sometimes be the most destructive of all attitudes.

There is little doubt that the Franks, who were able to provide themselves with so much, could have provided themselves with a gun or two had they wished. They could have shot down at least one or two of the "green police" who came for them. There was no surplus of such police. The loss of an SS with every Jew arrested would have noticeably hindered the functioning of the police state. The fate of the Franks wouldn't have been any different, because they all died anyway except for Anne's father, though he hardly meant to pay for his survival with the extermination of his whole family. But they could have sold their lives dearly instead of walking to their death.

There is good reason why the so successful play ends with Anne stating her belief in the good in all men. What is denied is the importance of accepting the gas chambers as real so that never again will they exist. If all men are basically good, if going on with intimate family living no matter what else is what is to be most admired, then indeed we can all go on with life as usual and forget about Auschwitz. Except that Anne Frank died because her parents could not get themselves to believe in Auschwitz. And her story found wide acclaim because for us too, it denies implicitly that Auschwitz ever existed. If all men are good, there was never an Auschwitz.

High time

At various places in this book I have mentioned how submitting to the total state leads to a disintegration of what once seemed a well integrated personality, plus a return to many infantile attitudes. At this point perhaps a theoretical speculation may be helpful. Years ago Freud postulated two opposite tendencies: the life instincts, which he called eros or sex, and the destructive tendencies, which he named the death instinct. The more mature the person becomes, the more he should be able to "fuse" these two opposing tendencies, making the resultant "ego" energy available for the task of meeting and shaping reality.

The more immature the person, the more these tendencies are apt to push the total personality, at one moment in one direction, at the next moment in the other. Thus the so-called childlike friendliness of some primitive people, followed in the next moment by extreme "thoughtless" cruelty. But the disintegration, or perhaps one should better say the "defusion" of ego energy under extreme stress—at one moment into pure destructive tendencies ("Let it be over, no matter how"), at the next moment into irrational life tendencies ("Let's get something to eat now, even if it means death in short order")[10]—was only one aspect of man's primitivization in the total state. Another was engaging in infantile thought processes such as wishful thinking in place of a more mature evaluation of reality, and an infantile disregard for the possibility of death. These led many to think that they of all others would be spared and survive, and many more to simply disbelieve in the possibility of their own death. Not believing in its possibility, they did not

---

[10] For example, those prisoners who ate the whole day's ration the moment they got it had nothing left for their faltering energies toward the end of the working day. Those who divided the little food they had and saved some for the moment when exhaustion threatened them most, fared much better in the long run.

prepare for it, including no preparation for how to defend their lives even when death became inescapable. Defending their lives before such time might have hastened their death. So up to a point, this "rolling with the punches" that the enemy dealt out was protective of life. But beyond that point it was destructive of both one's own life and that of others whose survival might be more certain too if one risked one's own life. The trouble is that the longer one "rolls" with the punches, the more likely it becomes that one will no longer have the strength to resist when death becomes imminent, particularly if this yielding to the enemy is accompanied not by an inner strengthening of the personality (which it would require) but an inner disintegration.[11]

Those who did not deny validity to death, who neither denied nor repressed its possibility, who embraced no childish belief in their indestructibility, were those who prepared for it in time as a real possibility. It meant risking one's life for a self chosen purpose and in doing so, saving one's own life or that of others, or both. When Jews in Germany were restricted to their homes, those who did not allow inertia to take over used the imposing of such restrictions as a warning that it was high time to go underground, join the resistance movement, provide themselves with forged papers, etc., if they had not done so long ago. Most of them survived.

An example out of the lives of some distant relatives of mine may further illustrate. Early in the war, a young man living in a small Hungarian town banded together with a number of other Jews and they prepared themselves for what to do when the Germans invaded. As soon as the Nazis imposed curfews on the Jews, his group left for Budapest since the bigger the city, the better the chances for escaping

---

[11] This, too, could be observed in the story of the Franks who bickered with each other over trifles, instead of supporting each other's desire to resist the demoralizing impact of their living conditions.

detection. There, similar groups from other towns converged and joined those of Budapest. From among them they selected typically "Aryan" looking men who, equipped with false papers, immediately joined the Hungarian SS so as to be able to warn of impending actions, to report in advance when a particular district would be searched, etc.

This worked so well that most of the groups survived intact. But they had also equipped themselves with small arms, so that when detected they could put up enough of a fight for the majority to escape while a few would die fighting to gain time for the escape.[12] A few of the Jews who had joined the SS were discovered and immediately shot, probably a death preferable to one in the gas chambers. But even among their special group the majority survived, hiding within the SS up to the last moment.

My young relative was unable to convince some members of his family to go with him when he left. Three times, at tremendous risk to himself he returned, pointing out first the growing persecution of the Jews, later the fact that their transport to the gas chambers had already begun. He could not convince them to move out of their homes, to leave their possessions. On each visit he pleaded more desperately, on each visit he found them less willing or able to listen to him, much less able to take action. It was as if each time they were more on their way to the crematoria where they all in fact died.

On each visit his family clung more desperately to the old living arrangements, the possessions they had accumu-

---

[12] Compare this to the Franks' selection of a hiding place that was basically a trap without an outlet, and that in all their months there no emergency escape route was constructed through which some of their group could at least have tried to escape while one or two of the men blocked and defended one of the small entrances with a homemade barricade. Compare also, Mr. Frank's teaching typically academic high school subjects to the youngsters, rather than how to make a getaway: a token of the same inability to face the possibility of death.

lated over a lifetime. It was like a parallel process in which their life energies were drained away while their possessions seemed to give them a pseudosecurity to replace the real assurance that no longer came from planning for their lives. Again like children, they preferred to cling desperately to some objects in which they had invested all the meaning they could no longer find in their lives. As they withdrew from the fight for survival, their lives began to reside more and more in these dead objects and the persons in them died piece by piece, little object by little object.

In Buchenwald, I talked to hundreds of German Jewish prisoners who were brought there in the fall of 1938. I asked them why they had not left Germany because of the utterly degrading conditions they were subjected to. Their answer was: How could we leave? It would have meant giving up our homes, our places of business. Their earthly possessions had so taken possession of them that they could not move; instead of using them, they were run by them.[18]

How the investing of possessions with one's life energy made people die piece by piece is also evident in the course of the Nazi attitude toward Jews. At the time of the first boycott of Jewish stores the whole external goal of the Nazis was the possessions of the Jews. They even let Jews take some of them out of the country if they would just go, leaving the bulk of their possessions behind. For a long time the intention of the Nazis, and of their first discriminatory laws, was to force undesirable minorities, including Jews, into emigration. Only when this did not work was the extermination policy instituted, though it also followed the inner logic of the Nazi racial ideology. But one wonders if the notion that millions of Jews (and later foreign nationals) would submit to extermination did not also result from

---

[18] The Franks, too, postponed going into hiding because they wished first to transfer more of their possessions to their hideout. They postponed it so long that it was nearly too late for Anne's sister, who was called to the SS.

seeing how much degradation they would accept without fighting back. The persecution of the Jews worsened, slow step by slow step, when no violent resistance occurred. It may have been Jewish acceptance, without fight, of ever harsher discrimination and degradation that first gave the SS the idea that they could be gotten to the point where they would walk to the gas chambers on their own.

Most Jews in Poland who did not believe in business as usual survived the second World War. As the Germans approached, they left everything behind and fled to Russia, much as many of them distrusted the Soviet system. But there, while perhaps citizens of a second order, they were at least accepted as human beings. Those who stayed on to continue business as usual moved toward their own destruction and perished. Thus in the deepest sense the walk to the gas chamber was only the last consequence of a philosophy of business as usual; a last step in no longer defying the death instinct, which might also be called the principle of inertia. Because the first step was taken long before one entered the death camp.

True, the same suicidal behavior has another meaning. It means that man can be pushed so far and no further; that beyond a certain point he chooses death to an inhuman existence. But the initial step toward this terrible choice was inertia.

Those who give in to it, who have withdrawn all vital energy from the world, can no longer act with initiative, and are threatened by it in others. They can no longer accept reality for what it is; having grown infantile, they see it only in the infantile perspective of a wishful denial of what is too unpleasant, of a wishful belief in their personal immortality. All this is dramatically illustrated in an experience of Lengyel's.[14] She reports that although she and her

---

[14] Lengyel, O., *Five Chimneys*, The Story of Auschwitz, Chicago: Ziff Davis, 1947, pp. 54-55.

fellow prisoners lived just a few hundred yards from the crematoria and the gas chambers and knew what they were all about, yet after months most prisoners denied knowledge of them.[15] Realization of their true situation might have helped them to save either the life they were going to lose anyway, or the lives of others. But that realization they could not afford. When Lengyel and many other prisoners were selected to be sent to the gas chambers, they did not try to break away, as she successfully did. Worse, the first time she tried it, some of the fellow prisoners selected with her for the gas chambers called the supervisors, telling them she was trying to get away. Lengyel desperately asks the question: How was it possible that people denied the existence of the gas chambers when all day long they saw the crematoria burning and smelled the odor of burning flesh? How come they preferred not to believe in the extermination just to prevent themselves from fighting for their very own lives? She offers no explanation except that they begrudged anyone who might save himself from the common fate, because they lacked enough courage to risk action themselves. I believe they did it because they had given up their will to live, had permitted their death tendencies to flood them. As a result they now identified more closely with the SS who were devoting themselves to destruction, than to those fellow prisoners who still had a grip on life and hence managed to escape death.

Human competence for what?

When prisoners began to serve their executioners, to help them speed the death of their own kind, things had gone beyond simple inertia. By then, death instinct running

---

[15] German gentile civilians denied the gas chambers, too, but the same denial in them did not have the same meaning. By that time, civilians who faced facts and rebelled, invited death. Prisoners at Auschwitz were already doomed.

rampant had been added to inertia. Those who tried to serve their executioners in what were once their civilian capacities were merely continuing if not business, then life as usual. Whereby they opened the door to their death.

Lengyel speaks of a Dr. Mengele, SS physician at Auschwitz, in a typical example of the "business as usual" attitude that enabled some prisoners, and certainly the SS, to retain whatever inner balance they could despite what they were doing. She describes how Dr. Mengele took all correct medical precautions during childbirth, rigorously observing all aseptic principles, cutting the umbilical cord with greatest care, etc. But only half an hour later he sent mother and infant to be burned in the crematorium.[16]

Still, having made his choice, Dr. Mengele and others like him had, after all, to delude themselves at times to be able to live with themselves and their experience. Only one personal document on the subject has come to my attention, that of Dr. Nyiszli, a prisoner serving as "research physician" at Auschwitz.[17] How Dr. Nyiszli fooled himself can be seen, for example, in his repeatedly referring to himself as a doctor, though he worked as the assistant of a criminal. He speaks of the Institute for Race, Biological, and Anthropological Investigation as "one of the most qualified medical centers of the Third Reich" though it was devoted to proving falsehoods. That Nyiszli was a doctor didn't at all change the fact that he, like any of the prisoner officials who served the SS better than some SS were willing to serve it, was a participant, an accessory to the crimes of the SS. How then could he do it and survive?

The answer was: by taking pride in his professional skills, irrespective of what purpose they were used for. Again and again this pride in his professional skill permeates his story of his own and other prisoners' sufferings. The im-

---

[16] *Op. cit.,* p. 147.

[17] Nyiszli, Dr. Miklos, *Auschwitz: A Doctor's Eyewitness Account,* New York: Frederick Fell, Inc., 1960.

portant issue here is that Dr. Nyiszli, Dr. Mengele, and hundreds of other far more prominent physicians, men trained long before the advent of Hitler to power, were participants in these human experiments and in the pseudo-scientific investigations that went with them.[18] It is this pride in professional skill and knowledge, irrespective of moral implications, that is so dangerous. As a feature of modern society oriented toward technological competence it is still with us, though the concentration camps and the crematoria are no longer here. Auschwitz is gone, but as long as this attitude remains with us we shall not be safe from the indifference to life at its core.

It is easy to see that achieving a subtle balance between extremes may be an ideal way of life. It is harder to accept that this holds true even in a holocaust. But even in extreme conditions, to give way only to the heart or only to the mind is neither a good way to live, nor the way to survive. Living only to keep his family intact, even all Mr. Frank's love did not keep them alive, as a better informed heart might have done. Dr. Nyiszli, carried away by his high level training as a pathologist, and against the prompting of the heart, lent himself to such debasement of his deepest pride, his medical science, that one wonders what can have survived except his body.

I have met many Jews, as well as gentile anti-Nazis, who survived in Germany and in the occupied countries, like the group in Hungary described earlier. But they were all people who realized that when a world goes to pieces, when in-humanity reigns supreme, man cannot go on with business

---

[18] Among the heads of clinics or chairmen of departments who participated knowingly in the experiments were Professors Sauerbruch of the University of Munich and Eppinger of the University of Vienna —teachers of whole generations of physicians before Hitler. Dr. Gebhardt, the president of the German Red Cross, was also among them. (Mitscherlich, A., and Mielke, F., *Doctors of Infamy,* New York: Henry Schuman, Inc., 1949.)

as usual. One then has to radically re-evaluate all of what one has done, believed in, stood for. In short, one has to take a stand on the new reality, a firm stand, and not one of retirement into even greater privatization.

If today, Negroes in Africa march against the guns of a police that defends *apartheid*—even if hundreds of them will be shot down and tens of thousands rounded up in concentration camps—their march, their fight, will sooner or later assure them of a chance for liberty and equality. Millions of the Jews of Europe who did not or could not escape in time or go underground as many thousands did, could at least have marched as free men against the SS, rather than to first grovel, then wait to be rounded up for their own extermination, and finally walk themselves to the gas chambers.

Yet the story of the extermination camps shows that even in such an overpowering environment, certain defenses do offer some protection, most important of which is understanding what goes on in oneself, and why. With enough understanding, the individual does not fool himself into believing that with every adjustment he makes he is protecting himself. He is able to recognize that much that on the surface seems protective, is actually self destructive. A most extreme example were those prisoners who volunteered to work in the gas chambers hoping it would somehow save their lives. All of them were killed after a short time. But many of them died sooner, and after weeks of a more horrible life, than might have been true if they had not volunteered.

Fighting back

Did no one of those destined to die fight back? Did none of them wish to die not by giving in but by asserting themselves in attacking the SS? A very few did. One of them was the twelfth *Sonderkommando*, prisoners working in the gas chambers.[19] Now all these *Kommandos* knew their fate since the first task of every new *Sonderkommando* was to cremate the corpses of the preceding *Kommando*, exterminated just a few hours before.

In this single revolt of the twelfth *Sonderkommando*, seventy SS were killed, including one commissioned officer and seventeen noncommissioned officers; one of the crematoria was totally destroyed and another severely damaged. True, all eight hundred and fifty-three prisoners of the *Kommando* died. But this proves that a position in the *Sonderkommando* gave prisoners a chance of about ten to one to destroy the SS, a higher ratio than in the ordinary concentration camp.

The one *Sonderkommando* that revolted and took such heavy toll of the enemy did not die much differently than all other *Sonderkommandos*. Why, then—and this is the question that haunts all who study the extermination camps— why then did millions walk quietly, without resistance, to their death when right before them were examples such as this *Kommando* that managed to destroy and damage part of their own chambers of death and kill almost 10% of their number in SS? Why did so few of the millions of prisoners die like men, as did the men of only one of these *Kommandos?* Why did the rest of these *Kommandos* not revolt, but march themselves willingly to their death. Or what did it take for the exception to do so?

Perhaps another rare instance, an example of supreme self assertion, can shed light on the question. Once, a group of naked prisoners about to enter the gas chamber stood lined up in front of it. In some way the commanding SS

---

[19] Nyiszli, *op. cit.* Scattered revolts in the death camps (Treblinka, etc.) are mentioned elsewhere in the literature, though I have not myself seen witnessed reports. Civilian uprisings began to occur with the turn of the war tide against Germany, but as in the case of the Warsaw uprising, the hour was far too late for the millions already dead.

officer learned that one of the women prisoners had been a dancer. So he ordered her to dance for him. She did, and as she danced, she approached him, seized his gun, and shot him down. She too was immediately shot to death.[20]

But isn't it probable that despite the grotesque setting in which she danced, dancing made her once again a person? Dancing, she was singled out as an individual, asked to perform in what had once been her chosen vocation. No longer was she a number, a nameless, depersonalized prisoner, but the dancer she used to be. Transformed, however momentarily, she responded like her old self, destroying the enemy bent on her destruction, even if she had to die in the process.

Despite the hundreds of thousands of living dead men who moved quietly to their graves, this one example, and there were several like her, shows that in an instant the old personality can be regained, its destruction undone, once we decide on our own that we wish to cease being units in a system. Exercising the last freedom that not even the concentration camp could take away—to decide how one wishes to think and feel about the conditions of one's life—this dancer threw off her real prison. This she could do because she was willing to risk her life to achieve autonomy once more. If we do that, then if we cannot live, at least we die as men.

---

[20] Kogon, *op. cit.*, p. 132.

7

Men Are Not Ants

Having discussed the direct impact of the German concentration camps on its inmates, there remains an equally important aspect of this institution: How it served less directly to intimidate German civilians at large and to modify their personalities. In this respect it fortunately failed of total success. Yet Americans, particularly, find it hard to understand how persons who once knew and enjoyed freedom later succumbed to the spell of National Socialism.

Perhaps I can best begin by referring to those victims of the Nazi state who perished under the weight of their earthly possessions. Similar events, though with less drastic results, also took place in France. Refugees fleeing the invading German armies were everywhere bogged down by the load of goods they were carting in wagons, barrows, bicycles or on their backs, because they could not bring themselves to face life without them. True, those possessions were still difficult to replace, but less so than their lives. Moreover, even in the brief years since then, technology has made great strides.

I have stated many times in this book that the success or failure of any mass society will depend on whether or not man so reshapes his personality that he can modify the society into one that is truly human; in our case, into one where we are not coerced by technology, but bend it to our human needs.

Thus only one of the needed adjustments to a new technological fact would be a clear recognition that dead objects are far less vital to man than they used to be, since it no longer takes a year's labor to acquire one good suit, or a good bed and mattress. Such recognition, if it is to deepen our freedom not our bondage, would have to mean investing these goods with little emotional attachment. On the other hand, perhaps the degree to which we are still beholden to our possessions may help Americans, so proud of their liberties, to understand the experience of the German under Hitler.

Nobody wishes to give up freedom. But the issue is much more complex when the decision is: how many possessions am I willing to risk to remain free, and how radical a change in the conditions of my life will I make to preserve autonomy.

When life is at stake and one is still in full possession of one's powers, making decisions and taking action is relatively easy. The same is nearly true for one's physical liberty. But in the case of one's personal independence, things seem less clear cut. Risking one's life to prevent small inroads into one's autonomy is not what most people would do. And when the state makes small inroad after small inroad, at which point is one to say: No more, even if it costs me my life? And pretty soon the many small inroads have sapped so much courage that one no longer has the nerve to take action. The same is true for anxiety generated by fear for one's life or one's freedom, or both.

To take action in the moment of the first onset of anxiety is relatively easy, because anxiety is a powerful motivating force to action. But if action is delayed, the longer anxiety lasts and the more energy is spent on binding it, that is, on not acting to relieve it, the more a person is drained of vital energy and the less he feels capable of acting on his own.

At the inception of the German tyranny, the longer action was delayed, the weaker grew the ability to resist. But once set in motion, this process had its own momentum. For a long time, many were still convinced that at the next inroad the state made on their autonomy, at the next infringement of liberty, at the next degradation, they would definitely take decisive action. Only by that time they could no longer act, and had to realize too late that the road to disintegration as persons, or worse, to the death camp, had been paved with intentions not acted on in time.

Again, my interest here is not in the importance of this process within a now defunct system, but that similar tendencies are present in any mass society and can be detected to some degree in our own time.

The concentration camps, too, affected the autonomy of civilians only step by step. In the first years of the camps (1933-1936) they were meant to punish and deter active anti-Nazis in the old sense—as individuals. But then came an important innovation: the systematic attempt to do away with individuals as such. How this was done in the camps I have already described. Here I want to show how it was achieved among the rest of the German population, and how heavily the Gestapo relied on well planned and effectively "advertised" techniques.

After 1936, with political opposition crushed and the Hitler state well entrenched, no individuals or groups remained inside Germany that could seriously threaten its existence. Although people were still sent to the concentration camps for individual acts of opposition, the overwhelming majority entering the camps in the next few years were singled out because of membership in a particular group. They were punished because for some reason the group had incurred the displeasure of the regime or was expected to in the future. No longer was it just the individual and his family who were being punished and intimidated, but large segments of the population. This shift in emphasis from the individual to the group, though it coincided with military preparations for war, had its main purpose in securing total control of a people not yet robbed of all freedom of action; that is, to force individualism to submerge itself within a total malleable mass.

The vast majority of Germans had by then accepted the Hitler government and its system, though some continued to grumble and were dissatisfied with this or that. Much of this acceptance was viewed as an act of free will, and by persons who still enjoyed considerable outer freedom and a sense of inner independence. A typical example was the authority still held by fathers within their own homes. No one who is truly and fully his own master within his family, and derives self respect and security from his work, can be said to have lost all autonomy.

So the next problem for the state was to do away with those factors blocking the development of a total society of depersonalized subjects. Occupational and social groups that accepted the ideology of National Socialism, but opposed the way it interfered with their personal sphere of interests, had to be kept in line and taught there was no room for personal concerns in the total mass state.

To destroy all groups still enjoying a measure of independence seemed impractical; that would have hampered the functioning of the state and interfered with vitally needed production for the coming war. Therefore, groups that showed any hesitation about falling in line had to be forced by intimidation. The Gestapo called these group punishments "actions," and applied them for the first time in 1937.

At first the system developed slowly and destroyed integrity more through a logic inherent in the total state than any deliberate planning. Only later, when these actions had proved effective, were they consciously planned to destroy the autonomy of large groups by deliberately wiping out a selected few of its members.

Control from below

During the first of these actions, only the leaders of a restive group were punished, since the Nazi system was built on the leader principle. That is, the leaders supposedly carried all responsibility; the rank and file had simply to obey without questioning. But this worked only as long as all leadership rested in one or a few persons, or in one small and well integrated group. It did not work for diffuse groups where no clear leadership existed. Although all decisions ultimately came from Hitler, modern society requires many subgroupings. Even state created subgroups have a tendency to assert their independence, to fight for their special interests against other state created groups.

So there was not only the problem of how to deal with older existing groups but how to subject the newly created groups to total control. Both were very useful and the state could not function without them. This the members realized and it fortified their independence. Moreover, if group members really obeyed their leader blindly, as they were told to, how could the state remain safe if some group leaders became subversive? So the issue was to find ways to subject all groups to total control, both leaders and membership, and to do that without nullifying the leadership principle on which subgroups were organized. The solution was to so intimidate group members that fear for their very lives would counteract the obedience to their leaders that was expected of them.

The method that could accomplish all this was control from below. But it had to be a control that did not confer strength, since that would run counter to the leadership principle and give the member independence. On the contrary, it had, if possible, to weaken him. This was achieved by using resentment and anxiety as chief motivating forces. Actions engaged in out of resentment, anxiety or both, do not confer strength and security, but tend to weaken the person, even if the action succeeds. In some groups, resentment of the leader was enough to secure state control from below. In other groups the interests of the members were so similar to those of the group leader that resentment alone was not a strong enough motivating force, so anxiety was added.

Among small groups, the family is not only the most important one, but in many ways it typifies all groups. We may therefore take it as an example of control from below through anxiety and resentment.

Inside the family the parents lead, the children are the rank and file. For historical reasons paternal authority in the German family was very great. Such a family group shared important common interests; but its definite class structure also generated a great deal of fear and resentment toward the parents. So in this group, if fear of the parents was eliminated, either by greater fear of the state, or support from the state against the parents, or both, then it was relatively easy to arouse and encourage the children's resentment of parental authority. By manipulating this resentment, the state could establish a complete and weakening control over the whole family.

Denunciation of parents by their children, or of one mate by the other was never widespread enough to do much damage to the integration of all parents, or to disintegrate all families as a source of inner security. But the few actual denunciations and their terrible consequences, made widely known, were enough to sow distrust. What was so destructive to all parents was having to dread the consequences of what they might do or say in front of their children.

This fear gripped most parents, and by weakening their security within the home, dried up a main source that could still have fed their self respect, given them a sense of worth and thus of inner autonomy. The fear, more than the fact of betrayal by children or mates, made it impossible to lower one's defenses even within one's own four walls. Unquestioned trust, which is the greatest value of an intimate relation, became a danger instead of the relief it should have been. It turned family life into an experience of continuous caution, of strain, of being on guard if not openly distrustful; it became a weakening experience when it should have given greatest security.

I might add that while relatively few children denounced their parents, many more threatened to do so. Nor did the child who went through with it gain strength from his self assertion: weakened by guilt, he had to justify his action to himself through even blinder allegiance to the superfather, the leader. Only by viewing the leader (or the state) as sacred could he justify having turned on his parents. So while little was gained in autonomy by asserting oneself vindictively, much chance for autonomy was lost by viewing the state's demands as overpowering, inescapable and absolute.

Praise by the secret police, or even public praise, as by announcement at Hitler Youth meetings or in the newspapers, brought elation at the moment. But it could not long compensate for the silent ostracism these informers were treated with by their families, and even less for the absence of the member sent to prison, or the hardships wrought on the whole family now without a provider. For all these, only the glorified state could compensate; so the effort to win independence from the parent ended only in still greater submission to the state.

What is here said of the family was also true to a lesser degree for other, less intimate group associations. There, a denounced leader was replaced by another one who owed his advancement not to respect from his colleagues or to professional achievements, but only to the state that appointed him. As likely as not, he was resented and secretly blamed by the friends of the man he replaced; even more reason for the newcomer to prove his usefulness to the state by greater compliance with its demands, since he could not count on his own group to support him. So much for the intimidation from below of group leaders in the Hitler state.

Group actions

As for the rank and filers, it was soon clear that just to intimidate restive leaders was not enough for them either. It created the impression that it was not very dangerous just to belong to such a group, as long as one took no personal action and expressed no definite opinion. So the Gestapo revised its system and instead of arresting only leaders, it began to send a cross section of the dissatisfied group to the concentration camps. This new tactic enabled them to punish and spread terror among all members, and also to destroy the independence of the group without even touching the leader if that happened to be troublesome.

At one time, for example, there was a movement opposed to the regimentation of cultural activities and to the ban on what was called decadent art. It centered around the noted conductor, Furtwaengler, who secretly encouraged it, though he himself took no open stand on the issue. He was never threatened but the group was destroyed, and all artists severely intimidated, by the imprisonment of a cross section of its members. Even if Furtwaengler had taken a more active role in the movement, he would have found himself a leader without followers and the movement would have collapsed. Interestingly enough, quite a few artists were punished who had nothing to do with the opposition movement. It made no difference. As long as all artists knew that some of their friends had been punished, few people asked why. All fellow artists felt terrorized, irrespective of what the politics of the victims had been.

At first only a few professional groups, such as lawyers and doctors, were thus decimated for not fully accepting their new role in society. Typically, they were groups that for a century or more had been proud of their special education and superior knowledge, their contributions to society and the position it gave them. For these and other reasons they felt entitled to certain privileges and considerations, most of all to being treated differently from the rest of the population. They felt that much of what the Nazi state did was necessary to win a mass following and to keep it in line. But they felt it could not and should not apply to their own group, since they were well able to think for themselves and decide what was best for them and for the nation. The "actions" against these two sophisticated and privileged groups brought them to heel, showed them how dangerous it was even for them to indulge in the luxury of private opinions, or to think of themselves as individuals.

Group actions proved so effective that soon they were used to do away with entire social or professional groups whose existence seemed needless or undesirable. Again, the first to meet such a fate were the gypsies—a group traditionally opposed to anything curbing their freedom of movement or action. When an effort to settle and control them failed, and when a part action, the imprisonment of a couple of hundred of them, did not sober the rest of them, all gypsies were sent to the concentration camp. Here, then, was a new warning. If sending a cross section of the group into the camps was not heeded, the whole group would be destroyed.

No such radical solution was therefore needed for other unwanted groups, such as nightclub entertainers or professional dancers. The latter were the first group warned beforehand, in the newspapers and through talks to their professional associations, to change their profession to one more useful to the state. After a number of them had been sent to the concentration camps, those still at liberty showed without delay that they had learned their lesson; they "voluntarily" disbanded their organizations and found themselves other jobs. From then on the warning to find a more "useful" calling was usually enough to bring about whatever changes in profession the state required.

It was somewhat harder to deal with groups less marginal within society than brothel keepers and pimps, entertainers, graphologists, or dancers. Labor was not yet strictly regulated. The worker still had some legal freedom to change places of work, to criticize poor labor conditions or ask for better wages; soon this kind of self assertion was curbed, less because of the small inconvenience it caused in industry or the labor market than because it was a piece of self assertion, a sign that some autonomy still remained. Unquestioning obedience to the state, on the other hand, was rewarded with tangible benefits, of which the special vacations offered by "Strength through Joy" *(Kraft durch Freude)* was merely the best advertised.

Fear of the concentration camps had spread among the German population as soon as they were instituted. But prior to these group actions the *kleine Mann,* the little man, had believed himself too unimportant to be bothered with. Up to that point, too, Nazi party members had felt free to express dissatisfaction or to permit themselves minor infractions of discipline.

But it is typical of the oppressive mass state that it soon finds it equally important to intimidate its own followers. Early adherents of National Socialism, acting on personal conviction, tried to carry out principles of the system "prematurely" or in ways the leaders disapproved of. Such persons were found just as dangerous to the state as its active opponents. Because here as elsewhere, danger consisted less in the particular opinion a man held than in his holding personal opinions at all. Group actions taught party members that they too were in constant danger. The hazards of the least deviation from norms set down by the Gestapo they already knew about. Now they learned just how dangerous it was to hold private convictions in the first place.[1]

Random terror

But members of organized groups were not the only ones cowed by group actions. They served equally well to destroy unorganized efforts at independence and self assertion such as listening to foreign broadcasts. At first these were only denounced but still permitted; only during wartime were they forbidden by law and then punished by civil imprisonment. Since the activity involved no organized groups, no random selection among members could intimidate, nor could all of them be put away. Therefore, the procedure was to collect evidence by denunciation on a few hundred of them and bring them all to the concentration camps at the same time. And again, if some of these had never listened

[1] This explains why, in 1934, Roehm and his immediate friends had to be destroyed and their followers intimidated, and why, up to the last years of the war, high Nazi functionaries, including SS officers, were sent into concentration camps. Roehm's guilt, in the eyes of the system, was not that he was opposed to it, which he was not, but that he wanted its principles realized at a speed different from that intended by the leader. He had to be destroyed for wanting a will of his own in a system whose central problem was to do away with individual wills. The analogy should be obvious between what happened to Roehm and what happened in communist Russia to some of its most prominent leaders. The so-called Moscow trials marked the destruction of persons who, though in agreement with the system's basic philosophy, retained individual freedom of critique and action. Those trials took place after the start of the German regime of terrorization through the concentration camps. The Russian forced labor camps also developed less radically than the German concentration camps, although they held many more laborers; terrorization was not initially the central issue of the Soviet system; it was an after effect of the system of slave labor.

to foreign broadcasts, it did not matter. The rest of the population was no whit less terrorized.

The action against listeners, long before it was illegal to listen, had the widest publicity and it increased the fear of denunciation at home by showing how often it happened, and with what fearful results. It certainly intimidated others who might have contemplated similar activities.

It is important to realize that "actions" of this type nearly always punished something that was not yet forbidden by law. It would have been very easy for the state to pass any laws it wished to. But that was not the purpose of the "actions." They were intended less to punish transgressors, than to force all citizens to do as the state wished, and to do it of their own volition. No doubt the motive for conformity was anxiety. Still, it was the person's own anxiety that forced him to conform, and not the letter of the law. Though this distinction may seem thin, it was psychologically important.

This psychological effect was not owing to the fact that in one case the man on the street could supposedly claim he had a legal choice, which in the other he did not. Such legal subtleties have no psychological impact, or only a negligible one. The great difference was that a law is made public, and thereafter everybody knows what is expected of him. But with group actions, the man on the street never knew what behavior was going to be punished next. For those persons who wanted to play it safe, group actions forced them to anticipate what the state might expect of them, long before the state made its expectations known. The subject's anxiety always made him dread many more "actions," entailing many more areas of behavior, than even the total state could afford to conduct without endangering its own functioning. So the subject had to behave himself in many more respects than were actually singled out for "actions."

To anticipate the nature of future events correctly, one must have intimate knowledge of the other person's (or group's) intimate thoughts, motives, desires. There was only one way for the man on the street to acquire this kind of "intuitive" knowledge; it was through total identification with the state, including its present and future purposes. The unexpectedness of "actions" that dealt extreme punishment for what persons not "in the know" had thought permissible or even safe, forced them to become persons who are "in the know"; it forced them for their own safety, and hence out of their own will, to become so much a part of the total state that they could anticipate and abide by what the state was likely to expect of them in the future.

The results were impressive. By about 1939 the number of serious dissenters was running so low that merely listening to foreign broadcasts became as great a political offense as the printing and distributing of leaflets inciting to revolt had been a few years earlier.

In 1938, for example, there was a widely publicized action against the so-called *"Meckerer,"* or mutterers, who had supposedly made critical remarks in private about their employers or the state. This, and the action against listeners to foreign broadcasts, were among the first in which state control of individual behavior invaded the privacy of the home.

True, on a smaller scale the actions against *"Rassenschaender"* (miscegenation) had come earlier, and established state control of the most private, the sexual relations. But since these actions were directed against Germans who had had intimate relations with Jews (and a negligible number with Negroes, etc.,), only a small group was intimidated. Those against homosexuals cut deeper into the private affairs of individuals, but since homosexuals were viewed as undesirables by most of the population, these actions too frightened only persons directly concerned.

All this changed with the action against the mutterers. Now no German could feel safe in his private life any more.

By the time actions had destroyed all privacy in Germany through its premium on denunciations of what people said or did at home, Hitler's youth organizations were well established. Children had been sufficiently indoctrinated to counteract fear or respect for their parents and were now capable of spying on their parents, and on friends of their parents. They were also capable of reporting to the police on the most intimate conversations and behavior of their parents, or of threatening to do so.

Soon the task of preparing for and waging total war received priority, and a new group was felt to warrant complete removal: those considered dangerous to the war effort. Nevertheless here too the measure was called a group action. Most important of those now arrested were the conscientious objectors, whose largest subgroup was the German Jehovah's Witnesses.

Newspaper notices had long made everyone aware of the concentration camp and its punitive character, but no detailed knowledge was available. This only heightened anxiety, because psychologically the individual can deal with even the worst torture as long as its character is known. Sometimes he can repress the knowledge, or else deny its threatening character. The unknown that threatens our lives is much more frightening; it is uncanny, it haunts us continuously. We cannot face it and cannot forget it, so it dominates our mental life either as conscious or unconscious terror. This may explain why the concentration camp was threatening not just to those who opposed the regime but even to those who never violated the smallest regulations.

But it was not just the threat of the concentration camp that spread enough terror to make many feel immobilized by anxiety. They were even more immobilized by the inability to reach vital decisions and to act upon them. No longer was just their self respect at stake, but their very life. The greater the anxiety, the greater the need to take action;

but anxiety is debilitating. As noted at the start of this chapter, taking action in the first moments of anxiety is relatively simple because anxiety is such a powerful incentive.

The particular anxiety generated by the threat of the concentration camp was, after the fear for one's life, anxiety about what might be called one's moral existence. It posed the question: If resisting the state deprives me of my social status in society and within the family, of my home and my earthly possessions, will I be able to make a go of life without what has always been my main source of security? Only those who knew for sure what was ephemeral and what essential, in themselves and their life, and that the essential would stay with them no matter what, could easily afford to take action toward ending their anxiety. They tried either to fight or to escape.[2]

Whether or not Germans realized it consciously, the longer they lived under threat, the more energy it took to manage anxiety, the less inner energy remained for the courage to act, and the more they were thrown back on externals that had formerly kept them going in times of stress. It was the same process that led to disintegration in many apolitical middle class prisoners, though in the camps it happened faster. For those still at liberty, the greater the pressure of anxiety, the more they felt driven to act while the less able they felt to take action.[3]

To some, therefore, the final call to present themselves at Gestapo headquarters came as a relief. Sometimes it was

[2] Many active Zionists managed to survive the Hitler system, partly because they had withdrawn their emotional attachment from the home environment and anchored it in their hopes for a new life in Israel. Having long ago decided that what they most wanted for themselves was an entirely new life, they found it quite easy to give up the old. That they shared this emotional attachment to the future with a circle of friends who supported them, and whom they supported, was a further source of strength.

[3] This was the process that immobilized Jews in the Nazi ghettos, for example, even as their anxiety mounted.

because anxiety increased so suddenly that fear won out over timidity and brought positive action. Sometimes it was because the final arrival of the Gestapo marked an end to mental agony. No longer did they have to ask themselves the painful question: What gives me strength: my inner convictions, or the job I managed to get for myself, the earthly possessions I managed to accumulate? The longer they had to ask themselves such questions without reaching decisive answers, the more their very existence as human beings was put into question. Even the repeated asking of the question was itself a debilitating experience. If to this was added doubts about how their wives and children would feel about them and act toward them if they were deprived of all the external symbols of status and security, there was little left to live for but externals, with very little remaining inner strength.[4]

Many Germans knew or feared that they were scheduled for questioning by the Gestapo, and plotted to escape. Yet they stayed where they were and waited to be called for, and when the notice finally came to present themselves at Gestapo headquarters on such and such a day they no longer had the inner strength to go through with escape. Some additional reasons that account for this paralyzing effect of the Gestapo on the German population are discussed in the remainder of this chapter.

Dear Lord, make me dumb

Like the prisoners in the concentration camps, almost all German citizens had to develop defenses against the threat of the Gestapo and the concentration camp. Unlike the prisoners they did not form organizations of their own. This,

---

[4] Returning to the *Diary of Anne Frank*, one may speculate whether such feelings motivated the Franks both to stay together as a family (so as not to have to test their emotional ties) and to take as many possessions as possible into hiding.

they felt, would only have made arrest a more likely fate. Prisoners inside the camps were quite aware of this, and said that the concentration camp was the only place inside Germany where one could discuss politics without immediate danger of betrayal and imprisonment. Because organized defense was extremely hazardous, German citizens relied mostly on psychological defenses. These were similar to the ones developed by prisoners, though not as deep reaching or elaborate.

Basically there was a limited choice of ways for German subjects to deal with the problem of the camps in the early years. They could try to deny their existence. This was difficult because the Gestapo itself publicized them. They could try to believe that the camps were not as bad as they imagined, and this many Germans tried to believe. But this too was difficult because again and again the newspapers warned them they could either behave or wind up in a concentration camp. The simplest way to deal with the problem was to assume that only the scum of society was sent there, and that what they got they deserved. But only a small segment of the population could make itself believe that.

Those Germans who were outraged by the terror they had to submit to, also had to admit to themselves that their own government was vile, which further undermined their self respect. To any person who clung to his morality or some self respect, recognizing the true character of the concentration camps implied an obligation either to fight a regime that created and maintained them, or at least to take a firm inner stand against it.

In the absence of effectively organized opposition, which appeared only after military defeat became obvious, open fight was both suicidal and pointless unless one's life was endangered. Nevertheless some few among the university students preferred the incredible odds against resistance to evading what they considered their moral obligation. Apart from open fight there were some things many people could do and a few did, such as hiding or tendering other help to anti-Nazis or Jews.

But even taking a decisive inner stand required readiness to give up present and future position; to risk economic security; in some cases to risk the emotional security that comes from living closely with one's family. Again only those few could run such a risk who felt secure in themselves about how little either possessions or status meant to them, and how secure they were in their emotional attachments to those closest to them, no matter what might happen. But this, until most of us have reached the higher integration needed for life in the mass state, is a security only few of us possess.

So it can readily be seen how living under such conditions weakens self respect and finally brings about the disintegration of the individual. It is less readily seen how this leads with near necessity to a deep split in the personality, and with it the destruction of autonomy.

The terror spread by the existence of the camps, and the various actions, made every German who was not deeply secure in himself wish to remain not just silent, but to show no action or reaction whatsoever that might displease those in power. It was just as in the camps: while the good child may be seen and not heard, the German citizen had to be unseen and also dumb.

It is one thing to behave like a child because one is a child: dependent, lacking in foresight and understanding, taken care of by bigger, older, wiser adults, forced by them to behave, but occasionally able to defy them and get away with it; most important of all, feeling certain that in time, as one reached adulthood oneself, all this would be righted. It is quite another thing to be an adult and have to force oneself to assume childish behavior, and for all time to come. The need to force it on oneself probably had deep psychological consequences that do not hold for the child's being forced to it by others.

It was not just coercion by others into helpless dependency; it was also a clean splitting of the personality. Man's anxiety, his wish to protect his life, forced him to relinquish what is ultimately his best chance for survival: his ability to react appropriately and to make decisions. But giving these up, he was no longer a man but a child. Knowing that for survival he should decide and act, and trying to survive by not reacting—these in their combination overpowered the individual to such a degree that he was eventually shorn of all self respect and all feelings of independence.

Amnesia again

One outward evidence of this disintegration amazed and outraged American public opinion after the conquest of Germany. I refer to an attitude found prevalent among the German population, namely their denial of having known of the existence and nature of the concentration camps.

Because of this widespread denial, military authorities of occupying nations decided to arrange for intensive publicity of the camps after the war. German citizens were forced to visit them because Allied officers were appalled at the horrors, and angered to hear Germans denying they had known of them. If this was the reason for forcing Germans to visit the camps, it was not the result of sound psychological deliberations.

For example, the most frequent statements about German guilt were based on the assertion that they must have known of the existence and the horror of the camps. But this was hardly the issue. The real issue was whether they were able to prevent it, and if so, why they didn't.

Of course the Germans knew of the existence of the

camps. The Gestapo saw to that. Again and again German citizens were cowed into submission by the threat of being sent to one. Some individual Germans tried to fight back; hardly any of them survived. Others made the attempt to organize resistance movements; they were among my fellow prisoners in the concentration camps. Certainly one can blame the average German for not having been one of those heroes, but not often has there been a people whose average citizen is a hero, unless under the special circumstances of serving in the army or when his life is clearly threatened.

No more than a very few Germans ever fought openly against the terror of the Gestapo. But I recall very well how elated the prisoners of Buchenwald were when they learned that soldiers of the Deathhead units of the Gestapo borrowed uniforms from other units when they visited Weimar, the town next door, because nice girls there refused to have anything to do with them. They called them "killer boys" because of their crimes against the prisoners. The Gestapo threatened the citizens of Weimar, but to no avail. Theirs was not a heroic way to fight back. As a matter of fact, it was no fight at all. But it was a clear expression of disgust on the part of citizens in a town that consistently voted the Nazi ticket before the Nazis gained power.

We cannot ascribe blame to the unarmed onlookers of the crimes of the Gestapo as long as we do not charge the unarmed onlookers of a holdup who do not stop the gunmen from assaulting the cashier. Even this comparison is inadequate. The witnesses of a holdup know that the police are on their side, a police with weapons even deadlier than the gunmen's. The German citizen knew that no armed force would protect him if he should interfere with the Gestapo.

With terror already in effect, what were most Germans to do? They could try to leave Germany; quite a few did and many more tried. The majority were soon too terrorized to leave or in no position to do so. Which country opened its borders and said: Come unto me, all you who are heavy-laden?

What was open to those who had to remain? They could think day and night of the terrors of the Gestapo that threatened them. The result would have been a state of permanent anxiety based not on delusion but on reality. They could have told themselves: My own country is an abyss of evil. What this does to the individual who has to keep living in it I have been trying to indicate.

Therefore, the method used by the Allied army of occupation was irrealistic. Of course the Germans were badly shaken at sight of the corpses in the camps. This indicates at least one thing: that twelve years of Nazi control was not enough to destroy all human feeling.

Probably the major impact of seeing the horrors was to show them how right they had been in the first place in not daring to oppose the Gestapo. Until then they may have thought the Gestapo exaggerated in its threats; now they knew that was just wishful thinking on their part, indulged in to keep some small independence of thought. Now they had their full justification for using repression and denial to forget the existence of the camps. Now they found justification for the dread that had forced them not to risk the slightest deviation. So the net effect of their visit to the camps was probably to convince them how right they had been all along in not opposing the Gestapo.

But there are other, more serious aspects of this effort to blame all Germans for the crimes of the Gestapo. To place responsibilities on groups instead of individuals is one of the most effective devices of an authoritarian regime, first to force the individual into submission, and then to destroy him as an individual. Those who do not want democracy deliberately avoid thinking in terms of individuals, but think instead in terms of groups. They blame the Jews, the Catholics, the capitalists. For them to blame individuals and not groups would imply a contradiction of their main thesis; it would mean accepting the concept of the autonomy of the individual.

One of the major conditions for the independent existence of the individual is his personal responsibility for his acts. When we select a group of German citizens, show them the concentration camps, and say to them "You are guilty," we are affirming a fascist tenet. Whoever accepts the doctrine of the guilt of a whole people helps to destroy the development of a true democracy which is based on individual autonomy and responsibility.

Applying psychoanalytic reasoning, one might say that exactly because the Germans were unconsciously only too aware of the camps, only very few were consciously able to face facts. Much as a soldier going into battle may be most apt to say he will come out all right and believe it (for without such conscious conviction he could not enter battle, exactly because deep down he knows how great the danger is), so the German most afraid of the concentration camp was most in need of believing it did not exist.

All we can conclude from the widespread denial is this: that the intensity of the denial (in the face of knowledge that was readily available and even deliberately forced upon Germans) was the exact counterpart of the degree and depth of anxiety that caused the denial. The conclusion should have been not that all Germans were simply liars, which on a moral level of analysis they were. On a deeper level, the conclusion should have been that issues of morality did not apply to them because their personalities were so disintegrated they no longer knew, nor were able to separate out,

what was fact and what was only conviction born of fear.[5]
The conclusion should have been that the personalities of
all these individuals were so disintegrated that they had lost
the autonomy that alone would have enabled them to evaluate facts correctly, and on their own.

Perhaps there were two levels even in the American reaction. Our annoyance, if not anger, was based on the tacit assumption that Germans lied for our consumption, that they
wanted simply to alibi, that they lied only to avert punishment. It is assumed that the denial was born at the moment
of questioning. But it may be that we overestimate ourselves
as a motive for the lying, important though we were to the
Germans as victors.

The small child who denies his misbehavior does not
simply lie to fool us; he is at least as anxious, or more so, to
fool himself. Afraid of punishment, and convinced we will
learn the truth sooner or later, what he is after is not to fool
us but to convince himself that his crime never even happened. Only then can he feel safe, both now and in the
future. Because he knows, from a certain age on, that if he
fools us and we find out, the punishment will be even stiffer.

This, incidentally, is one of the reasons why too severe
punishment is so often damaging to personality integration:
the child, if he is acutely anxious about punishment, is no
longer sure what he really did. When the anxiety is too great,
it often forces him to believe he did right when he did
wrong, as it sometimes forces him to think he did wrong

---

[5] Here, and at other places I cannot help discussing issues of morality.
But if I do so, my purpose is not to presume that I know what is right or
wrong for others. Nor can I tell others what they ought to do. I write as
a psychologist, trying to explain why what happened, happened. My
hope is that such analysis will help others to decide what reshaping of
their personalities they wish to effect to better meet the moral and emotional requirements for withstanding the pressures of a mass society;
or to put it differently, how to inform the heart in the service of
autonomy.

when he didn't. This inner confusion about what actually happened is much more destructive to personality development than the degrading character of punishment; that, by comparison, does only minor damage.

I have said that we may have taken ourselves too seriously in this matter. But with us too, if we were mistaken, it was not simply because we exaggerated our importance to the vanquished Germans. It was much more because we did not wish to recognize—and here I revert to a main thesis of this book—that a repressive regime can so disintegrate the personality of adults that out of pure anxiety they can firmly believe what they would know to be false if their anxiety permitted them to know it.

The Hitler salute

What was true of the inner responses of Germans to the concentration camps was also true for their overall reaction to total mass control. But in the Hitler state it was always more than fear for one's life that made it impossible to remain inwardly opposed to the system. Every nonconformist was subject to many contradictions. To cite the obvious dilemma: He could expose himself as a dissenter and thus invite persecution, or he could profess faith in something he not only did not believe, but hated and despised.

So the unwilling subject of the mass state had to begin to trick himself, to look for excuses and subterfuges. But in so doing he lost exactly the self respect he was trying to maintain. An example of the way this works may be seen in the Hitler salute. The salute was deliberately introduced so that everywhere—in the beer garden, the railroad, the place of work, and on the street—it would be easy to recognize anyone who hung on to the old "democratic" forms of greeting his friends.

To Hitler's followers, giving the salute was an expression of self assertion, of power. Each time a loyal subject performed it, his sense of well-being shot up. For an opponent of the regime it worked exactly opposite. Every time he had to greet somebody in public he had an experience that shook and weakened his integration. More specifically, if the situation forced him to salute, he immediately felt a traitor to his deepest convictions. So he had to pretend to himself that it did not count. Or to put it another way: he could not change his action—he *had* to give the Hitler salute. Since one's integration rests on acting in accord with one's beliefs, the only easy way to retain his integration was to change his beliefs. Things were made simpler by the fact that in most of us there is a great desire to conform. Everyone knows how hard it is to be deviant with even a casual acquaintance we meet on the street; it is infinitely more so when being different puts one's very life in danger. Thus many times a day the anti-Nazi had either to become a martyr or abandon self respect.

I once spoke with a young German psychologist who was a child at the beginning of the Hitler regime. Her father was a strong opponent of the Nazi movement and she felt as he did. But life went on and she had to go to school. At school she had to swear allegiance to the Führer, to give the Hitler salute repeatedly. For a long time she mentally crossed her fingers. She told herself that the oath and salute didn't count because she didn't mean them. But each time it became more difficult to hang on to her self respect and still keep up the pretense, until finally she gave up her mental reservation and swore allegiance like anybody else.

While this development was still going on, a parallel process was taking place in her inner relation to her father. At first his morality had given the girl strength to go on without wavering in her convictions. But as time went on, she felt herself more and more projected into a most difficult conflict. First she had sided with the father and simply resented the state that forced such a conflict on her. But eventually there came a time when she blamed her father for being the source of her difficulties. Once this happened, she also began to resent her father's values. But values we resent can no longer give us strength, nor can they motivate us strongly. So after this point in her inner development, the father's values which had fortified her resistance became weaker and weaker and what had once been an asset became a liability.

If a parent asks too much of us, we often end up complying even less than we might have done otherwise. By this time it was no longer a conflict between her and the Hitler state, with her father firmly on her side; the conflict was now within her, and her father could no longer support her because he was now a separate party in the conflict. Until she began to waver she took pride in his moral support; after that because she felt shame at her own behavior, he appeared to her as a critical figure, critical of her for doubting, for wishing to give in. So at the moment of indecision when she most needed to feel that her father respected her, he seemed to be pulling her still further apart. Here, then, is another example of how the personality splits under the impact of the coercive state if the individual tries to resist.

What was true for the Hitler salute was of course true for all other features of the regime. The inescapable power of the total state rests exactly on this: not only that it reaches the minutest and most private life activities of the individual, but more, that it splits the inner person if he resists.

To use another experience out of this young woman's student days: While attending *Gymnasium,* the girls in her school were asked to take a census of the population one day. To refrain from taking part would again have meant risking the well-being of herself and her family. Moreover, the request seemed innocuous enough. But in taking the census she suddenly found herself having to ask for private details from a Jewish family. She realized that these Jews saw her as a symbol of the regime and hated her. She resented this, and then realized that she was feeling just as the regime wanted her to: resentful of Jews. She also hated herself for helping to exterminate Jews. Certainly she hated the regime that forced the predicament on her, but she hated herself even more.

And the total state finds almost daily tasks that each subject must perform or risk destruction. Most persons, in fulfilling these requirements, start out hating the system that forces them, but then end up hating themselves more. Moreover, the regime can stand their hatred, but they cannot endure the self hate, which is so destructive to integration.

The appeal of tyranny

Life was no easier for parents who suddenly felt constrained in their own homes. Yet man does not change overnight. Expectations built up since early childhood remain with us as prime motivating forces even if they no longer match the changes in our life situation. It is not easy to stop finding security where for decades we have found it. So German parents continued to seek it in their homes and in their family relations even when they knew it was no longer there.

To hope for, to look for something so important as security, self respect and respect from others—in short for the experiences that breed autonomy—in situations that do not offer them, means only one thing. The person has to realize he is totally mistaken in the way he is going after what, after bare necessities, is most important to his survival as a human being. At this point we can see more clearly the psychological appeal of tyranny.

The stronger we are in ourselves, the more we can face even a hostile world without paralyzing fear. The less strength we find in ourselves—because our strength is no longer fortified by the respect of our family or the assurance and relaxation we experience at home—the less we are able to meet on our own terms a dangerous outside world. If we cannot achieve security in our homes, through our most intimate relations, we must make very sure that the world around us is friendly, supportive.

The tyranny of the oppressive mass state permits its subjects in one big sweep to solve all these difficulties and to re-establish security in both the inner and the outer spheres of life: by becoming the kind of subject the state wants them to be. Then the external world loses its dangers, it changes from being hostile to being friendly, and the intimate world becomes safe again. One can relax one's defenses at home, enjoy support from the family, and thus replenish one's emotional energy.

Perhaps these various appeals of tyranny can be summed up in a sentence: The more absolute the tyranny, the more debilitated the subject, the more tempting to him to "regain" strength by becoming part of the tyranny and thus enjoy its power. In accepting all this one can attain, or reattain, some inner integration through conformity. But the price one must pay is to identify with the tyranny without reservation; in brief, to give up autonomy.

In some people this inner conflict was so great that they committed suicide. But one did not have to kill oneself, because a careless remark achieved the same end. And many made such remarks. Others waited for the SS to come for them without trying to escape, because unconsciously they wanted an end to it all, even if it meant in the concentration camp.

Once in the concentration camp, survival was more precarious, but the inner split in the personality was not quite as great. For example, in the camps the Hitler salute was no longer required, nor any big show of love for the leader.

There one could vent one's hatred of the regime in words, without immediate anxiety of betrayal. Most of all, one was in the hands of the enemy against one's will, and powerless to do anything about it. In terms of my earlier example, it was now the situation of a child who is helpless to buck the will of the adult; before imprisonment, one had to voluntarily reduce oneself to a life of childlike dependence and obedience. True, the prisoner was forced into childlike behavior, and radically so. But he was forced by the guards, not by himself. If, even in the camps, a prisoner began to force himself into the childish position, then the difference disappeared; then he became an "old" prisoner, adjusted to life in the camps.

Whereas before imprisonment the split was in the self— one part of it demanding defiance, the other obedience— within the camps only the external world required obedience. What was wholly an inner conflict up to the moment of imprisonment, now became a conflict with the external world. In this sense, and only in this sense, did imprisonment offer momentary relief. But it was only momentary because very soon survival in the camps brought its own forms of unbearable conflict.

The nonconformist

Now the Hitler salute which I chose for an example was a very external thing. So was the Hitler picture on the wall, and so, for that matter, was the Stalin picture. They became tremendously important only because they reminded the nonconformist every minute of his conscious life that if he did not resist, neither could he afford to live by his inner convictions. Psychologically these mechanisms are rather crude but that should not blind us to the fact that they are extremely powerful. Because the power that can create such a tremendous inner conflict in man, that can force him to act against his convictions and desires, has a tremendous hold over him. Being subject to such an external power re-activates very childish attitudes and feelings. Only in infancy did other persons, our parents, have the power to throw us into desperate inner turmoil if our wishes conflicted with theirs.

It is not so much the actual power of the parent, how-ever, that makes him seem omnipotent to the child. In the beginning the infant feels quite free to be a nonconformist, to take candy out of the jar or money out of his mother's purse, or to explore out of sexual curiosity. The parent may inhibit these things, but the child will still try to do it sur-reptitiously, and with little inner conflict. But one day the child suddenly wakes up to find that the parents, without being present, have created a painful conflict in his mind, the conflict between his own desires and their past prohibi-tions. And at this point the parent begins to seem godlike, all-powerful, to be feared as potentially inimical.

This power for creating unmanageable inner conflicts in the child must be compared with the power of the total state to create similar conflicts in the minds of its subjects. The child, like the nonconformist, originally resented the power that controlled him. But any power that is strong also exerts tremendous appeal. After all, nothing succeeds like success. And successful power over the child has such great appeal that it becomes internalized as his standards and values.

This, some may argue, is valid only for the child and comes from his biological helplessness. Once the child has grown up and his values are well established, once he achieves personal identity, no external power will ever again fascinate him so much. There will be no need to internalize a new set of values.

But this argument overlooks the very essence of the total mass state: that *it sets out to destroy individual autonomy.*

The parent seems omnipotent because he has the power to withhold the substance of life—food. Under Hitler, the state had exactly the same power. Living in such a society, all citizens were as dependent as children for the substance of life. Or again, if the parent can inhibit his child's freedom of movement, the mass society can do the same to its recalcitrant citizens. And the parallels follow throughout.[6]

Fortunately, some differences remained. An important one was that a certain independence of thought was needed for making decisions at work. Therefore, workers could not be so externally controlled as the child. This, I think, was another reason for the slave labor camps. Workers who still retained too much independence were sent to dig ditches. They returned to factory work, for example, only after they had internalized the values of the state.

A reassuring thought

Thus most if not all Germans who were not convinced Nazis shrank severely in their own estimation for the following reasons: their denial of what they knew to be true; their living in constant fear; and their not fighting back where they felt it their duty to resist. These blows to their own image of themselves could be compensated in only one of two ways: through great satisfaction in their family lives, or through the rewards of achievement and recognition.

Both sources were closed to most Germans who rejected

---

[6] This, then, is another reason for the starvation diet of the concentration camps. The infant fears his parents' displeasure lest they withhold what he needs for his very existence; for the infant, this is symbolized by food. That fear is much more basic than his later fear of losing the love and respect of his parents. The SS reactivated this same basic fear by starving prisoners to such a degree that they lived in continuous anxiety about what food, and how much they would get. The results were very similar to those one can observe in the infant who is afraid his parents will stop feeding him. Conversely, it is difficult to deeply terrorize a people that is well fed and well housed.

National Socialism. Their family lives were seriously interfered with by the state. Their children were encouraged to spy on them and thus robbed the home of its intimacy. This wrecked even once stable and happy families. Status and social success were entirely dependent on party or state organizations. Even advancement in what many countries consider private enterprises or professions was subject to state control.

There was still one easy way for these Germans to fortify their badly damaged pride and preserve even the semblance of an integrated personality. It was by just being a German, the citizen of a country that was day after day winning political and military successes. The fainter their sense of pride the more insistent the need for some other source of strength to lean on. The appealing solution alluded to earlier, was to share power with the group one belonged to. And most Germans, both in and out of the concentration camps, availed themselves of this source of vicarious satisfaction and self respect.

Only a few German citizens could withstand all the pressures of tyranny and survive in virtual isolation. To succeed, they had to have a particularly well integrated personality to begin with, and had to keep it intact through a satisfying family life or such achievements as gave them pride and satisfaction even when no one else knew about them.

In all other Germans who were not convinced Nazis, the concentration camp produced personality changes, however indirectly. They may not have been as radical as those produced in the camps, but were far reaching enough to fit the needs of the state. The new integration that came to characterize almost every German citizen was on a very low level of personal dignity. But as yet most people, when they must choose between integration on a low human level and intolerable inner strain, will probably take the first and forego the second to regain peace. Yet there is much truth in the saying that the peace that reigns under tyranny is not the peace of human existence, but the peace of death.

And this may turn out to be a reassuring thought. I have stated my convictions before. As in all other great revolutions in the history of mankind, so too in this technological, industrial, and social revolution we live in: after some delay man will once again develop the requisite inner structures, and the greater ability to achieve inner integration, that must go with our new conditions of life. New social and technological developments often seem to subject man to new and greater slavery; hence my remarks on the attitudes and fears of nomads when faced with the task of settling down. Hence also the fears of Marx and other of his contemporaries as they experienced early forms of the industrial revolution; what they feared was that workers would now be permanently degraded and exploited in ever larger factories, while instead we have seen how greater mechanization of industry has brought an ever greater freedom from toil and ever higher standards of living.

Revolutionary developments do bring about periods of social crisis until such time as man learns to develop those higher steps in integration that permit not only adjustment but mastery. Often the adjustment is momentarily an empty one, as we seem to be witnessing a rather empty adjustment to the new opportunities of material abundance, and even more important, to a luxury of time. But in the past, man has eventually mastered the new achievements and made them serve higher human goals.

If these views seem too optimistic, those who cannot share them may take some comfort from what happened in the Hitler state where some of its victims dug their own graves and laid themselves into them or walked on their own to the gas chambers. All of them were the vanguard of a walk toward death, toward the peace of death I have just spoken of. Men are not ants. They embrace death rather than an antlike existence. That is a further meaning of these victims of the SS walking to their death. That the SS then killed them is of less import than the fact that they marched themselves into death, choosing to give up a life that was no longer human.

In times of great crises, of inner and outer revolutions in all phases of life, situations may occur in which men have only the choice between such a giving up of life, and the achieving of a higher integration. Because we have not yet achieved the latter is no proof we are going to choose the former. If I read the signs of our times correctly, we have taken the first steps toward mastering the new conditions of life in an age of atomic power. But let us not fool ourselves either; the struggle will be long and hard, taxing all our mental and moral powers, if we do not want a brave new world but an age of reason and humanity.

Index

FOR THE BEST IN PAPERBACKS, LOOK FOR THE

In every corner of the world, on every subject under the sun, Penguin represents quality and variety – the very best in publishing today.

For complete information about books available from Penguin – including Pelicans, Puffins, Peregrines and Penguin Classics – and how to order them, write to us at the appropriate address below. Please note that for copyright reasons the selection of books varies from country to country.

In the United Kingdom: For a complete list of books available from Penguin in the U.K., please write to *Dept E.P., Penguin Books Ltd, Harmondsworth, Middlesex, UB7 0DA*

In the United States: For a complete list of books available from Penguin in the U.S., please write to *Dept BA, Penguin, 299 Murray Hill Parkway, East Rutherford, New Jersey 07073*

In Canada: For a complete list of books available from Penguin in Canada, please write to *Penguin Books Canada Ltd, 2801 John Street, Markham, Ontario L3R 1B4*

In Australia: For a complete list of books available from Penguin in Australia, please write to the *Marketing Department, Penguin Books Australia Ltd, P.O. Box 257, Ringwood, Victoria 3134*

In New Zealand: For a complete list of books available from Penguin in New Zealand, please write to the *Marketing Department, Penguin Books (NZ) Ltd, Private Bag, Takapuna, Auckland 9*

In India: For a complete list of books available from Penguin, please write to *Penguin Overseas Ltd, 706 Eros Apartments, 56 Nehru Place, New Delhi, 110019*

In Holland: For a complete list of books available from Penguin in Holland, please write to *Penguin Books Nederland B.V., Postbus 195, NL–1380AD Weesp, Netherlands*

In Germany: For a complete list of books available from Penguin, please write to *Penguin Books Ltd, Friedrichstrasse 10 – 12, D–6000 Frankfurt Main 1, Federal Republic of Germany*

In Spain: For a complete list of books available from Penguin in Spain, please write to *Longman Penguin España, Calle San Nicolas 15, E–28013 Madrid, Spain*

FOR THE BEST IN PAPERBACKS, LOOK FOR THE

A CHOICE OF PENGUINS AND PELICANS

Asimov's New Guide to Science   Isaac Asimov

A fully updated edition of a classic work – far and away the best one-volume survey of all the physical and biological sciences.

Relativity for the Layman   James A. Coleman

Of this book Albert Einstein said: 'Gives a really clear idea of the problem, especially the development of our knowledge concerning the propagation of light and the difficulties which arose from the apparently inevitable introduction of the ether.

The Double Helix   James D. Watson

Watson's vivid and outspoken account of how he and Crick discovered the structure of DNA (and won themselves a Nobel Prize) – one of the greatest scientific achievements of the century.

Ever Since Darwin   Stephen Jay Gould

'Stephen Gould's writing is elegant, erudite, witty, coherent and forceful' – Richard Dawkins, *Nature*

Mathematical Magic Show   Martin Gardner

A further mind-bending collection of puzzles, games and diversions by the undisputed master of recreational mathematics.

Silent Spring   Rachel Carson

The brilliant book which provided the impetus for the ecological movement – and has retained its supreme power to this day.

Setting Genes to Work   Stephanie Yanchinski

Combining informativeness and accuracy with readability, Stephanie Yanchinski explores the hopes, fears and, more importantly, the realities of biotechnology – the science of using micro-organisms to manufacture chemicals, drugs, fuel and food.

Brighter than a Thousand Suns   Robert Jungk

'By far the most interesting historical work on the atomic bomb I know of' – C. P. Snow

Turing's Man   J. David Bolter

We live today in a computer age, which has meant some startling changes in the ways we understand freedom, creativity and language. This major book looks at the implications.

Einstein's Universe   Nigel Calder

'A valuable contribution to the de-mystification of relativity' – *Nature*

The Creative Computer   Donald R. Michie and Rory Johnston

Computers *can* create the new knowledge we need to solve some of our most pressing human problems; this path-breaking book shows how.

Only One Earth   Barbara Ward and Rene Dubos

An extraordinary document which explains with eloquence and passion how we should go about 'the care and maintenance of a small planet'.

FOR THE BEST IN PAPERBACKS, LOOK FOR THE 🐧

A CHOICE OF PENGUINS AND PELICANS

The Second World War (6 volumes)   Winston S. Churchill

The definitive history of the cataclysm which swept the world for the second time in thirty years.

1917: The Russian Revolutions and the Origins of Present-Day Communism
Leonard Schapiro

A superb narrative history of one of the greatest episodes in modern history by one of our greatest historians.

Imperial Spain 1496–1716   J. H. Elliot

A brilliant modern study of the sudden rise of a barren and isolated country to be the greatest power on earth, and of its equally sudden decline. 'Outstandingly good' – *Daily Telegraph*

Joan of Arc: The Image of Female Heroism   Marina Warner

'A profound book, about human history in general and the place of women in it' – Christopher Hill

Man and the Natural World: Changing Attitudes in England 1500–1800
Keith Thomas

'A delight to read and a pleasure to own' – Auberon Waugh in the *Sunday Telegraph*

The Making of the English Working Class   E. P. Thompson   ·

Probably the most imaginative – and the most famous – post-war work of English social history.

FOR THE BEST IN PAPERBACKS, LOOK FOR THE 🐧

A CHOICE OF PENGUINS AND PELICANS

The Apartheid Handbook Roger Omond

This book provides the essential hard information about how apartheid actually works from day to day and fills in the details behind the headlines.

The World Turned Upside Down Christopher Hill

This classic study of radical ideas during the English Revolution 'will stand as a notable monument to . . . one of the finest historians of the present age' – *The Times Literary Supplement*

Islam in the World Malise Ruthven

'His exposition of "the Qurenic world view" is the most convincing, and the most appealing, that I have read' – Edward Mortimer in *The Times*

The Knight, the Lady and the Priest Georges Duby

'A very fine book' (Philippe Aries) that traces back to its medieval origin one of our most important institutions, modern marriage.

A Social History of England New Edition Asa Briggs

'A treasure house of scholarly knowledge . . . beautifully written and full of the author's love of his country, its people and its landscape' – John Keegan in the *Sunday Times*, Books of the Year

The Second World War A. J. P. Taylor

A brilliant and detailed illustrated history, enlivened by all Professor Taylor's customary iconoclasm and wit.

PENGUIN CLASSICS

A Passage to India E. M. Forster

Centred on the unresolved mystery in the Marabar Caves, Forster's great work provides the definitive evocation of the British Raj.

The Republic Plato

The best-known of Plato's dialogues, *The Republic* is also one of the supreme masterpieces of Western philosophy whose influence cannot be overestimated.

The Life of Johnson James Boswell

Perhaps the finest 'life' ever written, Boswell's *Johnson* captures for all time one of the most colourful and talented figures in English literary history.

Remembrance of Things Past (3 volumes) Marcel Proust

This revised version by Terence Kilmartin of C. K. Scott Moncrieff's original translation has been universally acclaimed – available for the first time in paperback.

Metamorphoses Ovid

A golden treasury of myths and legends which has proved a major influence on Western literature.

A Nietzsche Reader Friedrich Nietzsche

A superb selection from all the major works of one of the greatest thinkers and writers in world literature, translated into clear, modern English.